The Sounds of Poetry Viewed as Music

LEONARD HASTINGS SCHOFF MEMORIAL LECTURES

UNIVERSITY SEMINARS

Leonard Hastings Schoff Memorial Lectures

The University Seminars at Columbia University sponsor an annual series of lectures, with the support of the Leonard Hastings Schoff and Suzanne Levick Schoff Memorial Fund. A member of the Columbia faculty is invited to deliver before a general audience three lectures on a topic of his or her choosing. Columbia University Press publishes the lectures.

Edward Mendelson, *The Inner Life of* Mrs. Dalloway

Robert Gooding-Williams, *Democracy and Beauty: The Political Aesthetics of W. E. B. Du Bois*

Robert G. O'Meally, *Antagonistic Cooperation: Jazz, Collage, Fiction, and the Shaping of African American Culture*

Herbert S. Terrace, *Why Chimpanzees Can't Learn Language and Only Humans Can*

Annette Insdorf, *Cinematic Overtures*

Paige West, *Dispossession and the Environment: Rhetoric and Inequality in Papua New Guinea*

Robert L. Belknap, *Plots*

Philip Kitcher, *Deaths in Venice: The Cases of Gustav von Aschenbach*

Douglas A. Chalmers, *Reforming Democracies: Six Facts About Politics That Demand a New Agenda*

Boris Gasparov, *Beyond Pure Reason: Ferdinand de Saussure's Philosophy of Language and Its Early Romantic Antecedents*

For a complete list of books in the series, please see the Columbia University Press website.

The SOUNDS *of* POETRY VIEWED AS MUSIC

FRED LERDAHL

Columbia University Press
New York

Columbia University Press
Publishers Since 1893
New York   Chichester, West Sussex
cup.columbia.edu

Copyright © 2026 Columbia University Press
All rights reserved

Library of Congress Cataloging-in-Publication Data
Names: Lerdahl, Fred, 1943–, author
Title: The sounds of poetry viewed as music / Fred Lerdahl.
Description: [1.]. | New York : Columbia University Press, 2025. |
Includes bibliographical references and index.
Identifiers: LCCN 2025021254 | ISBN 9780231221184 hardback |
ISBN 9780231221191 trade paperback | ISBN 9780231563604 ebook
Subjects: LCSH: Poetry—Musical settings—Analysis, appreciation |
Musical meter and rhythm | Music and language | Versification
Classification: LCC ML3850 .L45 2025 | DDC 782.02/24—dc23/eng/20250514
LC record available at https://lccn.loc.gov/2025021254

Cover design: Julia Kushnirsky

GPSR Authorized Representative: Easy Access System Europe,
Mustamäe tee 50, 10621 Tallinn, Estonia, gpsr.requests@easproject.com

Contents

	Preface	*vii*
1	Prelude	1
2	Prosodic Rhythm	10
3	Historical Approaches to Prosodic Rhythm	32
4	Generative Approaches to Prosodic Rhythm	56
5	Contour	83
6	Transcriptions and Analyses	101
7	Sound Color	128
8	Coda	152
	Appendix A: Cited Poems	*155*
	Appendix B: Metrical Grids and Time Signatures	*159*
	Appendix C: Rule Index	*161*
	Appendix D: Links to Recordings	*165*
	Notes	*167*
	Bibliography	*175*
	Index	*181*

Preface

The idea of analyzing the sounds of poetry from the viewpoint of music came to me in the late 1980s, not long after the publication of Ray Jackendoff's and my *A Generative Theory of Tonal Music* (*GTTM*), a book that appropriates linguistic methodology to address the cognitive organization of rhythmic and pitch structures in classical tonal music. At the time I was seeking to expand *GTTM*'s scope in several directions. One of them was to undertake a pilot study of timbral organization using synthesized vowels; another was to conceive the cognitive organization of atonal music (music without a pitch center) in terms of the relative salience of events as a complement to the intervallic methods of pitch-class set theory. Both the timbral study and the approach to atonal music pointed toward a study of the sounds of poetry because poetic sound structure depends on degrees of timbral similarity and syllabic prominence.

The ambition to pursue this line of inquiry crystallized after John Halle, son of renowned phonologist Morris Halle, became my composition student. By the early 1990s, we coauthored two articles, one outlining a musical treatment of poetic rhythm and the other proposing a formal model of text setting. After this promising start, the enterprise stalled as each of us turned to other endeavors. In the next decades, I returned to the poetry project intermittently with a few publications and many talks, but I was too busy composing and pursuing other music-theoretic interests to give it the attention it required.

An invitation to give the 2018 Leonard Hastings Schoff Memorial Lectures at Columbia University induced me to resume the project in earnest. The three lectures, intended for a general audience and titled "Reflections on Music and Language," covered a range of topics: the first lecture, a broad comparison of musical and linguistic organizations; the second, a musical treatment of the sounds of poetry; the third, a discussion of text setting and musical narrative. The present book sets aside the first and third topics to focus on an in-depth study of the second. It develops a musically conceived, rule-based theory of poetic rhythm, contour, and sound color, and it situates the theory in relation to relevant work in music theory, literary studies, and phonology.

My strategy throughout the book is to present components of the theory before discussing related approaches. After a short initial chapter introducing basic features of musical rhythm, the second chapter presents a model of poetic rhythm. Chapter 3 relates the model to traditional poetic scansion, and chapter 4 discusses relevant research on prosodic rhythm in generative phonology. Chapter 5 advances a model of intonational contour for poetic lines and then considers related work in intonational phonology. Chapter 6 compares predictions of the theory to transcriptions of aural readings by poets and actors. Chapter 7 proffers a hierarchical model of syllabic sound color and reviews its connection to work in music theory. The final chapter briefly summarizes the architecture of the overall theory and suggests future avenues to explore.

This study is inescapably interdisciplinary. In the hope of reaching readers of various backgrounds, I have attempted to avoid being overly technical without sacrificing rigor. I realize that the employment of musical notation to represent rhythms, contours, and sound-color connections will be an impediment for many readers, but unfortunately there is no way around this difficulty. Musical notation is a precise and efficient means to represent the sound structures under consideration, and any substitute for it would compromise the presentation. To understand fully what the theory describes, the reader should be able to follow the musical notation and internalize what it represents—indeed, to speak the poetic lines under analysis in accordance with the rhythms and contours that the notation conveys.

I am pleased to acknowledge those who have contributed, directly or indirectly, to this book. Much of it germinated through conferences and residencies. I first sketched my approach to poetic rhythm in a talk at the Wenner-Gren International Symposium on Music, Language, and Speech in 1990 in Stockholm. A residency in 1990–1991 at the Institut de recherche et coordination acoustique/musique (IRCAM) in Paris, initiated by Jean-Baptiste Barrière and assisted by Xavier Chabot, enabled me to explore the approach more fully in the context of attempting to create a computational platform for text setting. My 2001 article on the musical treatment of sounds of poetry grew out of a talk given at a conference on the biological foundations of music at the New York Academy of Sciences, organized by Robert Zatorre and Isabelle Peretz. A talk that I gave at a conference on words and music in 2003 at the University of Missouri, directed by Gilbert Youmans, led to an unpublished manuscript that sketched materials that appear in more complete form in chapters 2, 5, and 7. In 2006–2007, I was a Mind/Brain/Behavior Distinguished Faculty Fellow at Harvard University under the sponsorship of Marc Hauser, at which time I taught a seminar on music and language. In 2012, Philippe Schlenker invited me to give the LINGUAE lectures in Paris, including a talk at the Collège de France that presented work-in-progress on music and poetry. In 2013, the Strüngmann Forum in Frankfurt mounted a conference, organized by Michael Arbib, on language, music, and the brain. My contribution resulted in an article comparing musical and linguistic syntaxes.

In addition to these conferences and residencies, I have given many talks over the years at universities and conferences on the sounds of poetry treated from a musical perspective, and I taught several seminars on music and language at Columbia University. All these experiences paved the way toward the 2018 Leonard Hastings Schoff Memorial Lectures, given under the directorship of Robert Pollack and with the support of my Columbia colleagues Susan Boynton and Robert Remez.

There are a few specific debts. After the Stockholm symposium, Bruce Hayes tutored me on the prosodic hierarchy and stress grid. Aniruddh Patel and Adam Tierney applied the speech-analyzing program Prosogram to a poem by Robert Frost. Danuta Mirka advised me on eighteenth-century music treatises that employ linguistic concepts. A lively correspondence with Jay Keyser sharpened my thinking about differing prosodic theories. Jean-Baptiste Barrière's unwavering encouragement helped me bring the music-poetry project to a conclusion.

Peter Berek, John Halle, Ray Jackendoff, Jonah Katz, Jonathan Teram, and Gilbert Youmans read parts of the manuscript and made valuable contributions to its content and presentation. Louise Litterick helped edit the entire manuscript. I am most grateful to the anonymous reviewers solicited by Columbia University Press; their comments led to significant improvements and extensions. Finally, I thank Miranda Martin, Jennifer Crewe, and Kathryn Jorge at Columbia University Press for their assistance in bringing this project to publication.

The Sounds of Poetry Viewed as Music

1

Prelude

1.1 GOALS

A close relationship is often claimed between music and language. Both domains consist of organized sound in time. In their richest forms, they appear to be uniquely human, and they are culturally universal. Both domains employ rhythm and pitch contour, are organized hierarchically, and generate a potentially infinite output from finite principles of organization. There is neuroscientific evidence that storage and processing of music and language partly overlap in the brain (Peretz & Coltheart 2003; Patel 2008). Since Charles Darwin (1871), it has been argued that the two domains have a common ancestry. They come together in poetry and song. Unlike ordinary speech, much poetry shares with music the projection of metrical structure and patterned repetition.

Yet there are reasons to deny a close relationship between music and language. Music does not have anything corresponding to word meanings or sentential semantics. Music does not have parts of speech nor does it have a system of distinctive phonological features. Language does not have scales, harmony, or counterpoint. It does not have tonality, hierarchical pitch relations, or a multidimensional pitch space. It does not express tonal tension and attraction.

These similarities and dissimilarities can be viewed in terms of the standard linguistic subdisciplines of syntax, semantics, and phonology. For present purposes, "syntax" may be broadly defined as the hierarchical organization of a sequence of discrete objects. In this sense, music has syntax. But its hierarchical organization of events is one of elaboration—that is, subordination of one event to another, repeated at multiple levels. In linguistic syntax, in contrast, hierarchical nodes represent parts of speech and phrasal categories such as noun and noun phrase, verb and verb phrase. The absence of syntactic categories in music hinders attempts to seek parallels to linguistic syntax beyond the mere existence of hierarchical structure (Lerdahl 2013).

The situation of musical semantics is comparable. Linguistic semantics deals with phenomena such as reference, synonymy, truth conditions, and entailment. But music, although meaningful in a broad sense, is essentially nonreferential (except at its imitative edges).[1] As a result, any pursuit of musical semantics must take place at a level of abstraction that is at a remove from its linguistic counterpart.[2]

Ray Jackendoff's and my *A Generative Theory of Tonal Music* (Lerdahl & Jackendoff, 1983; hereafter GTTM) adapts some of the methodological framework of generative linguistics, but it does not pursue musical analogues to linguistic syntax or semantics.[3] These links are too remote. It does, however, find significant parallels between music and phonology, first, between its metrical component and the treatment of poetic meter in generative prosodic theory, and second, in its component of time-span reduction and, in phonological theory, the groupings of syllables and their stress hierarchies. That substantive phonological parallels to music exist is not surprising because phonology, like music theory, is concerned with the organization of sequences of sound objects.

This book continues and expands on connections between music and the sounds of language particularly with respect to poetry. I shall develop the correspondences summarized in figure 1.1. Musical grouping structure has a phonological counterpart, the prosodic hierarchy. Relative points of prominence or salience at a musical surface correspond to an organized system of syllabic stress. In both music and poetry, if stresses are sufficiently periodic, the perceiver infers a metrical grid of strong and weak beats. The relative duration of musical events corresponds to degrees of syllabic duration, in both cases measured by a metrical grid. The intonational contour of an utterance resembles the rise and fall of a melody.

Music		Poetry
Grouping Structure	⟷	Prosodic hierarchy
Surface salience	⟷	Syllabic stress
Metrical structure	⟷	Poetic meter
Duration of events	⟷	Syllabic duration
Melodic shape	⟷	Intonational contour
Linear structure	⟷	Sound similarity/dissimilarity

FIGURE 1.1 Correspondences between musical and prosodic structures.

Nested patterns of pitch recurrence are analogous to the sound repetition of rhyme and alliteration.

I shall propose procedures for deriving all these structures. The approach to prosodic analysis differs from that of much generative phonology. My aim is not to decide if a line is a well-formed instance, say, of iambic pentameter. *GTTM*'s musical grammar involves interactive preference rules that conflict with or reinforce one another, leading to structural descriptions that cohere in varying degrees. My methodology is to assign intuitively preferred structures along a gradient rather than along categorical lines.

The flowchart in figure 1.2 offers a complementary perspective. Imagine a neutral rendering of a poetic line in which every syllable has the same duration, amplitude, and pitch height. No one would speak in this robotic way. An utterance is spoken with syllables of differing loudness, length, and pitch height, not arbitrarily but within a range of acceptability depending on the phonological structure of the utterance. Rules that generate these structures can be viewed as converting the neutral input into a small set of preferred outputs, each of which represents sequences of durations, metrical accents, and pitch contours. The success of the model can be evaluated by how well these outputs model a normative reading of the poem.

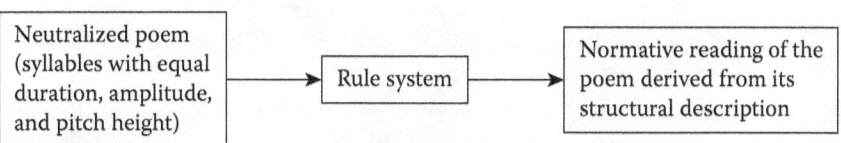

FIGURE 1.2 Flow chart for the theoretical model.

Issues of linguistic and poetic meaning and symbolism lie outside the scope of this book, although occasionally the analysis will impinge on points of poetic interpretation. My central purpose is to treat the sounds of poetry as music. I shall recast prosodic theory in musical terms.

1.2 MUSICAL GROUPING AND METER

Before proceeding to prosodic theory and analysis, it is useful to review two fundamental aspects of musical rhythm: grouping and meter.[4] Illustrations are from the beginnings of familiar national anthems, with words omitted to avoid issues of text setting.

A listener spontaneously groups a musical passage or piece into a hierarchy of motives, phrases, and sections. Groupings are typically represented by brackets beneath the notated music. Figure 1.3 gives the general form of grouping structure: events belong in groups, and groups nest within larger groups.

There are several principles by which listeners infer a grouping structure. Figure 1.4 presents the opening phrases of "The Star-Spangled Banner." At the smallest level, the music chunks into two-bar units, each beginning with a dotted eighth note plus a sixteenth note and ending with a half note. Two grouping principles trigger this assignment: parallelism and proximity. The units are parallel by virtue of their beginning with the same rhythm. The notes that are relatively proximate belong within a group; grouping boundaries form between notes that are relatively nonproximate, in this case, after the half notes. At the next larger level, these four segments group into two four-bar phrases. The principle here is symmetry: the grouping boundary divides the passage into phrases of equal length. Finally, the entire passage is a sectional group within the overall tune. The grouping principles of parallelism, proximity, and symmetry invoked here

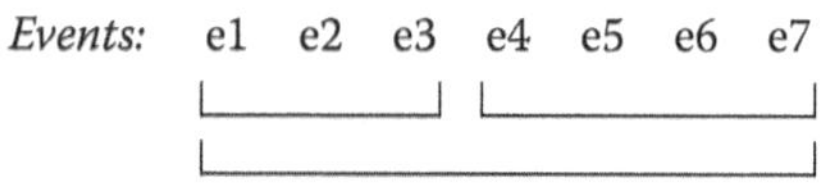

Events: e1 e2 e3 e4 e5 e6 e7

FIGURE 1.3 The format of grouping structure.

FIGURE 1.4 Grouping structure of the beginning of the "Star-Spangled Banner."

pertain not only to music but also to vision and other aspects of perception and cognition.

Meter is a cyclic pattern of strong and weak beats attributed by the listener to a musical passage. For this mental structure to come into play, events or patterns of events must occur with a degree of regularity at two or more levels of periodicity. (One level of beats yields equal rather than strong and weak beats.) As its name suggests, meter's essential function is to measure time as events unfold.

The traditional notation for poetic meter assigns "S" and "W" for strong and weak beats. Sometimes diacritics, borrowed from traditional prosodic scansion, are used instead, for instance "–" for strong and "⌣" for weak. Extra arbitrary symbols are needed to represent more than two degrees of beat strength. Such representations do not reveal the superimposed periodicities that are the source of the beat hierarchy. Thus, in contemporary rhythmic theory, meter is often represented by a grid format.[5] Figure 1.5 illustrates two metrical grids with time signatures and musically notated

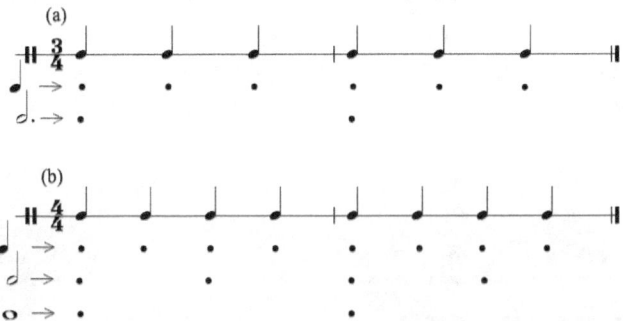

FIGURE 1.5 The grid format for metrical structure: (a) 3/4 meter; (b) 4/4 meter.

durations. Beats are represented by dots to convey that they are conceptual points in time. The grids are inverted to facilitate the layout in later figures in this book. To the left of each row of dots, the equidistant duration from one dot to the next is indicated.

If a beat is strong at one level, it is also a beat at the next larger level. In 3/4 meter in figure 1.5a, beats 2 and 3 are weak and receive one dot; beat 1 is stronger and receives two dots. In 4/4 meter in figure 1.5b, beat 3 is stronger than beats 2 and 4 and receives two dots; beat 1 is stronger than beat 3 and receives three dots. The more cyclic superimpositions on a beat, the greater its perceived strength.

The perceptual prominence of a metrical level depends on speed. The most salient level falls within the tempo region of seventy to one hundred beats per minute. This level is called the tactus. Beats at very fast speeds tend to run together, and the perceptual judgment of beats slower than thirty beats per minute become increasingly inaccurate and attenuated. Unlike grouping structure, which extends to the length of an entire piece, meter is a local phenomenon. The tactus rate is often explained as related to the human pulse rate. Recent research suggests rather that it is associated with an optimal rate of neural oscillations(Poeppel & Assaneo 2020).[6]

The time span from one beat to the next at a given level must be two or three times longer than at the next smaller level. Thus, the grid in figure 1.6a is ill-formed; a second level is required, as shown in figure 1.6b.

Depending on the musical idiom, beats can sometimes be two or three beats apart not only between levels but also within a given level, as shown in the middle level of figure 1.7. (Notice that beats at the top and bottom levels remain equidistant.) Whether in adjacent levels or within a level, the restriction to two or three beats apart ensures that a weak beat is always adjacent to a stronger beat. This restriction limits the number of possible meters.

A given idiom utilizes a subset of possible meters. A listener of that idiom intuitively selects a grid from this subset by identifying salient features of

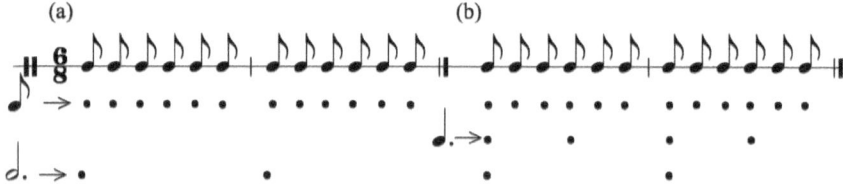

FIGURE 1.6 The two- or three-beat restriction: (a) ill-formed; (b) well-formed.

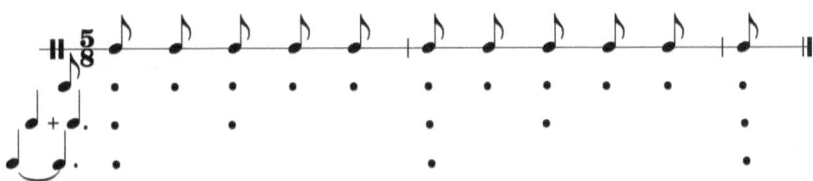

FIGURE 1.7 Metrical grid with two and three beats apart at the same level.

the auditory input. Several factors contribute to the perception that an event is salient. The event may be louder or longer than its adjacent events. It may be higher or lower. It may take place at a change in harmony. These diverse factors combine to produce a salience profile. The listener infers the grid that makes the best fit between salience strength and beat strength.[7]

Figure 1.8 displays the metrical grid and grouping structure for the first part of "God Save the King." (Dots for the eighth-note level are shown only where eighth notes appear.) Observe that beats are present under the dotted quarter notes and the dotted half note even where there is no pitch attack. This is part of how duration is measured. The tactus for this tune at a normal tempo is at the quarter-note level.[8]

The listener infers this grid by two principles: length and parallelism. The repeated C's in bar 1 and E's in bar 3 effectively extend their durations to half notes. Similarly, the dotted quarter notes in bars 2 and 4 are longer than the durations of their adjacent notes. Relative length increases salience, so these beats are heard as relatively strong. Because these strong beats are three smaller beats apart, triple meter results. The motivic repetition between bars 1–2 and 3–4 increases this assignment because parallel units generally receive parallel structures.

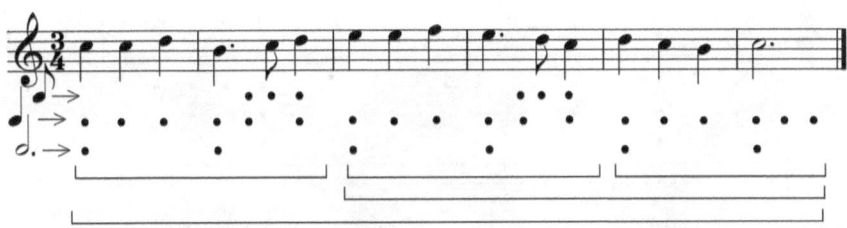

FIGURE 1.8 Metrical grid and grouping structure for the beginning of "God Save the King."

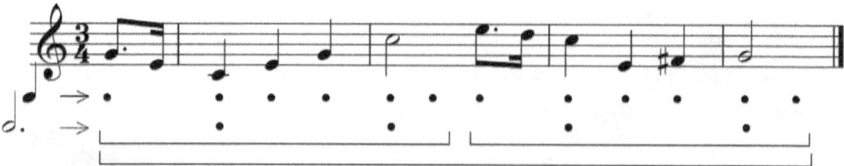

FIGURE 1.9 Metrical grid and grouping structure for the beginning of the "Star-Spangled Banner."

The grouping structure in figure 1.8 falls into three two-bar units, with the third unit an extension of the second. The meter and grouping are in phase in the sense that, at the dotted-half-note level, the time spans from one beat to the next align with the beginnings of each grouping unit. The groupings all begin on downbeats.

In "The Star-Spangled Banner," in contrast, each grouping unit begins on an upbeat or anacrusis, as shown in figure 1.9. (For visual convenience, dots are omitted for beats smaller than the quarter-note level.) In the figure, the meter and grouping are slightly out of phase.

The beginning of "La Marseillaise" in figure 1.10 illustrates another basic feature of musical rhythm. The events on the first beats of bars 1 and 2 are strong by virtue of relative length and, in the second case, pitch height. But the A on the first beat of bar 3 is much less salient than the F on the second beat, which is both long and high. The surrounding periodicity is well established, so the grid wins, and the salient F appears on a weak beat. The musical term for this is syncopation.

A conflict between salient events and metrical grid is common, more so in some styles than others. It is vital to rhythmic energy and tension.

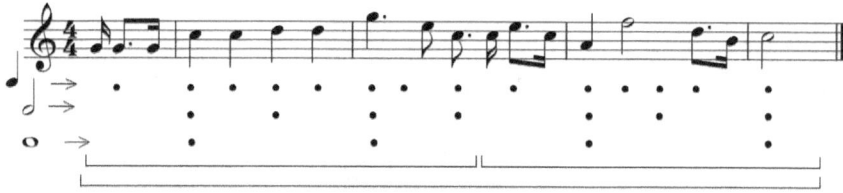

FIGURE 1.10 Metrical grid and grouping structure for the beginning of "La Marseillaise."

Usually, the inertia of the grid prevails, as in bar 3 of figure 1.10. But if there are enough aural cues that contradict the prevailing meter, the sense of syncopation gives way to metrical ambiguity and uncertainty. Metrical levels may fade and reemerge as part of the rhythmic experience. If salient events are highly irregular, the grid disappears altogether.

All the rhythmic features described in this chapter will play a role as we turn to the sounds of poetry viewed as music.

2

Prosodic Rhythm

2.1 INTRODUCTION

This chapter develops a theory of the rhythmic structure of verse without reference to traditional poetic scansion and its terminology.[1] There are two reasons for this approach. First and foremost, my intent is to explore what can be learned by treating poetry as music, and traditional scansion is basically irrelevant to music theory. Second, conceptual issues regarding traditional scansion are better addressed after the musical approach has been developed. Chapter 3 will turn to these issues.

The exposition begins with summaries of the prosodic hierarchy and stress grid and moves on to the metrical grid and syllable durations. I shall state rules periodically to summarize the discussion. They do not aspire to computational status but are precise enough to elucidate each step of an analysis.

To keep the scope of this enterprise within manageable bounds, all the poetic examples are in English. It suffices to begin with analyzing only a few lines from Shakespeare and Robert Frost. Later chapters treat a wider range of poetry.

A review of empirical support for the proposed poetic analyses in the form of authoritative spoken readings is deferred to chapter 6, after the rhythmic and contour components of the theory have been fully presented. But the reader is invited at any point to consult the readings, for which links are given in appendix D, and compare them to analyses in this and succeeding chapters.

2.2 THE PROSODIC HIERARCHY

The standard linguistic groupings of syntactic units are familiar: noun phrase, verb phrase, prepositional phrase, subordinate clause, and so forth. Less familiar is the prosodic hierarchy, a grouping of spoken sound units advanced by generative phonologists in the 1980s (Selkirk 1984; Nespor & Vogel 1986; Hayes 1989). This innovation was important not only on its own merits but also because it brought into mainstream linguistics a kind of hierarchy that relates to but is independent of syntax. It represents not grammatical constituency but a segmentation of perceived phonological units. They are analogous to phrases and subphrases in music.

The smallest levels of the prosodic hierarchy are the syllable and the word, which are determined lexically. A syllable breaks down into phonemes, but in the present context the atom of analysis is the syllable. Words fall into two categories: content words, which play a major semantic role and refer to some object, action, concept, or quality, and function words, which chiefly carry a syntactic role. A function word is pronounced as if it were part of a content word; that is, it is a clitic to the content word.

Consider the first two lines of Shakespeare's Sonnet 29:

When in disgrace with fortune and men's eyes,
I all alone beweep my outcast state,[2]

The clitic words are "in," "with," "and," "I," "all," and "my." Thus, "in disgrace" sounds as one word, with "disgrace" as clitic host. The combination of content words and function words joined to content words yields the second level of the prosodic hierarchy, the clitic group. The third level is a grouping of clitic groups called the phonological phrase—for example, "When in disgrace." Above that is the intonational phrase, which conveys the melody of speech. Each of the two lines in the sonnet is an intonational phrase. The largest level of the prosodic hierarchy is the utterance, which

```
[C When] [C in disgrace] [C with fortune] [C and men's] [C eyes] [C I all alone] [C beweep] [C my outcast] [C state]
[P When    in disgrace] [P with fortune    and men's    eyes] [P I all alone] [P beweep    my outcast    state]
[I When    in disgrace    with fortune    and men's    eyes] [I  I all alone    beweep    my outcast    state]
[U When    in disgrace    with fortune    and men's    eyes     I all alone    beweep    my outcast    state]
```

FIGURE 2.1 The prosodic hierarchy for the first two lines of Shakespeare's Sonnet 29.

corresponds to a sentence. The two Shakespeare lines together form an utterance (leaving out its extension beginning in the third line). A prosodic unit can repeat at successive layers. For example, an intonational phrase can also be an utterance.

Figure 2.1 arranges the prosodic hierarchy for the two Shakespeare lines into a single format. To save clutter and space, syllables and words go unmarked in the figure. Larger levels are bracketed, with clitic groups marked **C**, phonological phrases **P**, intonational phrases **I**, and the utterance level **U**.

The clitic and utterance levels are clearly defined, but a determination of the phonological and intonational levels can be ambiguous. In this case, it is generally preferable to observe the syntactic parsing. Each of the two Shakespeare lines has two phonological groups: in the first line, "When in disgrace" and "with fortune and men's eyes;" in the second line, "I all alone" and "beweep my outcast state."[3] These then combine into one intonational group per line.

Levels larger than the utterance belong to discourse structure and verse form. Their groupings rely on symmetry and parallelism. Symmetry divides a section into two or three parts of equal or almost equal length. Parallelism in music tends to be strongest at the beginnings of phrases, which often start with identical or similar motives. The same holds for alliterative poetry. In much poetry, however, parallelism is strongest at line endings because of the force of rhyme. This chapter deals only with levels from the syllable to the utterance within the confines of the poetic line.

This overview of prosodic grouping can be summarized as a set of steps for deriving the prosodic hierarchy in any given instance. In contrast, *A Generative Theory of Tonal Music* (*GTTM*) states its preference rules from the perspective of the listener. This could be done here, too, but a structure-building perspective better reflects the way the theory is framed at the outset (see figure 1.2).

Procedure for assigning the prosodic hierarchy

Let **S** = syllable, **W** = word, **C** = clitic group, **P** = phonological group, **I** = intonational phrase, and **U** = utterance. Then:

(1) Assign **S** and **W** lexically.
(2) Categorize **W**'s as either content or function words.
(3) Group function words with adjacent content words in their syntactic unit.
(4) Assign **C** to content words and to clitic groupings of function and content words.
(5) Assign **P** to a grouping of adjacent **C**'s that form a syntactic unit.
(6) Assign **I** to a grouping of adjacent **P**'s that form a syntactic unit.
(7) Assign **U** to a grouping of adjacent **I**'s that form a sentence.
(8) The grouping of **C**, **P**, or **I** can repeat at the next larger level.

2.3 THE STRESS GRID

Chapter 1.2 referred to salient events in music—events that are loud, long, high, or otherwise perceptually prominent in their immediate context. These factors are diverse and difficult to organize into a systematic account beyond their role in shaping metrical perception. In most music, salience is a secondary feature compared to the more highly organized components of tonal space, harmonic syntax, event hierarchies, and stylistic schemas. It has not been viewed as a musical component per se.

The comparable concept in linguistics is syllabic stress. It acts in a more orderly fashion than in music, perhaps because language does not have a multidimensional pitch structure and compensates through this mode of organization. Stress is a composite perception caused by three interacting acoustic features: a syllable is experienced as relatively stressed if it is louder, longer, or higher than adjacent syllables. One might suppose that loudness is the main factor, but it has been experimentally demonstrated that the stronger factors are pitch height and duration (Fry 1958; van Heuven & Turk 2020).

Stress in a polysyllabic word is determined lexically. One says "dis-gráce" and "fór-tune," not "dís-grace" and "for-túne." Figure 2.2 displays these distinctions with a grid notation. Each syllable receives an x, and the stronger

```
         x              x
   x     x         x    x        FIGURE 2.2  The grid notation for stress applied to
   dis-grace       for-tune      polysyllabic words.
```

```
       x              x                 x                 x            x
       x         x  x    x        x  x     x         x    x            x
   [C When]     [C in dis-grace]  [C with for-tune]  [C and men's]   [C eyes]
```

FIGURE 2.3 Stress assignments for the clitic groups in the first line of Sonnet 29.

syllable receives two x's. Stress is represented hierarchically: if a syllable is strong at one level, it has an x at the next larger level.[4]

This representation applies up the prosodic hierarchy from the syllable to the intonational phrase. Figure 2.3 lists the clitic groups for the first line of the sonnet. Function words are unstressed and receive one x: "in," "with," and "and." If a content word is monosyllabic, it receives two x's at the clitic level: "When," "men's," and "eyes." If it is polysyllabic, its stressed syllable (or syllables) receives two x's at this level: "-grace" and "for-" (as in figure 2.2).

A factor called nuclear stress enters at higher prosodic levels in English and many other languages: the strongest syllable of the last word of a prosodic unit receives extra stress, cyclically from level to level (Chomsky and Halle 1968). Figure 2.4a shows the phonological grouping for the opening

```
(a)
                          x                                    x
            x             x                  x           x     x
            x   x  x      x             x    x   x   x   x     x
            [P When in dis-grace]  [P with for-tune and men's eyes]

(b)
                                                               x
                          x                                    x
            x             x                  x           x     x
            x   x  x      x             x    x   x   x   x     x
            [I When in dis-grace with for-tune and men's eyes]
```

FIGURE 2.4 Stress assignments for the (a) phonological level and (b) the intonational level in the first line of Sonnet 29.

PROSODIC RHYTHM | 15

```
                                              x                                      x
              x                               x         x                            x
  x           x           x           x       x         x          x         x       x
  x         x x x       x x x        x x      x       x x x x     x x      x x x     x
[C When] [C in disgrace] [C with fortune] [C and men's] [C eyes] [C I all alone] [C beweep] [C my outcast] [C state]
[P When]  in disgrace] [P with fortune]    and men's   eyes] [P I all alone] [P beweep]    my outcast    state]
[I When]  in disgrace    with fortune      and men's   eyes] [I I all alone    beweep      my outcast    state]
```

FIGURE 2.5 The prosodic hierarchy and stress grid for the first two lines of Sonnet 29.

line of the sonnet. In the first grouping, "-grace" is the strongest syllable of the last word and receives a third x. Similarly, "eyes" receives a third x. Figure 2.4b applies nuclear stress at the intonational level: "eyes" receives a fourth x.[5] This factor could also be invoked for a fifth x at the utterance level, but it is difficult to distinguish five levels of stress. This theory restricts itself to four stress levels.[6]

Figure 2.5 combines these stress assignments with the prosodic hierarchy from figure 2.1, omitting the utterance level and including the sonnet's second line.

Nuclear stress can be overridden by either of two factors: focus and evenness. To illustrate them, consider the first couplet of Robert Frost's short poem "Nothing Gold Can Stay"[7]:

Nature's first green is gold,
Her hardest hue to hold.

Figure 2.6 supplies the prosodic hierarchy and stress analysis. At the lowest level, each syllable receives an x. At the clitic level, the first syllables in

```
                              x                                x
                    x         x                       x        x
  x         x       x         x          x            x        x
  x x       x       x        x x       x x x          x       x x
[C Nature's] [C first] [C green] [C is gold] [C Her hardest] [C hue] [C to hold]
[P Nature's] [P first]  green]  [P is gold] [P Her hardest]   hue]  [P to hold]
[I Nature's]   first    green    is gold]  [I Her hardest]   hue     to hold]
[U Nature's    first    green    is gold    Her hardest      hue     to hold]
```

FIGURE 2.6 Prosodic and stress analysis of the first couplet of Frost's "Nothing Gold Can Stay."

the polysyllabic words "Nature's" and "hardest" receive second x's, as do the clitic hosts "gold" and "hold." At the phonological level, nuclear stress adds third x's to "green" and "hue" and, at the intonational level, fourth x's to "gold" and "hold."[8]

Focus refers to a special prominence on a syllable to bring out a semantic nuance or contrastive emphasis. One ordinarily says "first gréen," observing nuclear stress. If, however, one says, "fírst green," the emphasis implies that nature's second green is not gold. This is an example of focus potentially modifying a stress grid.

Evenness encourages a regular temporal distribution of stresses by moving the first of two proximate stresses in a word or phonological phrase to the next strongest syllable to the left.[9] For instance, one says "con-sóle" but "cón-so-lá-tion," moving the stress on "so-" back to "con-" to avoid adjacent stresses on "so-" and "la-." In the Frost poem, one would normally say "Her hardest húe," but in the context of the entire line, the stresses on "hue" and "hold" are close: "Her hardest húe to hóld." Consequently, the first stress may optionally move to the left, giving three x's to "hard-" instead of "hue": "Her hárd-est hue to hóld." The evenness principle reflects a disposition toward the periodicities of metrical organization.

The following statement summarize this discussion of stress.

Procedure for assigning syllabic stress

Let the number of x's assigned to a syllable represent the syllable's relative stress. There are no more than four stress levels. To build a stress grid:

(1) Assign an x to each syllable.
(2) Add an x (or more, as required) to the lexically stressed syllable(s) in a polysyllabic word.
(3) Nuclear stress:
 (a) Add an x to a monosyllabic word if it is the rightmost content word in **C**.
 (b) Add a third x to the syllable with the most x's in the rightmost content word in **P**.
 (c) Add a fourth x to the syllable with the most x's in the rightmost content word in **I**.

(4) Nuclear stress can optionally be overridden by:
   (a) Focus: stress a normally unstressed syllable to convey a nuance or contrastive emphasis.
   (b) Evenness: distribute stresses to approximate periodicity.

2.4 THE METRICAL GRID

As discussed in chapter 1 with respect to music, a metrical grid represents superimposed periodicities that measure time at multiple levels. A particular metrical grid is heard with respect to a particular sequence of musical events by inferring the one that best aligns strong beats with salient events. Salient events that do not align with the grid are heard as syncopations. If salient events are highly irregular, the inference of a metrical grid may weaken or disappear. These features also apply to poetry.

Syllabic and phrasal durations and stresses in ordinary speech are typically too variable to induce metrical perception (Patel 2008). Yet it would be misleading to claim that beats and durations in music are invariable. Clock precision is impossible in human performance, and slight deviations from isochrony are indispensable to musical expression. Like meter itself, temporal precision is a cognitive construct, a matter of quantization. While durations and stresses in verse are usually more variable than in music, many poetic idioms, from nursery rhymes to sophisticated traditions, exhibit considerable regularity (Oehrle 1989). As in music, these idioms approach periodicity as a framework against which expressive deviations take place. At the opposite extreme, durations and stresses are quite irregular in musical styles such as Gregorian chant, Japanese shakuhachi, the alap of North Indian raga, opera recitative, and some contemporary art music. In these idioms, a metrical grid is marginal or not inferred at all. In short, there is a gamut from regularity to irregularity in both music and language. The differences between musical and poetic meter are those of degree rather than kind.

A related issue concerning periodicity is how flexible distances between beats can be without leading to perceptual confusions of beat structure. In general, extreme changes, such as a sudden and large increase in the distance from one beat to the next at a given level, confound beat categorization. Changes in distances between beats are more easily accommodated

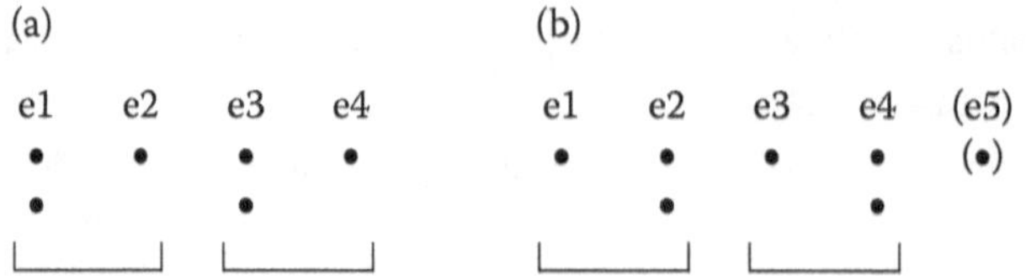

```
(a)                          (b)

e1    e2    e3    e4         e1    e2    e3    e4   (e5)
 •     •     •     •          •     •     •     •    (•)

 •           •                       •           •
 └─────┘ └─────┘             └─────┘ └─────┘
```

FIGURE 2.7 Interaction of grouping and meter: (a) in phase, (b) out of phase.

if they are part of a gradual rate of change, as in a musical accelerando or ritardando.

Meter interacts with grouping the same way in music and poetry. Spans from beat to beat can be in or out of phase with grouping spans. Figure 2.7 illustrates this abstractly with grouping brackets (whether musical or prosodic) beneath a sequence of four events (notes or syllables). In figure 2.7a, the metrical and grouping spans are in phase in the sense that the span from one strong beat to the next aligns with the grouping. That is, the metrical span from e1 to e3 coincides with the grouping span from e1 to e3. The second and fourth events are afterbeats within that grouping. In figure 2.7b, the spans are out of phase in the sense that the span from one strong beat to the next does not align with the grouping. That is, the metrical span from e2 to e4 does not coincide with the grouping spans, which are from e1 to e3 and from e3 to an anticipated e5. Thus, the first and third events are upbeats within the grouping structure.

Like stress grids, metrical grids in poetry align with syllables. A second, vertical constraint shared by stress and metrical grids is that a strong stress or beat at one level is also a stress or beat at the next larger level. It follows that a gap in the strength of a stress or beat cannot arise from one level to the next. For instance, if a stress or beat has three levels of strength, it cannot be a beat at levels 1 and 3 but not at level 2.

There are two significant differences, however, in well-formedness between the two grid types (aside from the trivial differences that here, metrical grids are inverted for visual convenience and stress grids are represented by x's and meter by dots). Both concern horizontal constraints. First, metrical grids specify cognitively equal time spans from beat to beat at the tactus level (the perceptually most prominent level, usually at a rate between seventy and one hundred beats per minute; see chapter 1.2) and at smaller levels. This principle is somewhat relaxed at levels larger than the

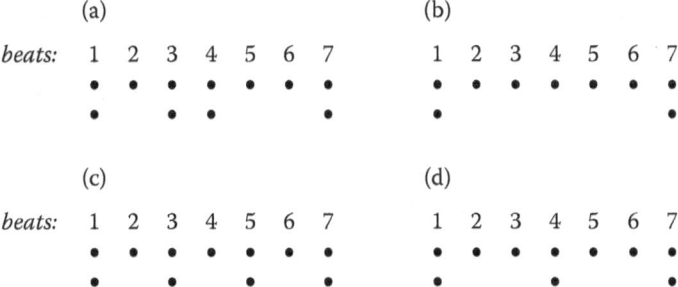

FIGURE 2.8 Permissible metrical patterns: (a) and (b) are ill-formed; (c) and (d) are well-formed.

tactus.[10] Stress grids, however, do not specify equal time spans. Linguists and poets refer to syllables as qualitatively long or short, but this distinction lacks temporal precision.

Second, in a metrical grid there must be either one or two weak beats between strong beats in a level. To illustrate, figure 2.8 gives a row of seven beats. In figure 2.8a, the adjacent strong beats 3 and 4 make the grid ill-formed. At the opposite extreme, the grid in figure 2.8b is not permitted because beats 2 through 6 are all weak. It must fill out as shown in figure 2.8c, in which beats 3 and 5 are strong, or as in figure 2.8d, in which beat 4 is strong.

There is no such restriction on stress grids. The beginning of the second line of Sonnet 29, shown in figure 2.9a, offers one example of consecutive

```
(a)                (b)
     x                            x
     x                            x
 x x x x          x  x x x x  x
 I all alone      But only so an hour

(c)                (d)
     x                            x
 x   x            x               x
 x x x x          x  x x x x  x
 I all alone      But only so an hour
```

FIGURE 2.9 Stress grids with more than two weak beats in a row: (a) Sonnet 29, line 2; (b) "Nothing Gold Can Stay," line 4; (c) focus on "I," giving it an extra x; (d) an extra x at "on-," by treating "only" as a content word.

weak syllables. The fourth line of the Frost lyric in figure 2.9b is another. In both cases, there is a tendency to fill in the stress gap either by focus, as at "I" in figure 2.9c, or by putting emphasis on a semi-function word, as at "only" in figure 2.9d. These choices reflect a propensity to approach a musical condition, but they are not obligatory. Accentual languages such as English do not favor long stretches of unstressed syllables.

The following summarizes this discussion of metrical well-formedness in verse.

Metrical well-formedness conditions

Definition: A beat is strong at any level L if it is also a beat at L + 1; if it is not a beat at L + 1, it is a weak beat at level L.

(1) Every syllable receives a beat.
(2) A beat at any level L is also a beat at L − 1 (except at the terminal level).
(3) At the tactus level, time spans between beats are equal.
(4) At sub-tactus level L, beats are equally spaced between beats at L + 1.
(5) Strong beats are spaced two or three beats apart within a level.

The absence of rules (3) to (5) in stress grids gives them greater horizontal flexibility compared to their metrical counterparts. As in music, a given poetic idiom has at its disposal a limited repertory of metrical grids. To hear a poem as metrical is to match its variable stress grid against an available periodic metrical grid that best fits it.

The basic strategy is to align strong stresses with tactus beats and place lesser stresses in the spaces between these beats. But it is rare for stress and beat to coincide at all levels. For a first approximation, the optimal fit is the one with the fewest mismatches between the two grids. However, mismatches at some levels matter more than at others. A mismatch at the tactus is more critical than at adjacent smaller or larger metrical levels, and mismatches at still smaller or larger levels are immaterial. A mismatch within a phonological phrase may be awkward, but a mismatch within a clitic group or polysyllabic word is unacceptable or nearly so. Thus, mismatches must be weighted in relation to the tactus, phonological and clitic groups, and word structure.

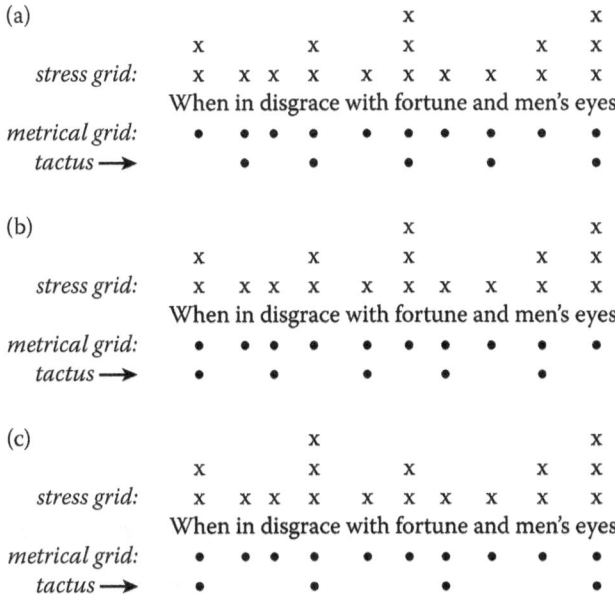

FIGURE 2.10 Three possible alignments of stress and metrical grids for the first line of Sonnet 29: (a) a weak-strong duple metrical pattern, (b) a strong-weak duple metrical pattern, (c) a triple metrical pattern.

Figure 2.10 illustrates this with three metrical grids for the first line of Sonnet 29. Three stress levels and two metrical levels are shown. Mismatches are counted where a stressed syllable appears on a relatively weak beat. The opposite, where an unstressed syllable appears on a strong beat, is perceptually less noticeable and is not counted. Figure 2.10a shows a weak-strong duple meter, with mismatches at "When" and "men's." Figure 2.10b shows the opposite, a strong-weak duple pattern. Here, there are three mismatches: within the polysyllabic words "disgrace" and "fortune" and at "eyes." This alternative is inadmissible. The triple meter in figure 2.10c gives a good match for "When in disgrace," but it fails badly at "fortune." Therefore figure 2.10a wins.

Figure 2.11 provides a similar analysis for the Frost couplet.[11] In figure 2.11a, there is an excellent fit except for the mismatch at "Nature's." In figure 2.11b and 2.11c, there are several mismatches. Therefore figure 2.11a wins.

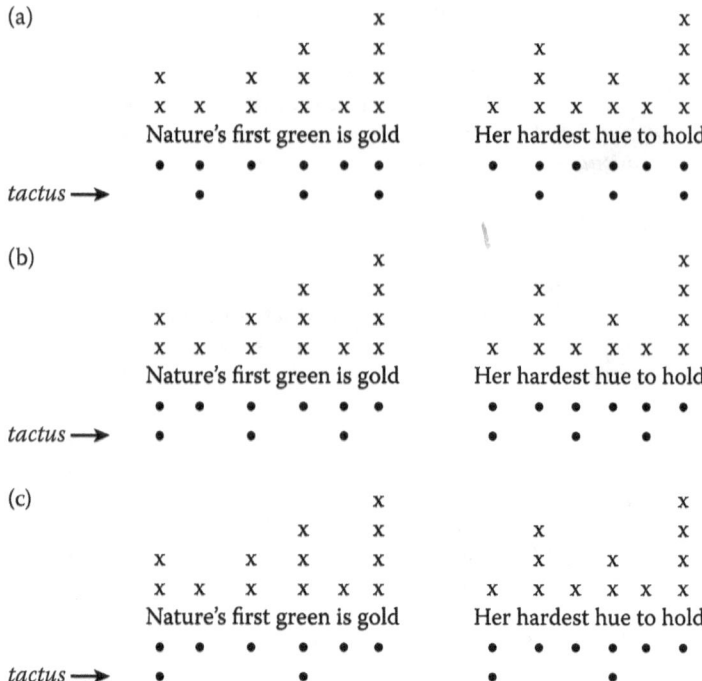

FIGURE 2.11 Three possible alignments of stress and metrical grids for the Frost couplet, using the same metrical patterns as in figure 2.10.

2.5 METER AND DURATION

Missing from the account thus far is the role of duration, a crucial factor neglected by both traditional and generative treatments of prosody. Metrical grids measure and represent cognitively equal time spans from beat to beat, but they do not show syllabic length. For this, musical notation is needed. To begin, figure 2.12 notates the syllable sequences of the Shakespeare and Frost lines by consecutive eighth notes, with a tempo of a quarter note equaling approximately eighty-five beats per minute. The time signature with an eighth note upbeat corresponds to figure 2.10a and 2.11a. No metrical level above the quarter note is assigned yet. It may be useful to read these lines with an imagined accent on the downbeat of each measure to bring out the minimal metrical structure represented here. Stress-metrical mismatches occur at "When ín," "and men's," and "Na-ture's."

PROSODIC RHYTHM | 23

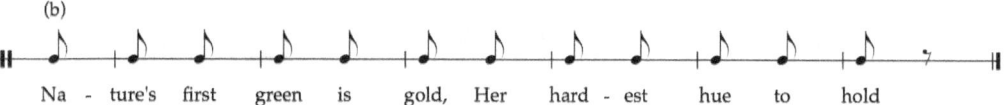

FIGURE 2.12 The opening lines of Sonnet 29 and "Nothing Gold Can Stay" notated in 2/8 meter.

Leaving these mismatches aside for the moment, no one would speak these lines in such a metronomic fashion. We say them in syllables of varying length. The steady tactus provides the framework within which local rhythmic variety takes place, so a durational derivation starts by aligning stressed syllables with tactus beats. Figure 2.13 does this by placing quarter notes under syllables with at least two x's in the Shakespeare and three in the Frost. The parenthesized x's indicate options with respect to focus and evenness.

Sub-tactus levels divide into two or three equal parts, as stipulated by metrical well-formedness rules 4 and 5. Figure 2.1a–c displays the three possible durational patterns if there is one weakly stressed syllable between

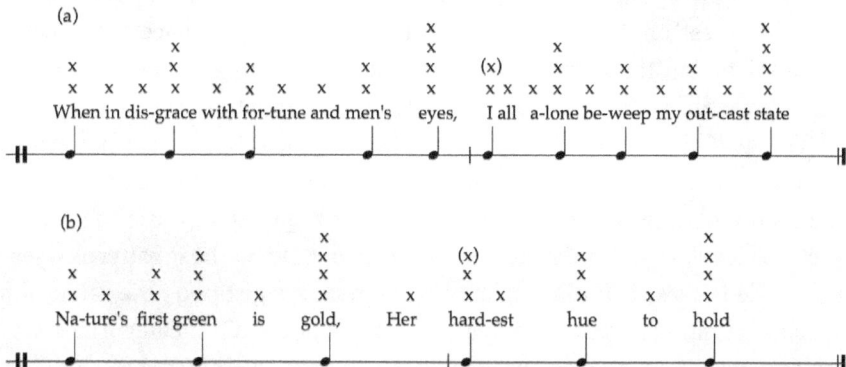

FIGURE 2.13 Alignment of primary stressed syllables with tactus beats in the Shakespeare and Frost lines.

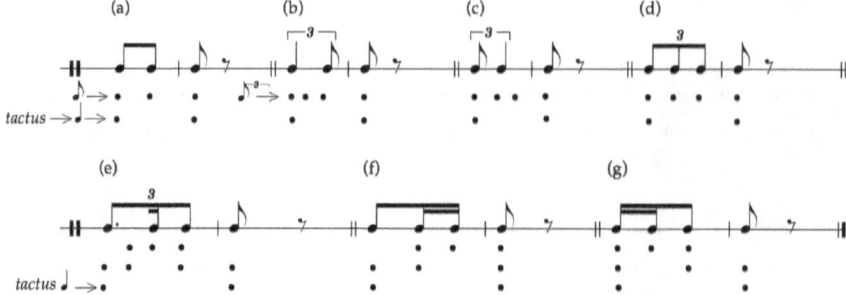

FIGURE 2.14 Repertory of durational patterns at sub-tactus metrical levels: (a–c) rhythms with one weak syllable between tactus beats, (d–g) rhythms with two weak syllables between tactus beats.

tactus beats: the duple-beat case of consecutive eighth notes in figure 2.14a, the triple-beat options of a quarter note plus an eighth note in figure 2.14b, and an eighth plus a quarter in figure 2.14c. Figure 2.14d–g shows candidates if there are two weak syllables between tactus beats: in triple meter, consecutive triplet eighth notes in figure 2.14d and a dotted eighth plus sixteenth and eighth in figure 2.14e; in duple meter, an eighth plus two sixteenths in figure 2.14f, and two sixteenths plus an eighth in figure 2.14g.

Two less common variants in duple meter are also worth mentioning: a dotted quarter plus a sixteenth and a string of four sixteenth notes. The former is effectively a nuance, in duple instead of triple time, of the rhythm in figure 2.14b. The latter can arise when there is a sequence of unstressed syllables spoken quickly. It is possible to invoke still other rhythmic divisions in quest of fine-grain durational nuances, for instance, employing quintuplets, but that would undermine the quantization inherent in hearing sub-tactus rhythms in duple or triple metrical patterns.

The grids in figure 2.14b–d show that a typical triple-beat pattern is simpler than a duple-beat pattern if the latter includes both eighth and sixteenth notes, as in figure 2.14f–g. The former requires only one sub-tactus metrical level, whereas the latter requires two. In triple-beat patterns—setting aside the less common figure 2.14e—there are just two note values for syllable durations: quarter notes and eighth notes. One categorizes syllables accordingly as long or short, even if, in a given instance, the long syllable is slightly longer or shorter than twice the duration of the short syllable. This is one reason why many poems are heard in triple meter.

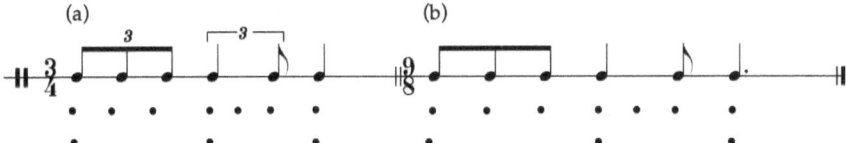

FIGURE 2.15 Conversion of triplets (a) into triple time (b).

A notational detail: If there is an ongoing triplet pattern, it is expedient to notate it in a 3/8 time signature or its multiples (6/8, 9/8, 12/8). For example, figure 2.15a maps into figure 2.15b. They have identical metrical grids.

The cases listed in figure 2.14 complete the main repertory of sub-tactus rhythms under the conditions described. That the repertory is small is an advantage in deriving normative rhythms for poetic lines.[12]

The metrical well-formedness conditions do not prohibit a shift between duple- and triple-beat patterns within a given metrical sub-tactus level if the tactus itself remains constant. For example, a poetic line might begin with a duple division of the tactus and move to a triple division. Rhythmic suppleness of this sort is common in music, and, as will be seen, in poetry as well.

In deriving metrical and durational assignments at sub-tactus levels, an initial constraint is to avoid mismatches between stress and beat within polysyllabic words and clitic groups. The first syllable of "Nature's" is stressed, so it should be on a stronger beat than the second syllable. In the clitic group "in disgrace," "in" as well as "dis-" are less stressed than "-grace," so "-grace" should be on a stronger beat than the previous two syllables. It is essential to achieve congruence between stress and beat at these prosodic levels.

Two perceptual principles, length and proximity, guide sub-tactus durational derivations. As noted in section 2.3, length and pitch height are the main acoustic factors in projecting degrees of stress. Thus, the assignment of greater length to stressed than unstressed syllables is preferred. As for proximity, objects that are close together tend to group together; boundaries tend to appear between nonproximate objects. (This is a Gestalt law that shapes visual as well as auditory perception.) To project the prosodic hierarchy, distances are generally larger between rather than

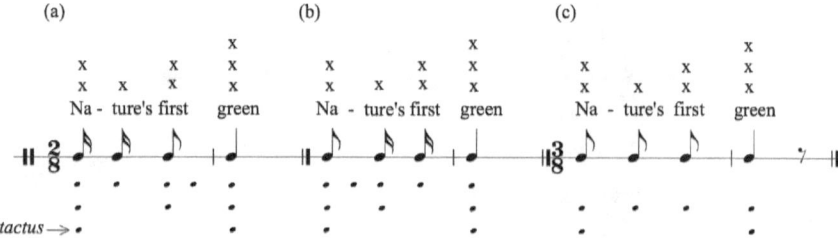

FIGURE 2.16 Possible metrical-durational realizations of "Nature's first green."

within prosodic units—the larger the prosodic boundary, the greater the inter-onset distance.

Let us apply these factors to the Frost couplet. The first two stressed syllables on tactus beats are "Na-" and "green" (see figure 2.13b), with two weaker syllables between. Figure 2.16 gives the three available durational realizations. The solution in figure 2.16a violates the proximity principle: "first green" is a phonological group, yet there is a greater distance between "first" and "green" than between "-ture's" and "first." Proximity is violated more seriously in figure 2.16b: "Nature's" is a word, yet there is a greater distance between "Na-" and "ture's" than between "-ture's" and "first." This leaves figure 2.16c as the preferred option because it evens out the durations in 3/8 time to neutralize the proximity factor.

Metrical periodicity continues by inertia unless contrary evidence intervenes. The rhythm of the Frost couplet remains in 3/8 meter. In figure 2.17a, downbeat quarter notes on "Na-," "green," "gold," "hue," and "hold" bring out the stresses on those syllables, leaving eighth notes on weak beats for the less stressed syllables "first," "is," "Her," and "to." These durational patterns also reinforce, by proximity, the clitic groups "is gold," "Her hardest," and "to hold." However, "hardest" is assigned an eighth plus a quarter note rather than the reverse, so that "-est" is closer to "hard-" than to "hue," again by the proximity principle. The moderate stress on "hard-" is projected not by length but by pitch height and by being on a stronger beat. But there is also another factor at play: "hard-" is a relatively long syllable to pronounce because of its two end consonants. In a case such as this, a duple treatment is optional to lengthen the duration of the short syllable. Figure 2.17b realizes "hardest" as two eighth notes spread equally throughout the measure.[13]

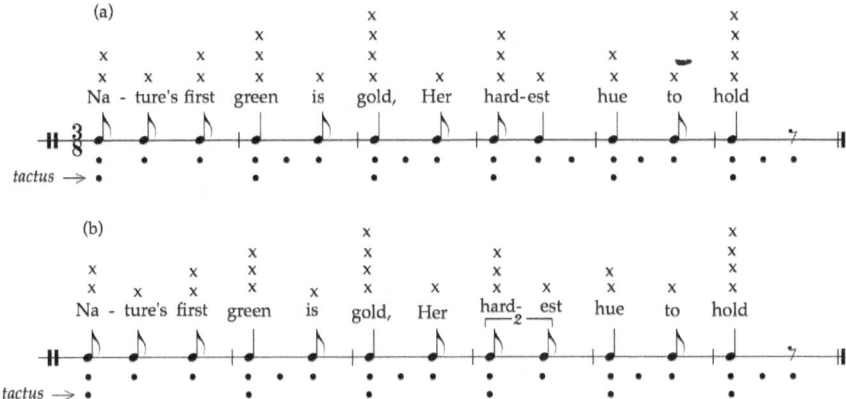

FIGURE 2.17 Metrical-durational realization in 3/8 of the first couplet of "Nothing Gold Can Stay": (a) a straightforward realization, (b) substitution of duple rhythm for "hardest."

Figure 2.18 presents a durational derivation of the two lines from Sonnet 29. In figure 2.18a, if we assume triple meter, the stressed syllables "When," "-grace," "for-," "men's," and "eyes" appear on downbeats. The remaining one-x syllables fill in the rhythm with eighth notes. Because the adjacent syllables "men's" and "eyes" are on downbeats, however, "men's"

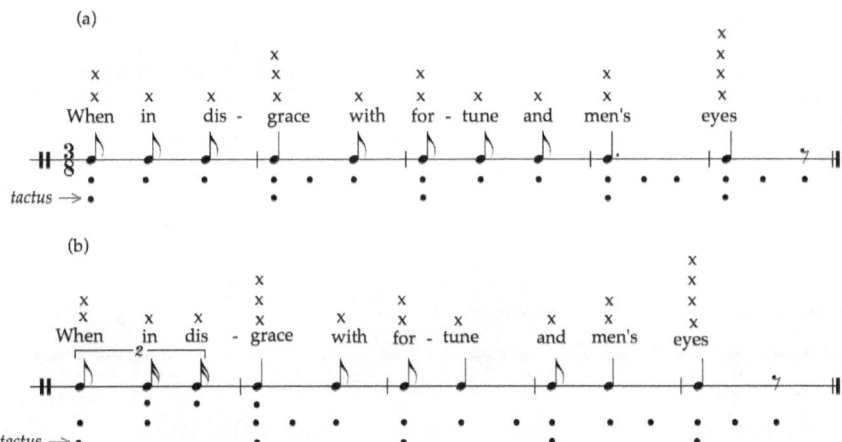

FIGURE 2.18 Metrical-durational realization of the first line of Sonnet 29: (a) initial version, (b) revised version.

is given an excessively long duration. The length of a dotted quarter note normally takes place at the end of a line, articulating its closure, or, if it takes place in the middle of a line, at a phonological or intonational prosodic boundary. But "men's eyes" occurs within a phonological phrase. The solution, shown in figure 2.18b, is to place "and" on the downbeat and project stress on "men's" not by its metrical strength but by its resulting quarter-note duration.

Figure 2.18b also offers an alternative realization for the beginning of the line. "When" and "in disgrace" are clitic groups, so lengthening "When" and shortening "in dis-" brings out the clitic boundary between "When" and "in." This is accomplished by rewriting these syllables in duple time, an eighth plus two sixteenths. This option comes at the price of greater complexity, however, by virtue of the change in sub-tactus metrical division.

Normative versions of the meter and duration of the Frost and Shakespeare lines are now achieved, but the analyses lack supra-tactus levels. Again, the procedure is to find the best fit between the stress grid and an available metrical grid. Consider the Frost poem. There are three main stresses per line, so the first option is a triple supra-tactus pattern per line, converting the 3/8 of figure 2.17 into 9/8. Figure 2.19a does this, omitting the metrical grid at levels below the tactus to avoid visual clutter. Conventional beat numbers appear beneath to supplement the grid.

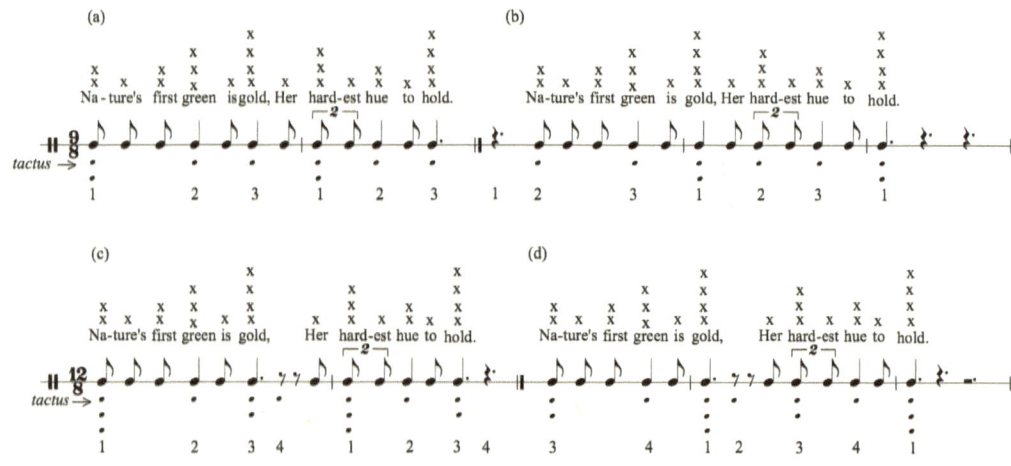

FIGURE 2.19 Supra-tactus levels in "Nothing Gold Can Stay." (a) and (b) are in triple meter; (c) and (d) are in duple meter at supra-tactus levels. In (a) and (c), grouping and meter are in phase; in (b) and (d), grouping and meter are out of phase, but the fit between stress and metrical grid is better.

The intonational grouping and metrical grid are in phase, but the match at "gold" and "hold" is not optimal. A good match is achieved in figure 2.19b, but now the grouping and meter are quite out of phase, with two upbeats for each intonational phrase. In both figure 2.19a and figure 2.19b the second line proceeds without pause from the first, running the two lines together.

Figure 2.19c–d alleviates these shortcomings by inserting a silent fourth beat at the end of each line, converting 9/8 into 12/8. This move is suggested by the fact that each line of the second quatrain is a short full sentence, and pauses are normal at the end of sentences. (There is also a nonprosodic reason for doing this: the theme of the poem is universal decline, and with the pauses each line falls into silence.) Of these two supra-tactus interpretations, figure 2.19c keeps the grouping and meter in phase at the cost of placing the heavily stressed "gold" and "hold" on only moderately strong beats. In contrast, figure 2.19d realizes a fine fit between stress and beat, but the grouping and meter are out of phase. Either option is viable. The decision is moot in any case because supra-tactus beats have weak perceptual force as a result of the long distances between them. Dividing each 12/8 bar into two 6/8 bars would circumvent this issue.

Note that, in both cases, a third x on "hue" shifts left to "hard-" in accordance with the evenness principle. In the triple meter of figure 2.19a or 2.19b, however, this step would not achieve greater evenness.

Supra-tactus levels for the Shakespeare sonnet are ambiguous because each line has five main stresses. Larger metrical time spans cannot be periodic from one line to the next unless a silent sixth beat is inserted at the line end, but this solution does not always suit the intricate syntax of the sonnet's flow. Thus, any supra-tactus metrical level is likely to be semiperiodic, in tactus time spans of either 2 + 3 or 3 + 2. Therefore, one may feel that there is no useful supra-tactus level. Yet if one accepts changes in time signature to go with a 2 + 3 pattern, as in figure 2.20, the supra-tactus fit is excellent.

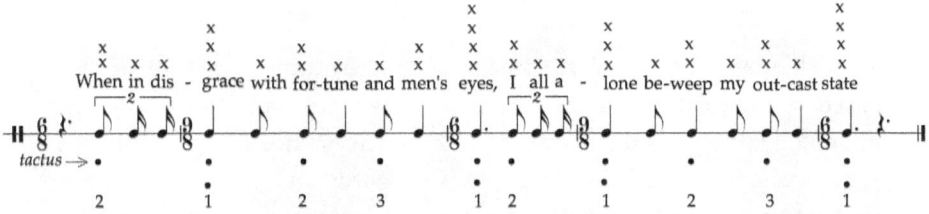

FIGURE 2.20 Supra-tactus analysis of the first two lines of Shakespeare's Sonnet 29.

The following summarizes this discussion of meter and duration.

Procedure for metrical and durational assignment

(1) Establish the tactus by finding the pattern of equidistant beats that causes the fewest mismatches with stressed syllables, preferably
   (a) At a tempo between seventy and one hundred beats per minute;
   (b) With one or two unstressed syllables between adjacent tactus syllables.
(2) An option is to insert a silent tactus beat at the end of an intonational phrase.
(3) Assign sub- and supra-tactus layers while observing the metrical well-formedness conditions.
(4) Of the available metrical grids, the preferred grid is one that yields the fewest syllabic mismatches with the associated stress grid.
(5) Congruence principle (corollary to [4]): Strongly avoid stress-meter mismatches within polysyllabic words and clitic groups.
(6) Proximity principle: assign longer durations between rather than within the constituents of the prosodic hierarchy.
(7) Length principle: assign greater length to syllables with stronger stress, unless doing so violates (6).
(8) Avoid long, tactus-length syllables within phonological phrases.
(9) An option is to move between duple and triple metrical subdivisions at a sub-tactus level in order to satisfy (6) better.
(10) An option is to assign greater duration to phonetically long syllables.

I do not claim that the metrical and durational readings realized by these rules are the only correct ones; they are normative readings, exemplars against which alternative readings can be evaluated. Chapter 6 will compare readings generated by the theory to recitations by poets and actors.

2.6 SUMMARY

This chapter proposed a treatment of the rhythmic structure of verse based on musical principles. It relied on two concepts from generative phonology: the prosodic hierarchy and the stress grid. The prosodic hierarchy assigns the perceived groupings of words and phrases. The stress grid designates the hierarchy of perceived syllabic salience. Stresses within polysyllabic words are assigned lexically. Function words have little stress and are clitic to adjacent, more stressed content words. At larger levels, strong stresses normally occur at or near the right edge of a group. Optional subsidiary factors focus on a particular word and the disposition toward a relatively even distribution of stresses.

A second type of grid represents the metrical hierarchy of strong and weak beats that the perceiver infers from a sequence of words if stresses are sufficiently regular. Unlike the stress grid, the metrical grid is periodic; it measures time. The first step in inferring a particular metrical grid from a pattern of syllabic stresses is to align the most prominent metrical level, the tactus, with strongly stressed syllables. Within that framework, smaller levels match the stress and metrical grids optimally, that is, with the fewest violations; mismatches within words and clitic groups are especially avoided.

The periodicity of the metrical grid enables the assignment of durations to syllables. Time spans between beats vary within limits but are perceived categorically. For example, "long" and "short" syllables can be realized by quarter and eighth notes. Usually, longer durations are assigned between rather than within the constituents of the prosodic hierarchy, and greater length is assigned to syllables with stronger stress. Silent tactus beats can optionally be inserted at the end of an intonational phrase. The rule system often permits more than one acceptable durational realization of a given poetic line.

The representation of poetic lines using time signatures and durational values makes a display of the metrical grid unnecessary because the grid is implied in the musical notation. In ensuing chapters, it will simplify the figures not to show the metrical grid except in special circumstances. Appendix B lists the main time signatures with their metrical grids and can be consulted as needed.

3

Historical Approaches to Prosodic Rhythm

3.1 INTRODUCTION

This chapter relates the theory set forth in chapter 2 to historical approaches to prosodic rhythm, beginning with the concepts of the poetic foot and poetic line that are standard in traditional scansion. Two musical treatments from the eighteenth and nineteenth centuries are then reviewed, after which the discussion turns to twentieth-century critiques of musical approaches.

3.2 THE POETIC FOOT

Traditional prosody relies on two concepts, the poetic foot and the poetic line. The term "iambic pentameter," for instance, refers to both: a poetic line with five feet, each with a weak-strong syllable pattern. Figure 3.1 gives

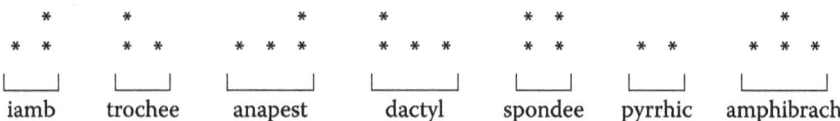

FIGURE 3.1 Repertory of poetic feet represented in grid notation.

the main repertory of foot categories translated into the grid notation of chapter 2. The grids are temporarily notated with asterisks instead of x's or dots to preserve neutrality about the status of "strong" and "weak" with respect to stress and metrical grids.

The core poetic feet are the iamb (weak-strong) and its reverse, the trochee (strong-weak). The anapest (weak-weak-strong) and the dactyl (strong-weak-weak) are trisyllabic versions of the iamb and the trochee, respectively. The spondee (strong-strong) and the pyrrhic (weak-weak) complete the possibilities for disyllabic feet. The amphibrach (weak-strong-weak) completes the possibilities for a trisyllabic pattern, assuming that the foot has only one strong syllable, but it is rarely invoked in the prosodic literature.

The ancient Greeks invented these terms as designations not for strong or weak syllables but for grouped patterns of syllable lengths, and they used them in conjunction with musical and dance movements. Theirs was a quantitative language in which syllables were classified as long or short, with two shorts equaling a long (West, 1992). (This 2:1 durational ratio reemerges in the present study through its characteristic notation of a quarter note for a long syllable and an eighth note for a short.) The Romans appropriated the poetic-foot classification from the Greeks. Scholars and poets in the Renaissance revived the poetic foot for modern European languages, even though their syllabic structures are accentual rather than quantitative.

From a musical perspective, the poetic foot, in its modern usage, is problematic in four ways.[1] First, foot boundaries frequently do not correspond to the prosodic groupings of words, clitic groups, and phonological phrases. This is evident in figure 3.2a, the first line of Thomas Gray's "Elegy Written in a Country Churchyard," a canonic example of iambic pentameter. The asterisks show only two levels of strong or weak syllables because poetic foot analysis usually specifies just two levels of strong and weak. The slashes mark iambic foot boundaries. Boundaries partition the syllables of "curfew" and "parting," in violation of the prosodic hierarchy at the word level.

```
        *     *     *     *     *
   *    *  *  *  *  *  *  *  *  *
The cur/few tolls/ the knell/ of part/ing day
```

FIGURE 3.2 Iambic feet for the first line of Thomas Gray's "Elegy Written in a Country Churchyard."

```
      *         *       *           *    *
   *  *  *  *   *  *  *  *     *    *
   When in/ disgrace/ with for/tune and/ men's eyes
```

FIGURE 3.3 Iambic feet for the first line of Shakespeare's Sonnet 29.

It is a rare iambic-pentameter line that does not have feet that somehow contradict the prosodic hierarchy. Far more common are lines that exhibit several complications. The first line of Shakespeare's Sonnet 29 in figure 3.3 is an example. At the word level, a foot boundary divides the syllables of 'fortune.' At the clitic level, "in" is a clitic to "disgrace," but a foot boundary intervenes between the two words. The same holds for "and men's."

These examples point to a second way in which the poetic foot is problematic. Do "strong" and "weak" stand for metrical beats or for relative stress? An immediate answer is beats: an iambic-pentameter line has five strong beats, as the term "pentameter" suggests. But the situation is not that simple. Two feet, the pyrrhic and the spondee, do not represent meter at all, the pyrrhic because it lacks the metrical minimum of two beat levels, the spondee because adjacent beats cannot both be strong. These foot types instead represent stress patterns, as in the pyrrhic "-tune and" and the spondee "men's eyes" in figure 3.3. "When in" is an instance of a line-opening foot that inverts the iambic weak-strong pattern to a strong-weak pattern, in accordance with the greater stress on "When." The prosodic literature calls this trochaic substitution. It occurs frequently because many utterances begin with monosyllabic content words or stress-initial polysyllabic words. As these instances reveal, "strong" and "weak" do double duty in foot analysis. The concept of the poetic foot obscures the distinction between beat and stress.

If we treat feet only as stress patterns within the prosodic hierarchy, the result is figure 3.4a for the Shakespeare line: an incomplete (or truncated or headless) monosyllabic foot, an anapest, an amphibrach, an iamb, and another incomplete foot. This may be a colorful description of stress patterns within prosodic groupings, but it is absurd from a metrical point of view; any sense of periodicity is lost. If instead we return to the framework of iambic feet in figure 3.4b, there are still only two iambs. The first line of Robert Frost's "Nothing Gold Can Stay," in figure 3.4c, manifests a similar foot pattern. Of its three supposedly iambic feet, two are substitutions.

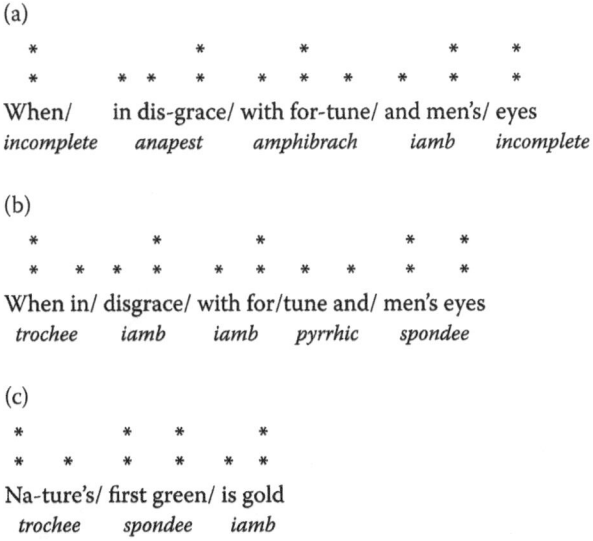

FIGURE 3.4 Foot labeling and substitutions: (a) the first line of Sonnet 29, with foot boundaries modified to match the prosodic hierarchy; (b) the same line with standard foot boundaries for iambic pentameter; (c) the first line of Robert Frost's "Nothing Gold Can Stay" with feet.

As these cases suggest, poetic foot analysis usually demands substitution, sometimes more substitutions than not. How then are these lines iambic? The first step is to separate meter from stress and give each its structural representation. Figure 3.5a discards the neutral asterisks in the above figures and replaces them with x's in the stress grid, as in chapter 2. Beneath is a metrical analysis employing a standard representation for metrical feet: W for a weak beat and S for a strong beat, with each assigned to one syllable. Foot divisions appear in the metrical analysis in a repeating W-S iambic pattern. The Greek foot types from figure 3.4b act as stress patterns within W-S metrical feet.

This metrical-foot analysis improves by replacing the W-S notation with the bracketed metrical grid in figure 3.5b. Now the grid shows the metrical hierarchy directly. But bracketing the metrical grid in this way makes perceptually inappropriate divisions within words and clitic groups. Here lies the third and deepest problem with the concept of the poetic foot: its confusion of the properties of grouping and meter. Grouping is

36 | HISTORICAL APPROACHES TO PROSODIC RHYTHM

(a)

```
stress           x         x      x            x   x
grid:        x   x x   x   x  x   x    x   x   x
             When in dis-grace with for-tune and men's eyes
metrical feet:  / W   S/W    S / W   S / W   S / W    S /
```

(b)

```
stress           x         x      x            x   x
grid:        x   x x   x   x  x   x    x   x   x
             When in dis-grace with for-tune and men's eyes
metrical     [ •   •][•   • ][ •   • ][ •   • ][ •     • ]
grid:        [     •][     • ][     • ][     • ][     • ]
```

FIGURE 3.5 The first line of Sonnet 29 analyzed with a stress grid and traditional metrical feet. For present purposes, only two stress levels are shown.

the hierarchical parsing of sequences of events into units. Meter is the periodic, hierarchical pattern of beats associated with sequences of events. Meter per se does not group; rather, it interacts with grouping. The poetic foot, however, merges metrical beat with grouping at its foundation, causing grouping divisions that are counterintuitive and formally unnecessary.

What is indeed necessary is a rhythmic system that assigns each syllable a place within a perceived grouping structure and, if the sequence is regular enough to induce the perception of meter, assigns each syllable a beat at two or more metrical levels. The prosodic hierarchy provides the requisite grouping, and the metrical grid without a priori foot groupings provides the requisite beat structure. The result is a flexible interplay between grouping, stress, and meter that can do justice to our fluctuating rhythmic intuitions.

Figure 3.6 illustrates this interplay. The five feet of traditional analysis are replaced by five strong beats—that is, by the tactus, as discussed in chapter 2. Groupings belong not to the metrical feet of figure 3.5 but to the prosodically grouped stress grid. The unbracketed metrical grid coordinates with these groupings to project upbeats and afterbeats. At the second grouping level, the monosyllabic words "When" and "eyes" frame the line. At "in disgrace" there is a weak-weak-strong metrical pattern, and at "with fortune" there is a weak-strong-weak pattern. A mismatch between the stress and metrical grids occurs at "and men's" because adjacent strong beats between "men's" and "eyes" are prohibited in a metrical grid.

```
stress grid with       [ x ] [       x ] [    x    ] [    x ] [ x ]
prosodic grouping:     [ x ] [ x  x  x ] [ x  x  x ] [ x   x ] [ x ]
                       When in dis-grace with for-tune and men's eyes
metrical               •  •  •     •    •    •   •    •   •    •
grid:                  •           •        •        •        •
```

FIGURE 3.6 The first line of Sonnet 29 analyzed with a prosodically grouped stress grid and an unbracketed metrical grid.

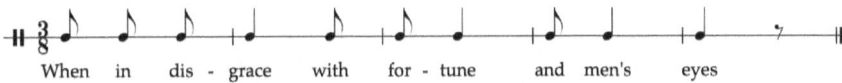

FIGURE 3.7 A normative metrical-durational realization of the first line of Sonnet 29.

The tactus-level beats in figure 3.6 point to a fourth problem in the concept of the poetic foot, the absence of duration as a factor in the analysis. (This is ironic given the origin of foot analysis in Greek quantitative prosody.) Chapter 2.4 reviewed durational issues in music and poetry, so its argument will not be repeated here. Without a durational framework, the structure in figure 3.6 could be realized rhythmically in any number of implausible ways, whether represented in musical notation or not. The procedures for assigning meter and duration set forth in chapter 2.5, however, constrain the options and convert the structure in figure 3.6 into the normative reading in figure 3.7 (compare to figure 2.18b).

In summary, the poetic foot divides words, clitic groups, and phonological phrases in counterintuitive places; mixes up stress and beat; confounds properties of grouping and meter; and lacks a durational component. It is too one-dimensional to represent the richness of poetic rhythm. A musical approach to prosody finds other, more comprehensive ways to represent prosodic features that the poetic foot purports to address.[2]

3.3 A NOTE ON THE POETIC FOOT IN MUSIC

In addition to its central role in poetic prosody, the poetic foot has played a peripheral role in the history of music theory and analysis. Briefly, the Renaissance revival of classical rhetoric and prosody infiltrated musical discourse, and by the eighteenth century, writers embraced the metaphor of music as a language. Musical treatises developed musical analogs to rhetorical tropes and linguistic-phrasal articulations, and attempts were made to reconcile poetic feet with musical measures (Mattheson, 1739). By the late eighteenth century, however, theorists retreated from the music-language metaphor and viewed musical meter in terms of strong and weak beats without dependence on linguistic analogies (Kirnberger, 1771–1776/1982). Poetic-foot notation denoted only strong and weak beats with the traditional macron (–) and breve (⌣) signs, without consideration of foot divisions.[3]

In the twentieth century, Cooper and Meyer (1960) revived poetic-foot analysis in search of a hierarchical rhythmic theory comparable in scope to Heinrich Schenker's (1935) pitch-oriented theory. Their theory has been critiqued on several grounds. It conflates metrical and grouping structures. They treat beats not as points in time but as having duration, indeed of considerable duration at larger levels of analysis. The function of strong and weak markings is unstable: sometimes they are metrical beats, sometimes moments of relative stress, sometimes structural harmonic arrivals, and sometimes relations between formal units (such as between antecedent and consequent phrases). Separate musical dimensions collapse into an undifferentiated analysis. Since the 1970s, the musical application of the poetic foot has fallen into disuse.[4]

So far as I know, nowhere in the history of the music-language analogy has a musical foot analysis been advanced that carves up the musical surface in ways contrary to motivic and phrasal groupings, as happens routinely to words and prosodic phrases in poetic foot scansion.

3.4 THE POETIC LINE

The poetic line is often likened to a musical phrase. The comparison is apt if the line corresponds to a major constituent of the prosodic hierarchy or if its end rhyme has a closing function somewhat like a musical cadence. All the lines in "Nothing Gold Can Stay" fulfill these criteria. There is a single exception in Sonnet 29, an enjambment in lines 11–12, where the phonological phrase "arising from sullen earth" crosses from one line to the next:

Like to the lark at break of day arising
From sullen earth, sings hymns at heaven's gate;

This change in rhythmic flow takes place at the sonnet's psychological turning point, after which a final rhymed couplet achieves closure.

An enjambment in the first quatrain of Sonnet 116 is particularly striking because it takes place at a major prosodic boundary, the utterance level. Only the interleaved rhymes project the line endings:

> Let me not to the marriage of true minds
> Admit impediments. Love is not love
> Which alters when it alteration finds
> Or bends with the remover to remove.

Extensive enjambment without the articulation of rhyme attenuates the perception of poetic lines, making them less a product of what the listener hears than of what the reader sees on the page. Figure 3.8 illustrates with the opening of John Milton's *Paradise Lost* (*PL*), first in the blank verse of the original and then as if in prose without line breaks.

A countervailing factor is cultural learning. The informed listener or reader of Shakespeare and Milton has absorbed so many lines in iambic pentameter that the expectation is of ten syllables, plus or minus one,[5] with five strong stresses associated with strong beats. Such expectations influence perception.

(a)

Of man's first disobedience, and the fruit
Of that forbidden tree whose mortal taste
Brought death into the world, and all our woe,
With loss of Eden, till one greater man
Restore us, and regain the blissful seat,
Sing heavenly muse, . . .

(b)

Of man's first disobedience, and the fruit of that forbidden tree whose mortal taste brought death into the world, and all our woe, with loss of Eden, till one greater man restore us, and regain the blissful seat, sing heavenly muse, . . .

FIGURE 3.8 The opening lines of *Paradise Lost*: (a) in the blank verse of the original, (b) without line breaks.

(a)	(b)
Some say the world will end in fire,	Some say the world will end in fire,
Some say in ice.	Some say [the world will end] in ice.
From what I've tasted of desire	From what I've tasted of desire
I hold with those who favor fire.	I hold with those who favor fire.
But if it had to perish twice,	But if it had to perish twice,
I think I know enough of hate	I think I know enough of hate
To say that for destruction ice	To say that for destruction ice
Is also great	Is also great and would suffice.
And would suffice.	

FIGURE 3.9 Robert Frost's "Fire and Ice": (a) the irregular lines of the original, (b) a regular iambic tetrameter pattern underlying the poem (eight syllables and four tactus beats per line).

Robert Frost's short lyric "Fire and Ice" offers a less extreme case of lines as a visual experience. Figure 3.9a reproduces the poem. The short final two lines both echo the short second line and bring out the rhyme of "great" with "hate." But behind the irregular line structure is the regular iambic tetrameter pattern in 3.9b, in which the second line's elided words are restored and the final two lines fuse into one. The layout in 3.9a suggests a short pause after "great," but Frost's own reading barrels through as if he had written "Is also great and would suffice" as one line. One sees the poem in one way and hears it in another.

As these examples imply, poetry has two simultaneous grouping structures, the grouping of prosodic constituents and the grouping of poetic lines. When the two kinds of grouping coincide, the distinction is hidden. When they do not, the present theory observes grouping by prosodic constituent rather than by poetic line. In most of the examples in this and later chapters, lines do not create enjambments but terminate at boundaries of intonational phrases or utterances so that any potential conflict between constituent and line can be set aside.[6]

Music does not have an analog to the poetic line as a visual-structural element independent of its grouping structure. The visual aspect of musical notation is mainly utilitarian, to convey information accurately and efficiently without adding an extra structural and aesthetic dimension.

In a poetic genre with lines of equal length, the number of syllables per line can be a more reliable stylistic feature than the number of tactus

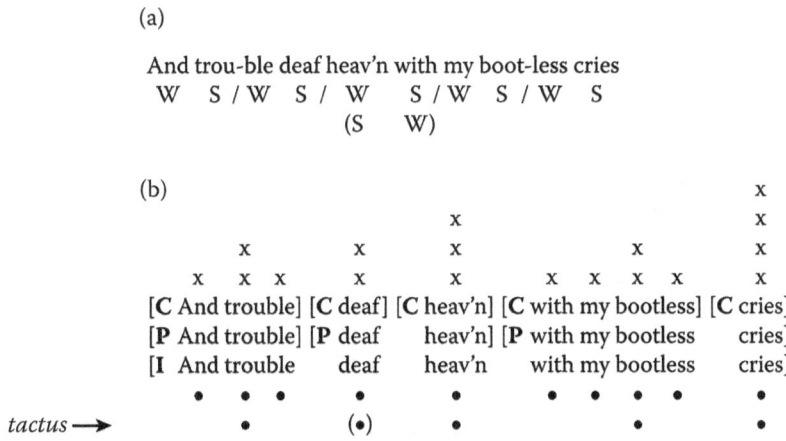

FIGURE 3.10 The third line of Sonnet 29: (a) a foot analysis; (b) an analysis with the prosodic hierarchy, stress grid, and metrical grid.

beats.[7] Consider the ten-syllable third line of Sonnet 29 in figure 3.10. The iambic foot analysis in 3.10a breaks up several prosodic units and falters at the third foot, for which a cumbersome trochaic substitution is needed. The analysis in 3.10b, derived from the prosodic hierarchy and stress grid, avoids these difficulties and highlights five stresses that provisionally serve as five tactus beats in the metrical grid, in conformity with the convention that a ten-syllable iambic line ought to have five strong beats. But adjacent strong beats on "deaf heav'n" cause a prohibited metrical clash. Therefore, the strong beat on "deaf," because it is less stressed than "heav'n," reduces to the status of a weak beat, indicated by the parentheses. The result is a line with four tactus beats.

The consequences of the problematic five-tactus solution become more visceral if, employing procedures from chapter 2, the analysis is converted into musical notation. In figure 3.11a, "deaf" must be a dotted quarter note so that it and "heav'n" can both be on downbeats. This duration is uncomfortably long in context—it is within a phonological phrase—and can be justified only on the dubious interpretation that "deaf" deserves exaggerated focus. In a four-tactus solution, however, "deaf" no longer needs to be on a downbeat. In the derivation in figure 3.11b, it is only moderately long, the same duration as "heav'n" but in a weaker metrical position. This is a natural as well as a well-formed solution.

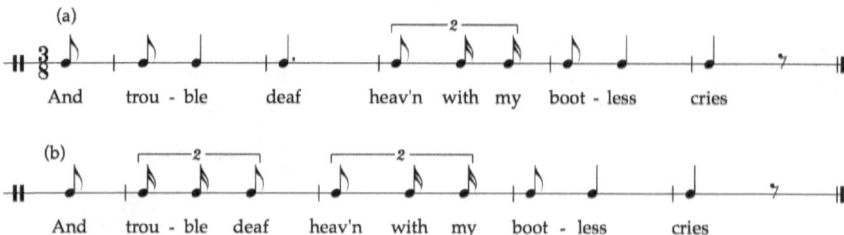

FIGURE 3.11 The third line of Sonnet 29 in musical notation: (a) an ill-formed solution with five tactus beats, (b) a well-formed solution with four tactus beats.

A recurring idea in the prosodic literature—for example, Wimsatt and Beardsley (1959)—is that some poetic lines project more tension than others, depending on how much they deviate from the established model. Figure 3.12a gives a version of the schema for iambic pentameter. There are ten syllables with weak stresses on odd-numbered ones and strong stresses on even-numbered ones, shown by the stress grid. In synch with the stress pattern are periodic beats in a weak-strong alternating pattern. But the grouping of these syllables is not specified, so the pattern could just as well be da/dá-da/dá-da/dá-da/dá-da/dá. Differentiation in syllabic

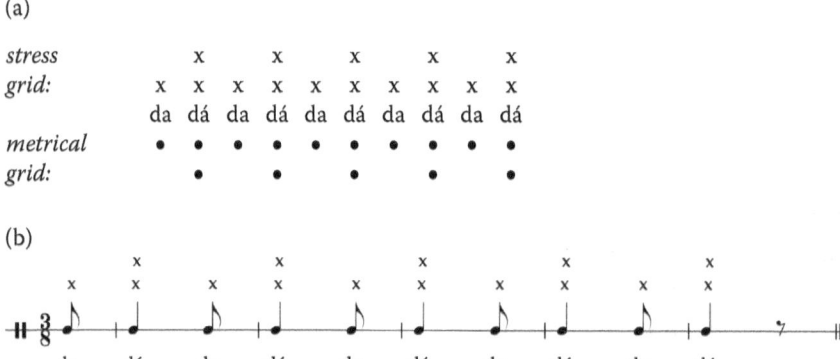

FIGURE 3.12 Template for iambic pentameter: (a) matching stress and metrical grids, (b) translation into musical notation with a 1:2 duration ratio of unstressed to stressed syllables.

duration resolves the ambiguity because grouping boundaries tend to form after longer durations. Suppose, then, that the stressed syllables are about twice as long as the unstressed syllables. Figure 3.12b realizes this iambic template in musical notation.

The first and third lines of Sonnet 29 are rhythmically tense because of their stress-beat conflicts, but the second and fourth lines do not bear such complications and are comparatively relaxed. Figure 3.13a illustrates with the fourth line. The stress and metrical grids match except for a possible suppression of the second-level stress at "-on." Figure 3.13b and c recasts the analysis in musical notation. If "-on" is slightly stressed, as in figure 3.13b, the result conforms to the template in figure 3.12b. But if "-on" is unstressed, as in figure 3.13c, as seems more natural, one tactus beat disappears, and the durations between "look" and "-self" contract to keep the tactus level regular. This alternative is rhythmically more tense than in figure 3.13b but less tense than the third line.[8]

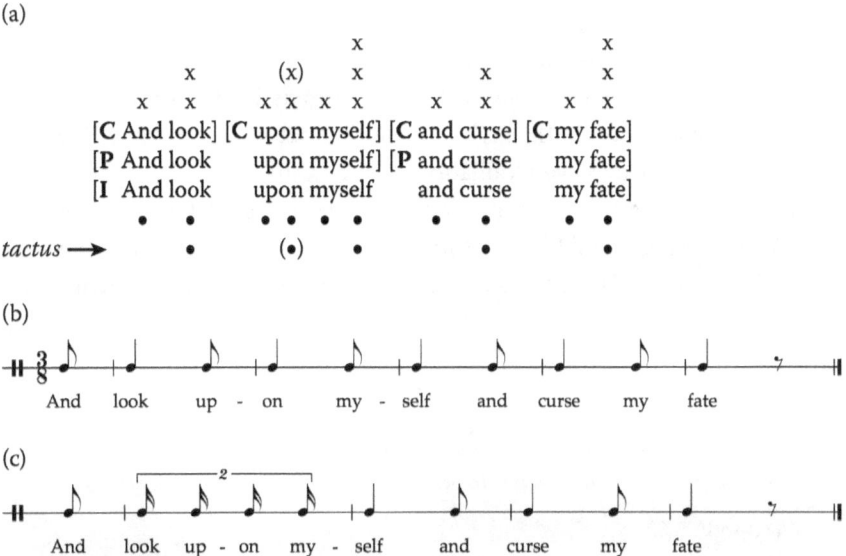

FIGURE 3.13 The fourth line of Sonnet 29: (a) its prosodic, stress, and metrical analysis; (b) its translation into musical notation; (c) its musical realization if "-on" is unstressed.

3.5 TWO EARLY MUSICAL TREATMENTS

Prosodic analysis has occasionally taken a musical turn. The classic instance is by the British writer Joshua Steele (1775). His remarkable tract analyzes poetic lines in terms of phrasing, duration, meter, contour, and dynamics. He diagnoses them as independent, interacting dimensions with their own modes of representation. For the following summary, I set aside contour and dynamics.

Steele does not develop separate representations for stress and meter. He writes in terms of light and heavy emphasis, but the analyses represent metrical structure, not stress. His idiosyncratic notation, properly interpreted, shows multiple metrical levels that can be converted intact into well-formed grids. In an approach compatible with the procedures of the present study, he places stressed syllables on downbeats and distributes unstressed syllables on weak beats. With these steps, he assigns durations to syllables in musical notation. He also allows for duple and triple metrical divisions within the same poetic line. In treating grouping structure, he rejects the poetic foot and considers only the phrase level, which he marks off by rests or even by bars of silent beats.

Figure 3.14a renders, not in Steele's symbols but in the notational form of the present study, his reading of the first line of Hamlet's soliloquy. The line-internal bars of rest respond to the commas in the written text. He notated the soliloquy "in the style of a ranting actor" (Steele, p. 47), which may explain the excessive elongation of "or" and "that." He subsequently witnessed the famous contemporaneous actor David Garrick perform *Hamlet* and transcribed Garrick's interpretation of the line into an equivalent of figure 3.14b. He reports that Garrick recited the soliloquy in a rather

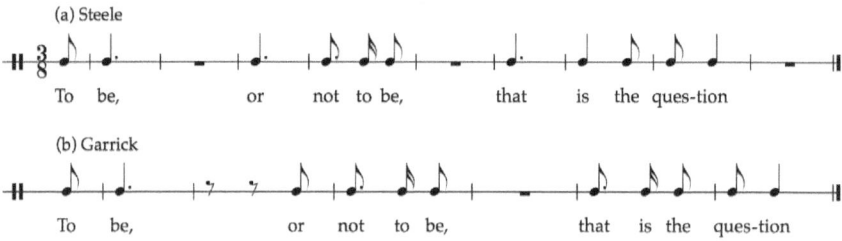

FIGURE 3.14 The first line of Hamlet's soliloquy: (a) Joshua Steele's version, (b) David Garrick's version.

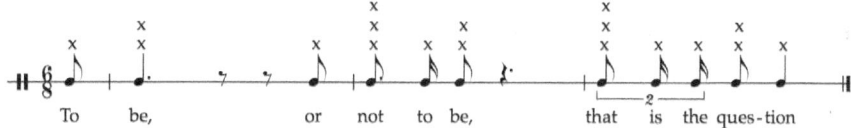

FIGURE 3.15 My modification of the transcription of Garrick's reading, with a stress grid included.

soft and even voice. Garrick accordingly gave "or" and "that" shorter durations than that shown in figure 3.14a.[9]

Notable in figure 3.14a and b is the emphasis on "not" over the second "be," which occurs on a weak beat. The dotted eighths on "not" and "that" bring out the contrastive emphasis on those words by their slightly extra length. In 3.14b, the jig-like rhythm of these two bars works well for "not to be" but not for "that is the," because "the" does not have greater stress than "is" and therefore should not be longer. I suspect that Garrick's reading of "that is the" was closer to the duple rhythm in the last bar of figure 3.15, in which "is" and "the" are equally short. The 6/8 time signature provided here adds another metrical level and places the most stressed syllables on downbeats. A stress grid is included to show that the second "be" has two x's and "the" just one, in contrast to their equivalent metrical placement in figure 3.14b.

Steele's overall intention is to show "that by means of these characters, all the varieties of enunciation may be committed to paper and read off as easily as the air of a song tune" (p. 48). It could be argued, however, that his analyses are mere performative transcriptions and that he does not really advance a theory. Such a view underestimates how much structure there is in a performance. Even silent beats reflect implicit knowledge. By representing phrases and metrical structure and by introducing a method for assigning durations to syllables according to their degree of emphasis, Steele indeed has a theory in embryo. His analyses are more precise than afforded by traditional scansion, and, as the discussion about figures 3.14 and 3.15 suggests, they enable detailed consideration of interpretive decisions and the structural factors behind them.[10]

Another well-known treatise on the musical treatment of prosody is by the American poet and musician Sidney Lanier (1880). It is both more extensive than Steele's essay and more problematic. Lanier classifies sounds by the dimensions of duration, intensity, pitch height, and timbre and goes on to develop successive levels of rhythmic grouping. The first level is syllabic duration, which, in contrast to the practice of traditional prosody, he records in specific values employing musical notation. The second level is a periodic grouping of syllables into the foot, which he equates with the musical bar—apparently on the visual analogy of a bar line corresponding to a foot division, even though there are only two or three syllables per poetic foot but typically many more notes in a musical measure.[11] The third level is the phrase, which corresponds in present terms to a phonological or intonational phrase. His phrases typically differ in length and provide rhythmic variety to offset the rigidity of the feet/bars. The fourth level (overlapping with the third) is the poetic line, which he strangely calls "meter;" it is often punctuated by a rest.

Lanier's taxonomy is persuasive at the first, syllabic level in his advocacy of precise duration as the bedrock of prosodic analysis. He rounds off the variance of actual syllabic durations into simple ratios, usually 1:2, and considers this operation to be a mental construction in search of simplicity. But he goes badly astray starting at the second level. By equating the foot with the musical bar, he makes foot analysis more vexed than it already is in standard scansion. A musical bar normally corresponds to one level of a metrical structure, and it interacts flexibly with the motives and phrases of grouping structure. But in his system, meter as an independent component is swallowed up by the foot/bar so that there is effectively no distinction between grouping and meter. There are only foot groups and syllabic stress. He has no way to represent grouping and meter as out of phase, as must be the case in iambic patterns.

Ratios of 1:2 usually give rise to ternary foot patterns, so my illustration will be from Lanier's examples of bars in 3/8 time. In a disyllable trochaic foot pattern, he places a quarter note on the first syllable and an eighth note on the second, as in figure 3.16a, with the result that the first syllable is emphasized by both metrical accent and duration. He avoids the reverse, an eighth plus a quarter note, presumably because the latter's longer duration would imply an iambic pattern. In a trisyllable trochaic (or dactylic) foot, he assigns straight eighth notes, as in figure 3.16b. Figure 3.16c displays his trochaic repertory with his invented line "Rhythmic roundelays wav'ring downward."

In an iambic pattern, however, the identification of foot with bar means that the iamb cannot be analyzed in the usual upbeat-downbeat way, for which an out-of-phase relationship is requisite between metrical and grouping time

HISTORICAL APPROACHES TO PROSODIC RHYTHM | 47

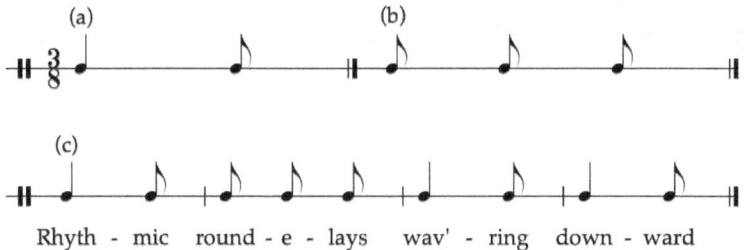

FIGURE 3.16 Sidney Lanier's trochaic foot/bar: (a–b) the trochaic repertory, (c) his illustration.

spans. As a result, to project the iambic foot, Lanier puts extra stress on the second syllable, which he notates by an accent mark, as in figure 3.17a. This treatment of the iamb leads to a bizarre analysis, in 3.17b, of the first line of Hamlet's soliloquy. When confronted with the trisyllable foot "the question," he is forced to cram the last weak syllable into a sixteenth note.

Figure 3.17c converts his analysis into a musically notated foot analysis in which the time spans between feet and downbeats are out of phase. This analysis corresponds to the template of figure 3.12b plus an extra weak syllable at the end. The reading may be boring, but at least it makes sense.

The suppression of an independent metrical component at the foot/bar level and the consequent inadmissibility of upbeats is surprising coming from a practicing musician. Roughly half the popular tunes that Lanier

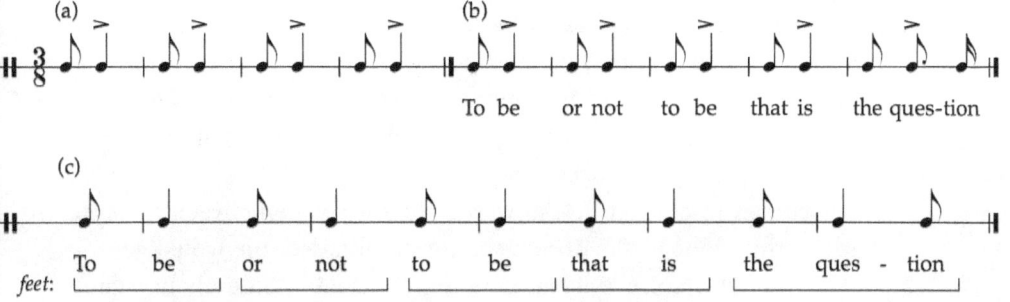

FIGURE 3.17 Lanier's iambic foot/bar: (a) the iambic pattern, (b) his analysis of the first line of Hamlet's soliloquy (p. 172), (c) conversion of his analysis into a prototypical iambic pattern.

would have known have phrase-beginning upbeats, for instance "The Star-Spangled Banner" (see figure 1.9), "Amazing Grace" ("Amazing Grace, how sweet the sound"), and "My Old Kentucky Home" ("The sun shines bright in the old Kentucky home"). He only had to consult his musical experience, but his fealty to the foot/bar got in the way.[12]

3.6 CRITIQUES OF MUSICAL APPROACHES

More recent poets and literary scholars have shied away from a musical treatment of prosody. Sometimes the barrier comes from a misunderstanding. Corn (2008, p. xvii) compares the poetic line to a musical bar; finds the analogy problematic because a bar begins on a strong beat, contrary to an iambic line; and decides that a musical approach is inappropriate. But a poetic line is a matter of grouping, not meter, and its proper analogy is to the musical phrase.

Other times the skepticism is indeterminate. Fussell (1965) begins his text on traditional scansion by citing T. S. Eliot's statement that his creative concerns "are more those of a quasi-musical nature, in the arrangement of metric and pattern, than of a conscious exposition of ideas" (Fussell, p. 4), but a few pages later Fussell dismisses a musical approach on unspecified grounds.

More informative is Wimsatt and Beardsley's (1959) influential article, which defends traditional scansion against the encroachments of the two disciplines, linguistics and music theory, that are best situated to rejuvenate the prosodic tradition. Their comments on linguistics deal mainly with a phonemic model (Trager and Smith, 1951) that predates generative linguistics. They view its use in prosodic analysis as merely transcriptive and performative. They oppose a temporal, musical approach on similar grounds and argue that musical and poetic meters are incommensurate because the former is rigidly metronomic while the latter is not. They recognize that meter means measurement but claim that broadly approximate temporal measurement suffices.

As discussed in chapter 2.4, however, the difference between musical and poetic durations is one of degree, not of kind. No one would accept a rendition in which, say, syllabic durations fluctuate randomly in values between a quarter of a second and a quarter of a minute, so the question becomes, How large a temporal window is tolerable without distorting the perceived structure? The best representation for duration is musical notation, which reduces the issue to the deviation range of specified note values. The deviation varies according to poetic style, as it does in musical styles. Nursery rhymes and limericks have narrow windows; blank verse has wider ones.

Against the surface representations and measurements that they ascribe to linguistic and musical approaches, Wimsatt and Beardsley maintain the centrality of an abstract level of alternating stressed and unstressed syllables grouped into feet. They see trochaic foot substitutions and other metrical variations as artful, tension-inducing deviations from this norm. Indeed, their description broadly resembles the iambic template in figure 3.12a but without grouping or grid representations. But the version of the template in figure 3.12b would not be to their liking because it assigns durations.

This notational dispute should not obscure the shared conception of abstract levels for prosodic rhythm beyond the observation of surface features. The argument then shifts to the status of the abstraction and what its grammar is. For Wimsatt and Beardsley, the grammar is an unsystematic version of traditional scansion. In the present framework, it is the prosodic hierarchy, stress grid, and metrical grid and how these components interact.

A few examples will help clarify the issues. As shown in figure 3.18a, Wimsatt and Beardsley shoehorn Percy Bysshe Shelley's line "Hail to thee, blithe spirit" into iambic trimeter with an incomplete first foot and an added weak syllable closing the third foot. Single strokes indicate moderate stress, and added strokes signify progressively greater stress. They draw attention to the ramping up of stress in the second and third feet: one stroke on "thee," two on "blithe," and three on "spir-." If cast in grid format, this analysis would violate the evenness principle. Figure 3.18b gives the line's prosodic hierarchy and stress grid using the present system. There are no feet. The stress pattern for "to thee, blithe spirit" is not a continuous crescendo but a parallel rising pattern: one x to three x's for "to thee," two x's to four for "blithe spirit." Figure 3.18c adds meter and duration to the analysis.

Figure 3.19a–b renders Wimsatt and Beardsley's scansion of two virtuoso lines from *Paradise Lost*. Iambic pentameter normally yields five main stresses, but in these ten-syllable lines, they allot as many as eight main stresses, as shown in 3.19a, and just three, as shown in 3.19b. To the unbroken sequence of six monosyllabic nouns in 3.19a, they assign

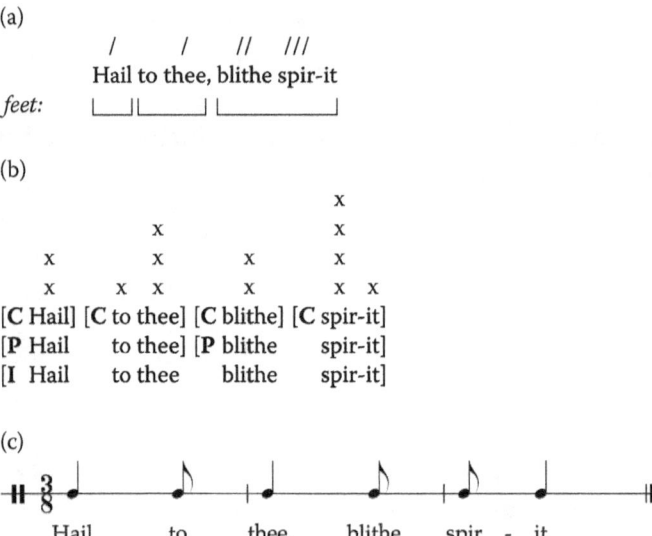

FIGURE 3.18 The first line of Percy Bysshe Shelley's "To a Skylark": (a) Wimsatt and Beardsley's scansion, (b) grouping and stress analysis from my model, (c) the derived meter and durations in musical notation.

an opening trochaic substitution followed by iambs to project a familiar pattern for lines in iambic pentameter. In 3.19b, the feet break up all three polysyllabic words.

Figure 3.20a submits the first Milton line to a grouping and stress analysis by the present system. The sequence of six consecutive nouns lacks

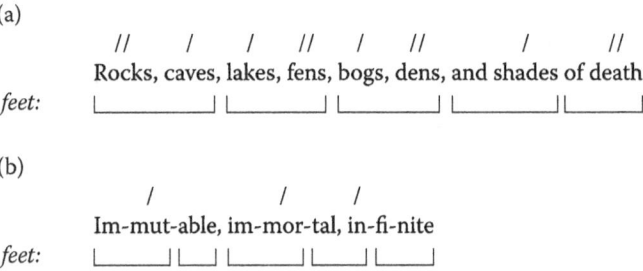

FIGURE 3.19 Wimsatt and Beardsley's scansion of lines from *Paradise Lost*: (a) *PL*, 2.621; (b) *PL*, 3.373.

HISTORICAL APPROACHES TO PROSODIC RHYTHM | 51

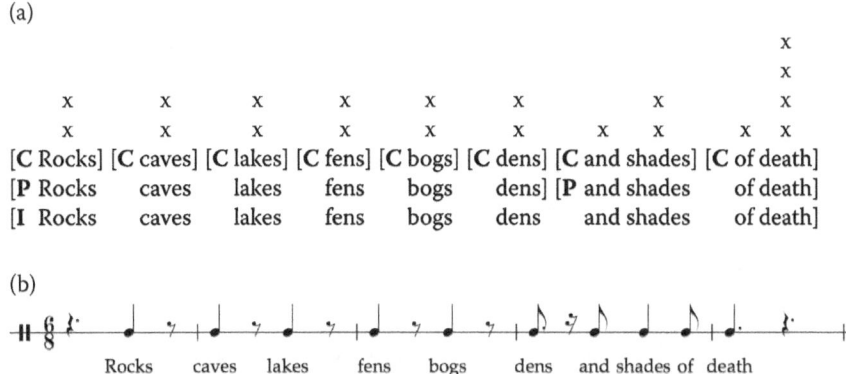

FIGURE 3.20 Treatment of *PL*, 2.621 by the present system: (a) prosodic grouping and stress grid, (b) the derived meter and durations.

internal grouping, causing equal stress on each word. (By the nuclear stress rule, "dens" would receive an extra x, but because this phonological phrase is just a list, the rule appears not to apply.) There cannot be parallel metrical treatment because strong beats are required every two or three beats apart (metrical well-formedness condition 5; see chapter 2.4). Of the available metrical options, the most direct is to assume the iambic template that readers of *Paradise Lost* would expect, with stronger beats on "caves," "fens," and "dens." This choice leads, in figure 3.20b, to the metrical-durational realization in 6/8 with an initial anacrusis.

Figure 3.21 analyzes the second Milton line. The rests between words are in response to the commas. The only complication is the slight stress on the last syllable of "infinite," which is finessed by a parenthesized x. This leads to the dotted rhythm in figure 3.21b, with "-fi-" shorter and metrically weaker than "-nite."

These cases demonstrate that there is no prosodic feature that Wimsatt and Beardsley discuss that the present system does not engage more completely. And it does so without the baggage of the poetic foot. The claim cannot be the superiority of the abstractions of traditional prosody.

Yet Wimsatt and Beardsley would be right if they argued that the present model has a performative dimension. This aspect is evident in the rests in figure 3.21b, but it is also implicit in some durational choices. In figure 3.18c, "thee, blithe" could be realized in duple eighth notes, giving the

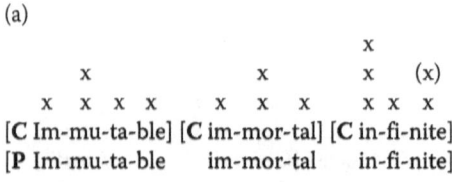

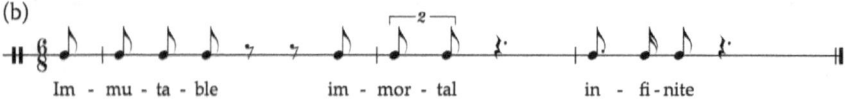

FIGURE 3.21 Treatment of *PL*, 3.373 by the present system: (a) prosodic grouping and stress grid, (b) the derived meter and durations.

relatively long syllable "blithe" its due. In figure 3.20b, an option could be taken of a tactus-length pause before "and shades of death." In figure 3.21b, "infinite" could be realized more simply by three equal eighth notes. The theory is, after all, a preferential system that accommodates a limited range of interpretations. It would be a mistake, however, to denigrate this performative aspect as merely transcriptive. All the assigned structures are based on principles that the theory sets forth.

In contrast to Fussell and Wimsatt-Beardsley, Prall (1936) rejects foot scansion as artificial and approaches the rhythms of poetry through a phenomenological analysis of elementary temporal patterns. He sees equal durational units, hence periodic beats, as essential to temporal measurement and from there sketches a hierarchy of beat divisions. Groupings of objects, in this case, syllables, interact independently with beat hierarchies. Main stresses align with strong beats. In all these respects, his approach echoes that of Steele (whose treatise he surely did not know) and, broadly speaking, anticipates the theory developed here.[13]

Figure 3.22a gives Prall's analysis of an iambic-pentameter couplet:

So eat your cake and have it too, say I;
That's really beating fate and living high.

The single-digit numbers above the vowels count beat numbers in 6/8 time, and the vertical lines demarcate quasi-musical bars; thus "6" indicates an

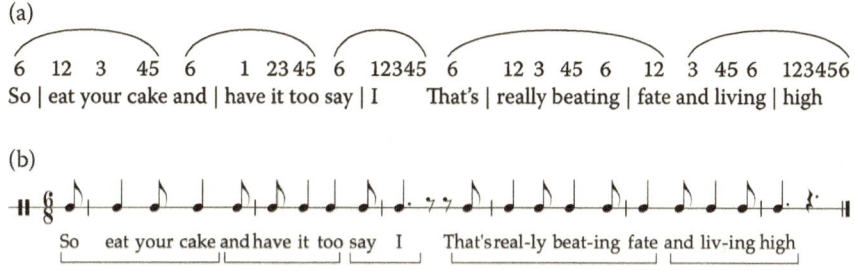

FIGURE 3.22 A couplet from Prall (1936): (a) his notation, (b) a musical transcription.

upbeat and "1" a downbeat. Numbers bunched together, for instance, "12" over "eat" (1 and 2, not the number 12), mean that a syllable lasts more than one beat; thus "eat" takes place over beats 1 and 2. The slurs above the numbers represent phrase boundaries and are slightly out of phase with the bar boundaries. Syllabic stresses are taken as understood rather than shown, and the metrical and prosodic hierarchies are incomplete, but the diagram is in the spirit of the present theory. Figure 3.22b casts his representation in musical notation.

Northrop Frye argues that many lines in iambic pentameter really have only four main accents (Frye, 1957a, 1957b, p. 251).[14] He illustrates with scansions of the opening lines of Hamlet's soliloquy (compare figure 3.15, which, ignoring the rests, has four tactus beats) and of *Paradise Lost*, and he speculates that a psychological inclination toward metrical periodicity lies behind the prevalence of four-accent lines in most English poetry, from Old English accentual verse to ballads and nursery rhymes. His description anticipates the present theory:

> We need a principle of accentual scansion, a regular recurrence of beats with a variable number of syllables between the beats. This corresponds to the general rhythm of the music in the Western tradition, where there is a regular stress accent with a variable number of notes in each measure (Frye, 1957a, p. xvii).[15]

Wimsatt and Beardsley contend that Prall's and Frye's musical approaches undervalue poetic feet and their substitutions, which they regard as fundamental to an understanding of poetic rhythm. Chapter 4.5 will revisit this issue from another angle.

Skepticism toward musical approaches to prosody has abetted the general neglect of prosody in the current literary landscape.[16] Many introductions to poetry concentrate on meaning, symbolism, and applications of philosophical or cultural studies, with scant attention to prosody. When they do attend to it, it is typically in the form of a rote account of foot scansion. One cause of this imbalance, I believe, is an uninterrogated acceptance of this tradition.

An exception is Attridge (1982), who covers musical and linguistic connections extensively, as they stood circa 1980. The analytic system that he advances in place of traditional prosody, however, is excessively stripped down, consisting of beats and offbeats without further metrical hierarchy or grouping structure, plus rules both for demotion or promotion of strong or weak syllables and for double-filled and empty syllable slots. These transformational rules replace substitutions in traditional scansion.

Another exception is Cureton (1992), who advances a theory of poetic rhythm inspired by a combination of *A Generative Theory of Tonal Music* (*GTTM*) and Cooper and Meyer's (1960) theory of musical rhythm. He develops three interactive rhythmic components: meter, grouping, and prolongation. His metrical component adopts *GTTM*'s dot grid with its equally spaced beats at multiple levels, but he does not take the further steps of assigning duration to syllables or proposing rules for deriving metrical analyses. Grouping, the most developed part of his theory, merges *GTTM*'s grouping structure and time-span reduction into a single component in which each group has a most prominent element. At the initial level, the prominent elements are syllables, but at larger levels, they become units comprised of words and phrases. Groups of units contained within superordinate groups are designated as strong or weak with respect to one another, from level to level, guided by a variety of preference rules. These criteria go well beyond what is usually thought of as rhythmic to include semantic and narrative dimensions. The assignment of strong and weak designations not only to syllables but also to groupings of words and phrases resembles Cooper and Meyer's (1960) methodology more than it does that of *GTTM*. His briefly sketched prolongational component is inspired by a *GTTM* component that assigns hierarchical patterns of tension and relaxation to sequences of pitches and chords. His version identifies patterns of poetic tension and relaxation not as in Wimsatt and

Beardsley's metrical deviations from the norm by foot substitutions but at a conceptual level of narrative anticipation, arrival, and extension.[17]

Cureton's grouping and prolongational components address issues well beyond the cognitive organization of the sounds of poetry, the concern of the present volume. From my perspective, the main strength of his study is its redirection of traditional prosody's fixation on poetic feet toward a multifaceted treatment of phrase rhythm.

4

Generative Approaches to Prosodic Rhythm

4.1 INTRODUCTION

My musical treatment of the sounds of poetry falls broadly within the framework of generative linguistics, above all by its adoption of the theoretical aims and rhythmic components from *A Generative Theory of Tonal Music* (*GTTM*). *GTTM* develops a strictly music theory, not a linguistic theory applied to music, but it shares with generative linguistics the goal of a rule-based explication of the intuitions of a perceiver experienced in the domain in question. The present study intersects with generative phonology and prosody in numerous ways. So far, I have invoked only the prosodic hierarchy and the treatment of syllabic stress from generative phonology. This chapter will review further points of convergence and divergence. It will then resume discussion of line templates (see chapter 3) and consider how useful generalizations made in the generative-prosodic literature might be represented in the present framework.

4.2 GRIDS, SLOTS, AND TREES

Generative prosodic theory, pioneered by Halle and Keyser (1966, 1971), initially sought to develop a rule system that identifies lines of verse as metrical or unmetrical. This goal reflects the program of early generative

```
        x     x   x    x      x
  x    x x    x   x  x x x x  x
  How many bards gild the lapses of time!
  W   S W  S    W   S W S W  S
```
FIGURE 4.1 Stress grid and standard W S analysis of the first line of a John Keats sonnet.

linguistics to generate all and only grammatical sentences of a language (Chomsky, 1957). Halle and Keyser take as given a pattern of strong (S) and weak (W) beats against which to evaluate a poetic line's syllabic stresses. They discard poetic feet. For instance, the iambic pentameter metrical pattern is five iterations of W S per line. The pattern is not / W S / W S / W S / W S / W S/ but W S W S W S W S W S, with a single syllable in a W or S position or slot. Their stress maximum principle counts an iambic pentameter line as unmetrical if these conditions are met: a stressed syllable is on a weak beat, adjacent unstressed syllables are on strong beats, and all three syllables are in the same syntactic unit. Thus, they judge the first line of a sonnet by John Keats, given in figure 4.1, to be unmetrical because "lap-" is a stress maximum. (They suggest that Keats made this line unmetrical to exemplify lapses of time.) In contrast, "gild" adds complexity to the line by being on a weak beat, but it is not a violation because the preceding syllable is not unstressed.

Kiparsky (1975, 1977) offers a counterproposal to sort metrical from unmetrical lines. His monosyllabic word constraint prohibits strong stresses in W positions for polysyllabic words unless preceded by a phrase boundary. This rule is compatible with the development, a few years later, of the prosodic hierarchy, hence my incorporation of it in the congruence principle stated in chapter 2.5. The monosyllabic word constraint agrees that the W S positioning of "lapses" makes the line unmetrical.

The unacceptability of this line, assuming the ten standard W S syllable slots, is palpable when cast in musical notation. Figure 4.2a does this in straight duple-meter eighth notes, and 4.2b inserts it into the triple-meter template from figure 3.12b. Neither solution is feasible. But if the assumption of W S slots is dropped and the line is treated by the procedures of the present theory, the result is figure 4.2c, a perfectly acceptable reading of a ten-syllable line with five main stresses. The long duration on "bards" enables "gild" and "lap-" to shift to the right and fall on downbeats. The shift flows smoothly because, unlike the comparable cases of "men's eyes" and "deaf heav'n" in Shakespeare's Sonnet 29 (discussed in

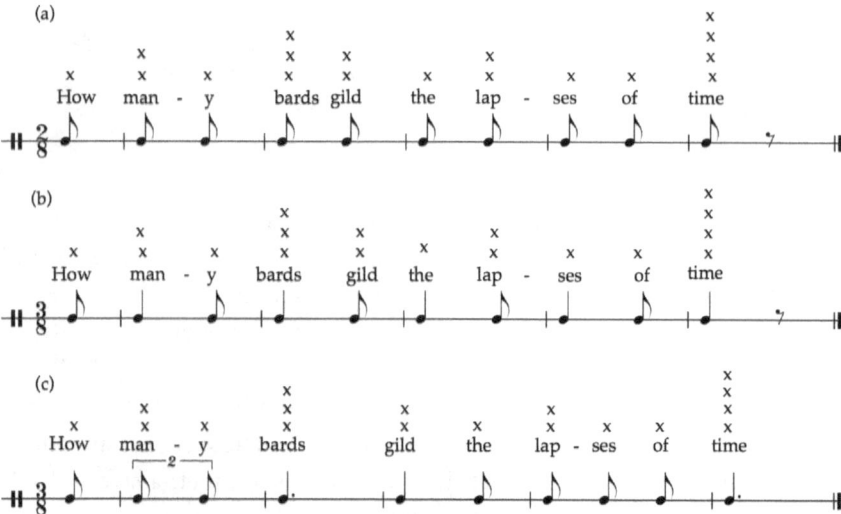

FIGURE 4.2 The Keats line rendered in musical notation: (a) following the traditional W S framework in duple meter, (b) fitting the line to the template of figure 3.12b, (c) realizing the rhythm by the procedures in chapter 2.

chapters 2 and 3, respectively), "bards" and "gild" are in different phonological phrases.

This analysis raises several fundamental issues. First is a point of convergence. Although Halle and Keyser (and Kiparsky) identify iambic-pentameter lines as metrical or unmetrical, they supplement their classifications by ranking the tension of lines on a gradient—that is, not by black-and-white categorization but in shades of gray along a continuum. Unlike earlier invocations of line tension, Halle and Keyser's analysis is derived step by step. This treatment anticipates Lerdahl and Jackendoff's (1977) and *GTTM*'s introduction of preference rules, which in turn anticipate optimality theory, a gradient approach to deriving phonological structures that has dominated phonological theory since the 1980s (Prince and Smolensky, 1993/2004). From this perspective, the Keats line is rhythmically complex but not unmetrical.[1]

Halle and Keyser present the following constructed line as an egregiously unmetrical instance of putatively iambic pentameter: "Ode to the West Wind by Percy Bysshe Shelley." Is it unmetrical from a gradient perspective? Figure 4.3a provides its prosodic hierarchy and stress grid. Stress

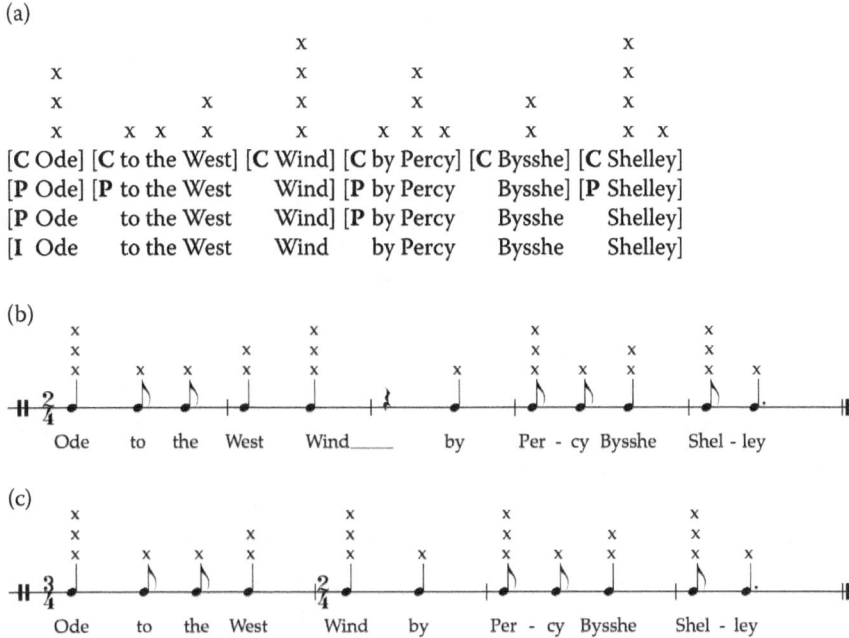

FIGURE 4.3 Halle and Keyser's constructed example of an unmetrical line of iambic pentameter: (a) its prosodic and stress analysis, (b) a musical realization with syncopated "Wind," (c) a realization with a change in time signature.

clashes take place at "West Wind" and "Bysshe Shelley." Figure 4.3b–c offers two musical realizations. In 4.3b, heavily stressed "Wind" is syncopated; only the elongated time span between "Wind" and "by" projects the stress. (Such is also the case, to a lesser extent, with "Bysshe.") "Wind" can arrive on a downbeat only if, as in 4.3c, there is a change in time signature from 3/4 to 2/4. Either way, there are just four tactus downbeats. These factors in combination plausibly push the line so far on the gradient that it might better deserve to be called an unmetrical iambic pentameter line.

Now to a significant point of divergence. I have already argued against the validity of the poetic foot. Now, and more deeply, I challenge the validity of fixed sequences of alternating W S slots—or S W slots if the pattern is trochaic—even if, as in Halle and Keyser, there are no foot boundaries.[2] Both traditional and generative prosodists assume a priori slot sequences against which to juggle stress patterns, the former by foot substitutions and the latter by rules that assign metrical or unmetrical status and degrees of tension. But finding the beat structure of a poetic line—or, for that matter, of a musical phrase—is a constructive mental act; it does not exist a priori. As discussed in chapter 2, the perceiver finds the best fit between a line's main stressed syllables and a stylistically available sequence of periodic beats at a moderate tempo. Within this tactus framework, the rest of the line's syllables fill in the gaps between tactus beats by an optimal fit of their stress patterns with sub-tactus beat patterns. From this perspective, W S slots—not to mention / W S / feet—are unnecessary and unwanted.

The essentials of this method are already present in Halle and Lerdahl (1993), a study of text setting that focuses on the chantey "The Drunken Sailor." The lyrics vary from verse to verse in the number of syllables and the distribution of secondary stresses per line, yet singers intuitively place primary stresses on strong beats and adjust local rhythms to fit within this framework.[3]

This procedure circumvents problematic features of the W S slot approach. There is no need for a special rule—the stress maximum principle or the monosyllabic word constraint—to adjudicate main stresses on weak beats because the derivation starts by placing them on strong beats. Nor is there any need for "extra-metrical" syllables, a notion whose sole purpose is to allow more than one unstressed syllable in a W slot.

Figure 4.4a gives an example from Halle and Keyser, the third line of John Donne's holy sonnet 14. The underlined syllables "me, and" are obliged in their analysis to fit into a single W slot that leaps across an intonational phrase boundary. As a result, "and" is dubbed extra-metrical, even though it, like any other syllable, necessarily has a certain stress, metrical location, and duration. The method developed here, by contrast, easily finds a place for "and." Figure 4.4b shows the line's atypical prosodic hierarchy and stress grid. In the derived metrical-durational version in 4.4c, the words "me, and" are on weak beats between "-throw" and "bend."

A root problem of the W S slot approach is that it ignores duration. Without duration, there is no periodicity, and without periodicity, there is no genuine meter. From a musical perspective, traditional scansion, including its generative counterpart, is in fact not metrical. In a true metrical context, it is an ordinary step to lengthen the distance between two adjacent stressed syllables to avoid a metrical clash, as in figure 4.2c, or to fit two adjacent unstressed syllables between periodically stressed syllables, as in figure 4.4c.

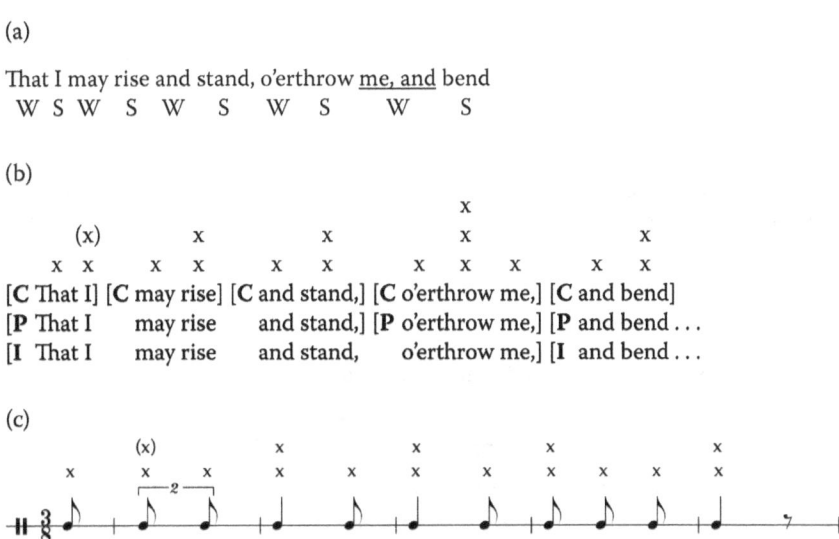

FIGURE 4.4 Line 3 of John Donne's holy sonnet 14: (a) in the alternating W S slot model, with "me, and" filling a single W slot and "and" counted as extra-metrical; (b) the line's prosodic hierarchy and stress grid; (c) a metrical-durational realization.

Musical metrical grids and phonological stress grids came into theoretical practice at about the same time (Lerdahl and Jackendoff, 1977; Liberman, 1975; Liberman and Prince, 1977).[4] Liberman and Prince proposed their grid notation to explicate the avoidance of adjacent strong stresses (referred to in the literature as the rhythm rule). Their grid representation resembles *GTTM*'s, although the objects of analysis—beats in music, stresses in language—are not the same. Unfortunately, Liberman and Prince called their stress grids "metrical grids." This misnomer has caused ongoing confusion. If "metrical grids" represent levels of stress, there is little conceptual space left to recognize that a sine qua non of meter is the inference of constant temporal units of measurement at multiple beat levels. It is easy to fall back instead on some version of traditional scansion.[5]

Liberman and Prince (1977) introduce tree structures to represent syllabic stress by relational hierarchies rather than by integers denoting stress levels (as in Chomsky and Halle 1968). *GTTM* (pp. 314–30) demonstrates

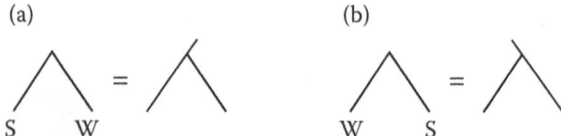

FIGURE 4.5 Mapping between Liberman and Prince's stress trees and *GTTM*'s time-span reduction trees: (a) an S W branching converted into a right-branching time-span tree, (b) a W S branching converted into a left-branching time-span tree.

in detail that Liberman and Prince's trees are isomorphic to the trees in time-span reduction, a component of generative music theory that represents pitch-event hierarchies within nested rhythmic units obtained from a combination of grouping and metrical structures.[6] Again, the objects of analysis are different, but the formalisms are alike. Figure 4.5a–b gives the mapping. An S W branching can be represented by a time-span tree in which the branch on the right is subordinate to the branch on the left, and conversely for a W S branching.

Figure 4.6a–b illustrates the mapping in the context of stress hierarchies by repeating Liberman and Prince's tree analysis of the word "reconciliation" together with *GTTM*'s translation of it. In figure 4.6b, italicized letters are added to label branches by level, following *GTTM*'s practice for time-span reduction.[7] *GTTM* also offers an equivalent bracket notation for time-span trees (as Chomsky [1957] does for syntactic trees). In figure 4.6c, correspondingly, level *d* lists the syllable sequence of "reconciliation"; level *c* eliminates its unstressed syllables, leaving a residue of "re-," "ci-," and "a-." Levels *b* and *a* repeat the process until only "a-," the most stressed syllable, remains. Finally, figure 4.6d represents 4.6c in musical notation, showing durations from syllable to syllable at multiple hierarchical levels. At level c the stressed syllables are a quarter note apart, and at level b the remaining stressed syllables are a half note apart.

Figure 4.7 performs the same procedure on the first lines of Robert Frost's "Nothing Gold Can Stay" and Shakespeare's Sonnet 29. The tree levels in figure 4.7a–b correspond to levels in the bracket notation in 4.7c–d. They also correspond to the number of x's in figures 2.5 and 2.6. These are different ways to represent the same hierarchical relationships. The format of figure 4.7c and d will prove particularly useful when combined, in chapter 7, with the hierarchical analysis of syllabic relatedness.

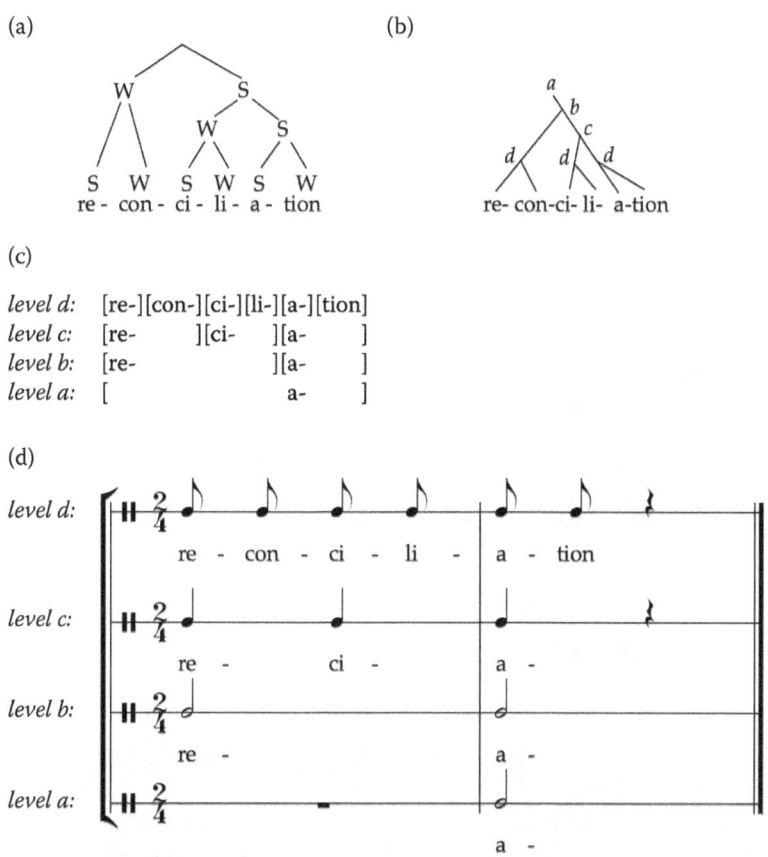

FIGURE 4.6 Hierarchical stress analysis of the word "reconciliation": (a) Liberman and Prince's representation; (b) mapping of (a) into time-span tree notation, with labeling by level; (c) mapping of (b) into a bracket notation; (d) representation of (c) in musical notation, as in *GTTM*'s and Lerdahl's (2001b) representation of time-span reduction.

Although the different representations in figures 4.6 and 4.7 all describe the same relationships, there is an important respect in which they are not equivalent. The cases employing musical notation—figures 4.6d and 4.7a–b—include time signatures and durations, while the others only show nonmetrical, nondurational sequences arranged hierarchically. Here again is a basic difference between the prevailing phonological conception of syllabic rhythm and the musical one developed in this study.

64 | GENERATIVE APPROACHES TO PROSODIC RHYTHM

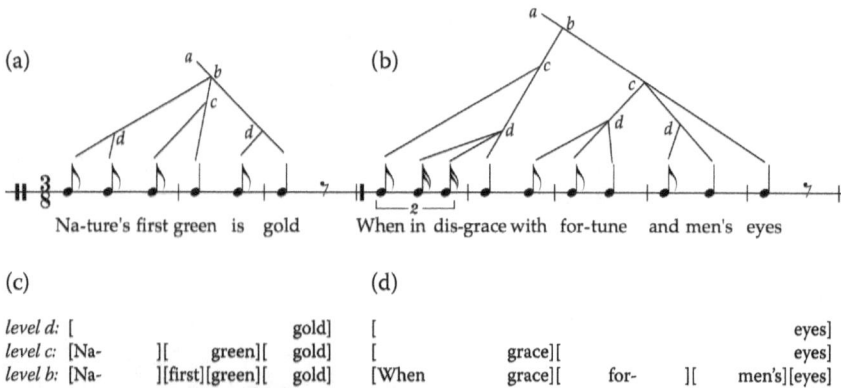

(c)
level d: [gold]
level c: [Na-   ][green][gold]
level b: [Na-   ][first][green][gold]
level a: [Na-][ture's][first][green][is][gold]

(d)
[eyes]
[grace][eyes]
[When   grace][for-   ][men's][eyes]
[When][in][dis-][grace][with][for-][tune][and][men's][eyes]

FIGURE 4.7 Equivalent representations of hierarchical stress relationships in the first lines of Frost's "Nothing Gold Can Stay" and Shakespeare's Sonnet 29: (a–b) in time-span reduction tree notation, (c–d) in bracket notation.

4.3 BRACKETED GRIDS AND TEXT SETTING

The central concept in Hayes's (1995) book on phonological stress theory is the bracketed grid—that is, a stress grid associated with nested groupings of syllables. Figure 4.8 shows the Frost and Shakespeare lines in his notation (slightly modified).[8] It corresponds to the representations in figure 4.7c–d. Thus, from my perspective, Hayes's bracketed grids are, like Liberman and Prince's trees, a nonmetrical, nondurational form of time-span reduction.

Hayes enumerates several formal properties shared by the present approach. First is the continuous column constraint for stress grids. A well-formedness condition in chapter 2.4 states it in terms of metrical grids, but

(a)
level a: (x)
level b: (x   ) (x) (x)
level c: (x   ) (x) (x) (x)
level d: (x   x) (x) (x) (x)(x)
         Na-ture's first green is gold

(b)
(x)
(x) (x)
(x) (x) (x   ) (x) (x)
(x) (x x   x) (x   x   x) (x   x) (x)
When in dis-grace with for-tune and men's eyes

FIGURE 4.8 Hayes's notation for the stress hierarchies in figure 4.7(c–d).

the same concept applies to stress grids: a syllable that is stressed at level L is marked at level L + 1. This precept ensures that no gap occurs from one stress level to the next. A second property, the faithfulness condition (adapted from Halle and Vergnaud, 1987) means that each bracket contains a single stress mark. *GTTM* states this principle in terms of a headed hierarchy; that is, each time span has a single dominating element, or head. This principle can be readily observed not only in figure 4.8 but also in figure 4.7c–d. It can also be read off the time-span trees in figures 4.6a–b and 4.7a–b. A corollary is what Hayes refers to as a lack of assimilation: weak syllables do not inherit strength from adjacent strong ones. The labeled levels in figure 4.6b–d convey this property clearly. Yet another shared property is a tendency to distribute stresses evenly at multiple levels. This is a feature of metrical grids, but it also applies more flexibly to stress grids.

As mentioned in chapter 2, the present study employs the prosodic hierarchy and stress grid along lines presented in Hayes (1989). However, Hayes proposes rules relating grouping and stress patterns to the schema of W S slots posited by Halle-Keyser and Kiparsky. As in their work, the purpose of his rules is to decide whether a given line is grammatical.

Conclusions from Hayes's analysis include avoidance of stressed syllables in W positions, especially within words and clitic groups; free stress treatment at beat positions at left edges of prosodic groupings; and strict alignment of strong stresses with S positions at right edges of prosodic groupings. But the W S schema is not needed to arrive at these conclusions. The congruence principle (see chapter 2.5) imposes stress-meter matching within words and clitic units. Clitic words in English typically precede their clitic hosts, and the nuclear stress principle (see chapter 2.3) emphasizes the ends of prosodic units. These criteria place stresses at right edges and leave left edges unencumbered.

Hayes and Kaun (1996) brings Hayes's (1989) methodology to bear on text setting in sung and chanted verse. As in the present theory, the goal is to align syllabic stress and metrical beats in an optimal way, but with the added provisos that, in sung and chanted verse, trochaic substitutions are preferably suppressed, and stressed syllables at line endings are stretched to fill empty tactus beats. Figure 4.9 illustrates with a couplet from *Mother Goose*. In terms of traditional scansion, as shown in 4.9a, the couplet is iambic but with an incomplete foot at the beginning and an extra weak syllable at the end. There is a trochaic substitution in the third foot; in everyday speech, one says "wént up the híll," not "went úp the híll." This

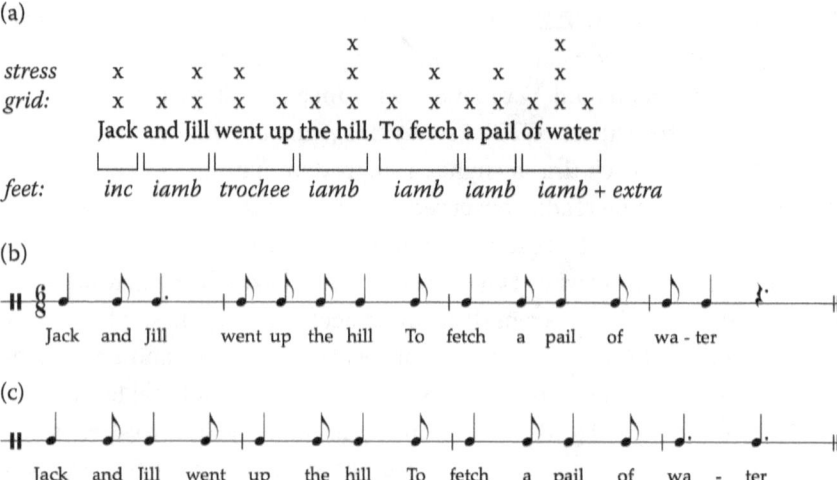

FIGURE 4.9 Analysis of a couplet from *Mother Goose*: (a) in traditional scansion, (b) metrical-durational realization of (a), (c) revised metrical-durational realization observing the text-setting factors of no trochaic inversions and filling of empty tactus beats.

analysis converts into the metrical-durational realization in figure 4.9b. A phonological phrase boundary after "Jill" licenses the long duration on that word. The syllable "wa-" in "water" is short, leaving an empty tactus beat at the end of the phrase. But given a text-setting context that promotes regular rhythms and phrase lengths, as Hayes and Kaun argue, neither the substitution nor the empty beat is favored. Their preferred realization in that context, translated into my representation, is figure 4.9c: relative stress transfers from "went" to "up," maintaining the iambic pattern, and "water" stretches to fill the empty tactus beat.

Hayes and MacEachern (1998) extend the methodology to preferred patterns of line structure in folk-verse quatrains and use optimality theory (OT) to reconcile conflicting rule applications and quantify predictions. Preferred patterns maximize the projection of grouping boundaries at the end of lines, couplets, and quatrains by what the present study calls the proximity principle (see chapter 2).

Hayes (2009a) reviews and evaluates Halle and Lerdahl's (1993) text-setting model. He accepts our method of first assigning main stresses and then filling in the interstices, but he convincingly demonstrates that an OT approach that includes additional factors such as evenness and a normative number of main stresses achieves better results than does the one-dimensional algorithm that we employed. The rules presented in chapter 2 are more in the spirit of both *GTTM*'s preference rules and the procedures of OT than are those of the 1993 article, and presumably they could be quantified in comparable terms. However, OT derives a winner-take-all solution, whereas in the present model there is often more than one preferred solution. Hayes, Wilson, and Shisko (2012) rectify this OT shortcoming by introducing grammars that rank solutions probabilistically on a gradient. This is a computational advance beyond anything attempted in this book—albeit on a theoretical foundation of poetic feet and W S slots that is not shared by the present theory.

A curious feature of these prosodic and text-setting articles is that they use both metrical and stress grids yet do not explicitly say so. In Hayes (1995), stress grids appear routinely. But in these articles, if the metrical grid is notated, the stress grid is represented in a nongrid way, for instance, by employing accent marks on main stresses. As a result, differences in well-formedness between the two grids are not examined. Nor is a direct comparison of paired grids explored as part of a potential formalization in which the number of stress-beat mismatches could be tabulated and ranked in strength according to prosodic level.

These articles also assume their metrical grids as given. They present a duple-beat grid with at least three levels, often with an upbeat. This may be a satisfactory choice for the verse corpus studied in Hayes and Kaun, but as a general assumption, it is not justified. Many folk lyrics are in ternary meter (as in figure 4.9). And a metrical grid does not exist a priori; its context generates it by finding a best fit between typically irregular stresses and a limited repertory of periodic beat patterns.

4.4 THE IAMBIC-TROCHAIC LAW AND LINE TEMPLATES

The minimal bracketed stress grids in Hayes (1995), out of which all other bracketed grids are built in his theory, are two feet, the trochee and iamb, shown in figure 4.10. Unlike typical applications of the poetic foot, they are phonological concepts that need not violate word, clitic, or phonological boundaries. They could be extended logically to groupings of three syllables, but Hayes abjures dactylic and anapestic groupings and assigns

(a)   (b)

(x   )   (x)
(x x)   (x x)   FIGURE 4.10 Hayes's core feet: (a) trochee, (b) iamb.

extra-metrical syllables to avoid ternary bracketed grids. From a musical point of view, there is no justification for extra-metrical syllables. The insistence on binary grouping and branching is a recurring theme in generative linguistics, in syntactic as well as phonological theory. The present model parts company in this respect because ternary groupings, grids, and trees are not unusual in representations of musical structure.

Hayes advances a principle underlying his foot inventory, the so-called iambic-trochaic law (Hayes, 1995, p. 80):

Intensity condition: Elements contrasting in intensity [loudness] naturally form groupings with initial prominence.

Duration condition: Elements contrasting in duration naturally form groupings with final prominence.

This principle was first articulated by early experimental psychologists (Bolton, 1894; Woodrow, 1909). Wagner (2022) argues that, rather than an iambic-trochaic characterization, it is better understood as an orthogonal interaction of the Gestalt factors of figure-ground prominence and grouping by proximity. This view suits my musical perspective better, but because this chapter is concerned with intersections with generative linguistics, I shall continue to refer to it as the iambic-trochaic law.

Figure 4.11 illustrates the intensity condition with steady eighth notes to neutralize duration and with accents to represent greater intensity on

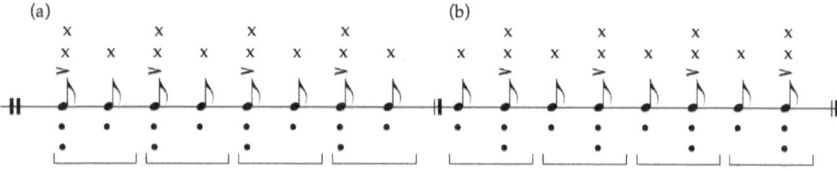

FIGURE 4.11 The intensity condition of the iambic-trochaic law: (a) in-phase trochaic pattern, (b) out-of-phase iambic pattern.

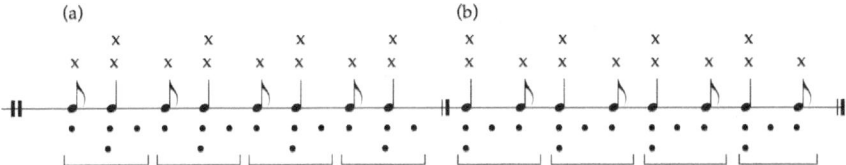

FIGURE 4.12 The duration condition of the iambic-trochaic law: (a) upbeat-downbeat iambic pattern, (b) nonpreferred grouping pattern.

alternating attacks. In 4.11a, strong beats are inferred on the accented notes, so the metrical grid lines up with the stress grid; the grouping is in phase with the grids. This is a trochaic pattern. In 4.11b, the accent-grid pattern is the same, but the grouping is out of phase with it, yielding an iambic pattern. Listeners naturally gravitate toward 4.11a instead of 4.11b because they prefer, all else being equal, interpretations in which the time span from one grouping segment to the next is not in conflict with the time span from one strong beat to the next.

Figure 4.12 describes the law's duration condition with alternating durations in a 1:2 ratio and with uniform intensity. In 4.12a, grouping boundaries arise after the quarter notes by the proximity principle: events that are close together group together. Strong stresses and beats are inferred on the longer quarter notes. The result is an upbeat-downbeat iambic pattern. In 4.12b, the duration-grid relationship is the same, but the grouping boundaries are placed after the shorter durations, in conflict with the proximity principle. This makes 4.12b difficult to sustain as a hearable interpretation. Condition 4.12a is preferred.[9]

The iambic-trochaic law grounds the treatment of stress and duration in general perception beyond its musical or linguistic instantiation. The minimal iambic unit in figure 4.10b is the nucleus of all iambic lines and can expand to two, three, four, or five iterations. It is the basis of the template in figure 3.12b and is repeated in figure 4.13a in tetrameter form. Similarly,

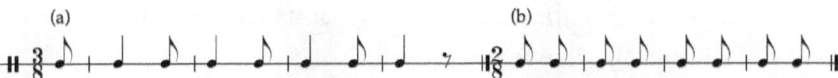

FIGURE 4.13 The (a) iambic and (b) trochaic templates with four downbeats per line.

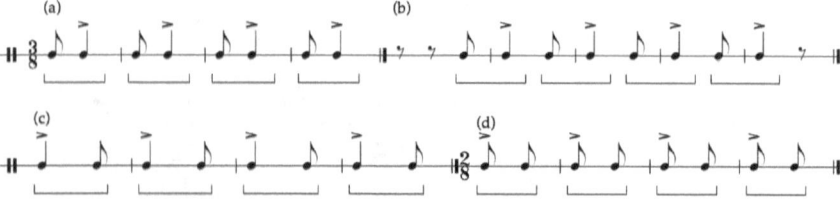

FIGURE 4.14 Conflicts in the trochaic template: (a) if durations are in a 1:2 ratio, conflict between downbeat and accent; (b) realignment of (a) into an iambic pattern; (c) if durations are in a 1:2 ratio, conflict between durations and grouping; (d) trochaic pattern with durations in a 1:1 ratio.

figure 4.11a is an expansion of the minimal trochaic unit in figure 4.10a and is repeated in figure 4.13b with a 2/8 time signature.

Another way of looking at the trochaic template is to consider the alternatives if the durations are in a 1:2 instead of a 1:1 ratio. In figure 4.14a, the downbeats and intensity accents are in conflict, pushing the listener to realign the rhythm into the upbeat-downbeat iambic pattern of 4.14b. In 4.14c, the proximity principle creates a conflict between duration and grouping, pushing a realignment of the grouping from a downbeat-afterbeat pattern again into the upbeat-downbeat pattern of 4.14b. The only way to avoid these perceptual conflicts and preserve a functional trochaic pattern is to neutralize durations to the 1:1 ratio of figure 4.14d.

This review of consequences of the iambic-trochaic law does not imply that a rhythmic realization of a nominally iambic or trochaic line ought to match its template. Deviations from the iambic template have been amply documented in this and previous chapters. For the trochaic template, consider the beginning of Edgar Allan Poe's "The Raven": "Once upon a midnight dreary, while I pondered, weak and weary." It is in trochaic octameter, or two lines of trochaic tetrameter written as one. Figure 4.15a shows its grouping and stress analysis, and 4.15b fits it to the trochaic template. (This monotonous reading could be somewhat alleviated by inserting a silent quarter rest after "dreary," separating the two intonational phrases.) Figure 4.15c shows a metrical-durational realization using the present model. The stress grid is included to bring out its relationship to the metrical and durational assignments.

The difference between figure 4.15b and c is considerable, above all because of the clitic groups "a midnight," "I pondered," and "and weary."

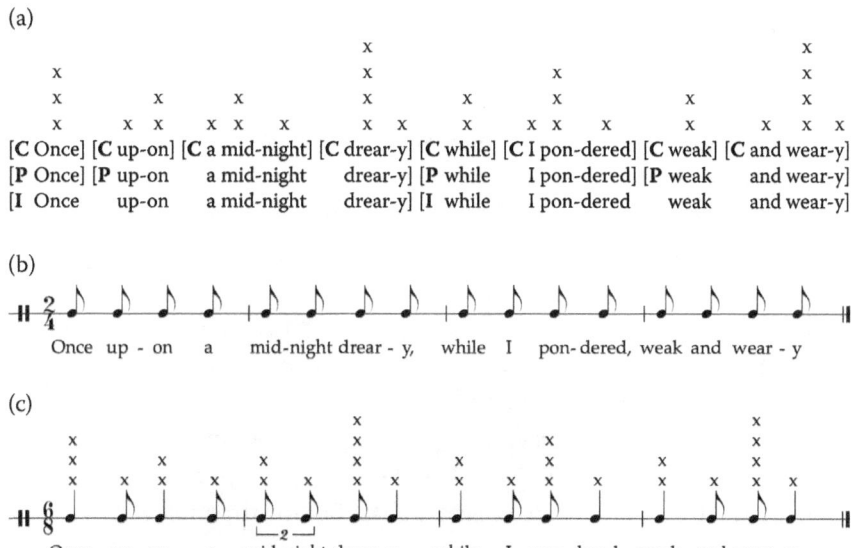

FIGURE 4.15 The first line of Edgar Allan Poe's "The Raven": (a) its prosodic hierarchy and stress grid, (b) its realization in the trochaic template, (c) a realization employing the present model.

As mentioned, clitic words in English usually precede the clitic host, and this fact of the language makes upbeat-downbeat iambic patterns far more common than downbeat-afterbeat trochaic patterns. (The situation might be otherwise in another language.) The only reliable indicators of a trochaic line are a stressed initial syllable and an unstressed final syllable. But these occur not infrequently in iambic lines as well, described in traditional terms by an initial trochaic substitution and an added weak final syllable. The upshot is that rhythmic realizations of nominally trochaic lines rarely conform to the trochaic template. Often, as in Poe's line, they are equally close to the iambic template.

4.5 LINE COMPLEXITY

The trochaic and iambic templates, as the simplest versions of their types, can serve as benchmarks for the tension or complexity of a trochaic or iambic line.[10] They serve neither as a priori rhythmic forms modified by substitutions, as advocated by Wimsatt and Beardsley (1959), nor as preordained W S slots, as posited by Halle and Keyser. Rather, they are useful points of reference without further theoretical baggage.

A line can be complex in various ways. Consider the first quatrain of Sonnet 29 in figure 4.16. The upper staff in each system supplies the iambic-pentameter template with accompanying words, and the lower staff shows derived versions of the lines, taken from figures 3.7, 2.20, 3.11b, and 3.13c, respectively. The first line is complex only in its syncopated treatment of "and men's." The second line is also close to the template. The third line is more complex, however, because it combines duple and triple subdivisions and is one bar shorter than the template. The fourth line continues this pattern. Viewing the four lines together, the juxtaposition of these rhythms against the template brings out the parallel metrical-durational values of lines 1–2 and of lines 3–4, and this despite their contrasting syntactic structures. The rhyme scheme is abab, but the rhythmic form is aabb.

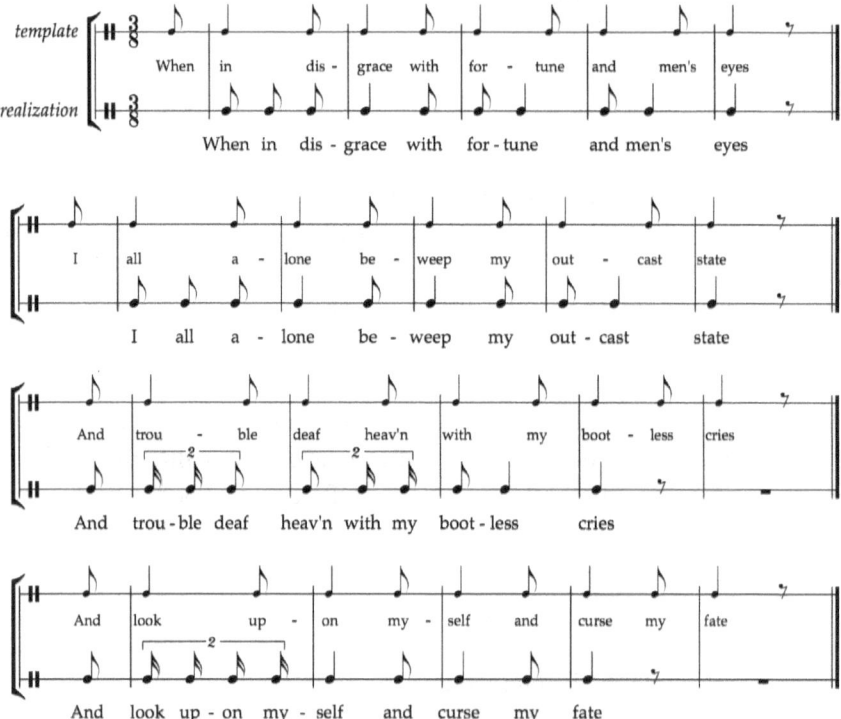

FIGURE 4.16 The first four lines of Sonnet 29 with their iambic-pentameter templates paired with their proposed metrical-durational realizations.

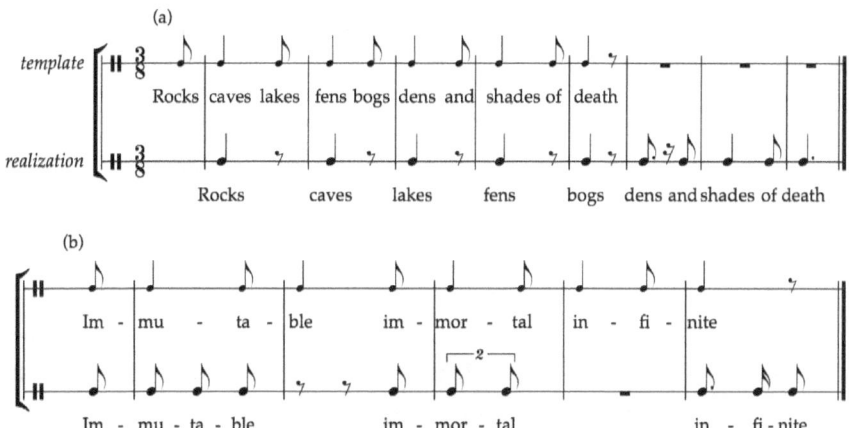

FIGURE 4.17 Lines from John Milton's *Paradise Lost*: (a) line 2.621 in the iambic template and in its metrical-durational realization, (b) line 3.73 in the same.

For more extreme cases of complexity, consider figure 4.17. The realization in 4.17a is repeated from figure 3.20b. The setting of the string of nouns, all on downbeats, differs markedly from the iambic template. Further, the realization has eight downbeats to the template's five. A contrasting complexity occurs in figure 4.17b, repeated from figure 3.21b. Here, the line lengths are the same (counting in downbeats), and the variance comes instead from the number of main stresses, three instead of five.

The iambic template resembles Youmans's (1989) iambic metrical prototype. Both constructs act as reference points from which actual poetic lines diverge in gradient fashion. There are two differences, however. First, his prototype is built on fixed W S positions and feet (following Kiparsky, 1977), whereas the present model specifies a metrical-durational pattern and leaves grouping to the prosodic hierarchy, the details of which vary from line to line. Second, his prototype has multiple hierarchical levels, all the way up to the line: feet are organized in a 2 + (1 + 2) grouping—or, alternatively, a (2 + 1) + 2 grouping. In contrast, the present model shows the metrical hierarchy only up to the level of a 3/8 bar. It would be feasible to extend the metrical hierarchy one level farther, as in figures 2.19 and 2.20, but not as far as the entire line because metrical grids fade perceptually at spans greater than a few seconds.

Even a slight hierarchical extension of the iambic template comes up against the variability of prosodic boundaries within a line. For example, in

When in disgrace/ with fortune and men's eyes,	*[4 + 6 syllables]*
I all alone/ beweep my outcast state,	*[4 + 6 syllables]*
And trouble deaf heav'n/ with my bootless cries,	*[5 + 5 syllables]*
And look upon myself/ and curse my fate,	*[6 + 4 syllables]*

FIGURE 4.18 The distribution of syllables separated by phonological phrase boundaries in the first four lines of Sonnet 29.

the first four lines of Sonnet 29, the phonological phrases divide into two 4 + 6 syllables per line, then 5 + 5, and then 6 + 4, as shown in figure 4.18. Given such variability, it seems dubious to posit hierarchy to the template beyond the minimal iambic unit and its sequential iterations.

Halle and Keyser (1971) quantify the complexity or tension of a poetic line by counting the number of stress mismatches in W S slots. Kiparsky (1977) adds foot bracketing and prohibits mismatches within polysyllabic words and clitic groups. Youmans (1989) observes that a given mismatch is stronger or weaker depending on its line position. He uses the number of S nodes in his hierarchical iambic prototypes to weight mismatches according to foot position.

Unlike Halle-Keyser's, Kiparsky's, and Youmans' approaches, the present theory does not quantify degrees of line complexity. But it could do so up to a point and in a manner parallel to what they propose. For example, Youmans's weightings for a given syllable could be approximated by tabulating the syllable's number of x's in the stress grid against its number of dots in the metrical grid. The weightings would come from syllabic stress and the prosodic hierarchy rather than from a hierarchical foot prototype. However, the present theory engages complexity in more ways than stress-beat mismatches. It assigns syllable lengths that often deviate in different degrees from the template, for instance, short-long instead of long-short within a 3/8 bar or shifting from triple to duple subdivisions within a constant tactus. Sometimes it derives line lengths that contract or expand in the number of downbeats. It shuns transgressions of phonological phrase boundaries and, as will be seen shortly, it disfavors double anacruses at line beginnings. It is difficult to compare and quantify such diverse dimensions of complexity. This is a scaling problem beyond the scope of this book.

The analogous situation in music is more tractable because tonal tension derives in large part from the components of tonal space and tonal

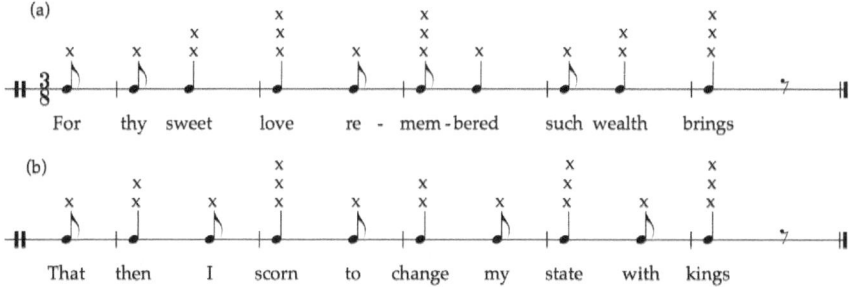

FIGURE 4.19 The closing couplet of Sonnet 29 in its metrical-durational realization.

attraction, which are relatively amenable to quantification. There is enough data on musical tension to guide the strength of the respective contributions of its structural components and to generate composite tension curves that are experimentally testable. The tonal model yields a tension curve over an entire musical passage or piece.[11]

I doubt, by contrast, the feasibility of attributing a tension curve over more than a few consecutive poetic lines. At larger distances, meaning and narrative overwhelm the factor of line complexity. The parallel is imperfect: in tonal music, the reference point is the tonic, a fundamental feature that is absent from language. The simplest version of a line type—its template—is hardly a tonic. Yet there is something to the analogy. Resolution on a tonic achieves relaxation and closure. Consider the final couplet of Sonnet 29 in figure 4.19 from this perspective. The figure includes stress markings to guide the metrical-durational realization. The rhythm of 4.19a resembles that of the sonnet's first line, particularly in their penultimate bars (compare the rhythm of the first line in figure 4.16). This somewhat tense line relaxes into 4.19b, which achieves rhythmic closure by fully fitting the iambic template. The effect of the two lines in sequence is broadly analogous to cadential relaxation in music.[12]

4.6 RHYTHMIC PATTERNS AS EVIDENCE

A strength of the generative-metrics school is its accumulation of evidence in support of generalizations about prosodic rhythm. I propose to engage such generalizations instead through evidence from metrical-durational patterns. To simplify the options, the following discussion deals only with iambic pentameter, and it assumes that line endings coincide with intonational phrase boundaries, setting aside issues of enjambment.

One generative-metrics generalization, as discussed earlier, is that stresses at left edges of prosodic units are free but at right edges are strict (Hayes, 1989). The degree of strictness depends in gradient fashion on grouping level (Youmans, 1983). Thus, mismatches between stress and W S positions are avoided in polysyllabic words and in clitic groups unless phonological phrase boundaries directly precede them. This is a version of the congruence principle (see chapter 2.5). But according to the generalization, mismatches are increasingly acceptable at the left edges of larger prosodic units, from phonological phrases to intonational phrases and utterances. At right edges of larger prosodic levels, however, they are avoided.

Figure 4.20 gives options in the present model for left-edge generalization, assuming three adjacent syllables that do not violate the congruence principle. Figure 4.20a shows a typical iambic pattern. Also acceptable is 4.20b, which corresponds to traditional trochaic substitution at line beginnings and after medial caesuras; 4.20c gives a duple variant of 4.20b. But the double anacrusis in 4.20d is not preferred because here the grouping is well out of phase with the metrical spans between strong beats, as illustrated in 4.20e.[13]

Figure 4.21 gives options for right-edge generalization. The most preferred is figure 4.21a, in which the arrival of a stressed syllable on a downbeat is reinforced by its greater duration, inducing closure. The longer anacrusis in 4.21b slightly weakens the effect. Figure 4.21c achieves closure because the final syllable is understood as an elaboration of the stressed penultimate syllable; it is a variant of 4.21a. In a time-span representation as in figure 4.6d, the final syllable in 4.21c would reduce out at the

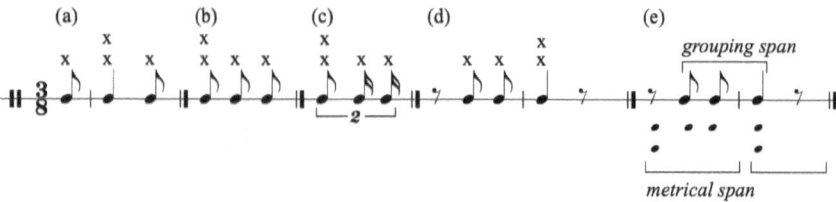

FIGURE 4.20 Left-edge cases of abstract rhythmic patterns in (a–d); (e) shows how out of phase the relationship is in (d) between its grouping and metrical spans.

FIGURE 4.21 Right-edge cases of abstract rhythmic patterns: (a–c) are preferred and (d) less so; (e) is strongly avoided.

next level. Figure 4.21d is less preferred because the repeating eighth notes imply further continuation. Figure 4.21e is strongly avoided because of the mismatch between stress and downbeat; it sends the rhythmic gesture forward instead of articulating closure.

Just as a musical phrase has a beginning, middle, and end, so the preferred left- and right-edge rhythmic patterns in figures 4.20 and 4.21 can be said to have beginning and ending line functions separated by variable middle functions. In this respect, the opening lines in figure 4.22 of "Nothing Gold Can Stay" and Sonnet 29 are alike: they begin with the pattern of 4.20b, followed by a middle, and end with the pattern of 4.21a or b. The only functional difference is that the middle is short in figure 4.22a and long in 4.22b.

The first line of Hamlet's soliloquy is functionally more complex. If the unadorned realization in figure 4.23a is chosen, the line has two beginning-ending functions, the first starting with "To be" and ending with the second "to be," the second starting with "that is" and ending with "the question." But if, as in figure 4.23b, pauses are taken in response to the punctuation and "not to be" is compressed rhythmically, the second "to be" takes a middle function, thereby projecting the line forward over the caesura to the second beginning at "that is . . ." This is a more dynamic reading.

A second generalization is that the standard transformation from the iambic prototype, trochaic substitution, is restricted. Kiparsky (1977)

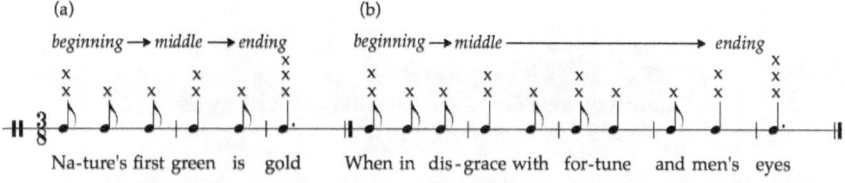

FIGURE 4.22 Phrase functions in the opening lines of "Nothing Gold Can Stay" and Sonnet 29.

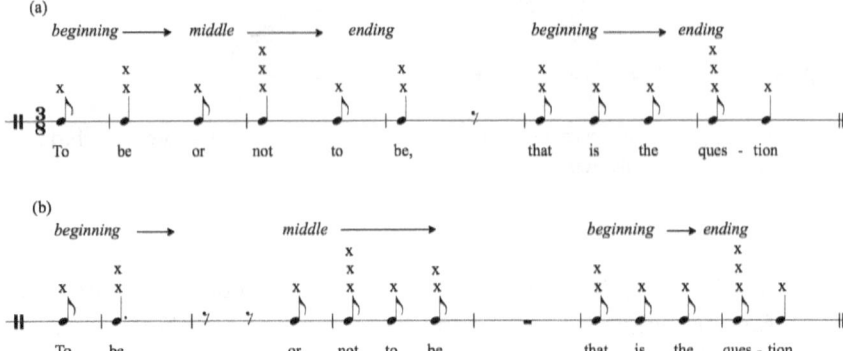

FIGURE 4.23 Phrase functions in the first line of Hamlet's soliloquy: (a) a straightforward realization, (b) an elaborated version.

observes that most poets writing in the iambic-pentameter tradition avoid it in a disyllabic word if the stressed syllable is in a W slot and the word crosses a foot boundary. That is, disyllabic word and foot boundaries normally coincide. Thus, the within-foot trochaic substitution at "image" in figure 4.24a is acceptable, but neither Shakespeare nor Milton would have written Donne's line in 4.24b, with its cross-foot mismatch at "behold."

Kiparsky uses the distinction between in-foot and cross-foot trochaic substitution to argue that the poetic foot Is a necessary construct in prosodic analysis. In the present theory, there are no feet, so an in-foot versus

(a)
```
         x        x         x         x
x x x    x     x x       x x    x     x
Creat/ed thee,/ in the/ image/ of God
W  S/W   S  /  W  S / W  S / W  S
```

(b)
```
              x              x          x
x      x  x      x      x    x     x
x x    x    x    x x x   x   x     x
Shall be/hold God,/ and ne/ver taste/ death's woe
W   S/W    S  /  W  S/W    S  /  W    S
```

FIGURE 4.24 Trochaic substitution and foot boundaries: (a) within a foot at "image" in *Paradise Lost*, 7.527; (b) crossing a foot boundary in "behold" in Donne's holy sonnet 7, line 8.

cross-foot account is not available. The intuition behind the distinction shows up instead in degrees of metrical-durational complexity. Figure 4.25 illustrates by adapting figure 4.24 to the present model. The iambic template in 4.25a shows conventional feet in brackets. The first metrical-durational realization modifies the grouping brackets in order not to violate word or clitic boundaries and compresses the line into four 3/8 bars. The second realization alternatively reinstates a five-bar length in response to the comma after "thee." In neither case does "image" cause a problem. In 4.25b, however, "behold" causes serious rhythmic complications. The first realization realigns the metrical-durational structure so that beats and

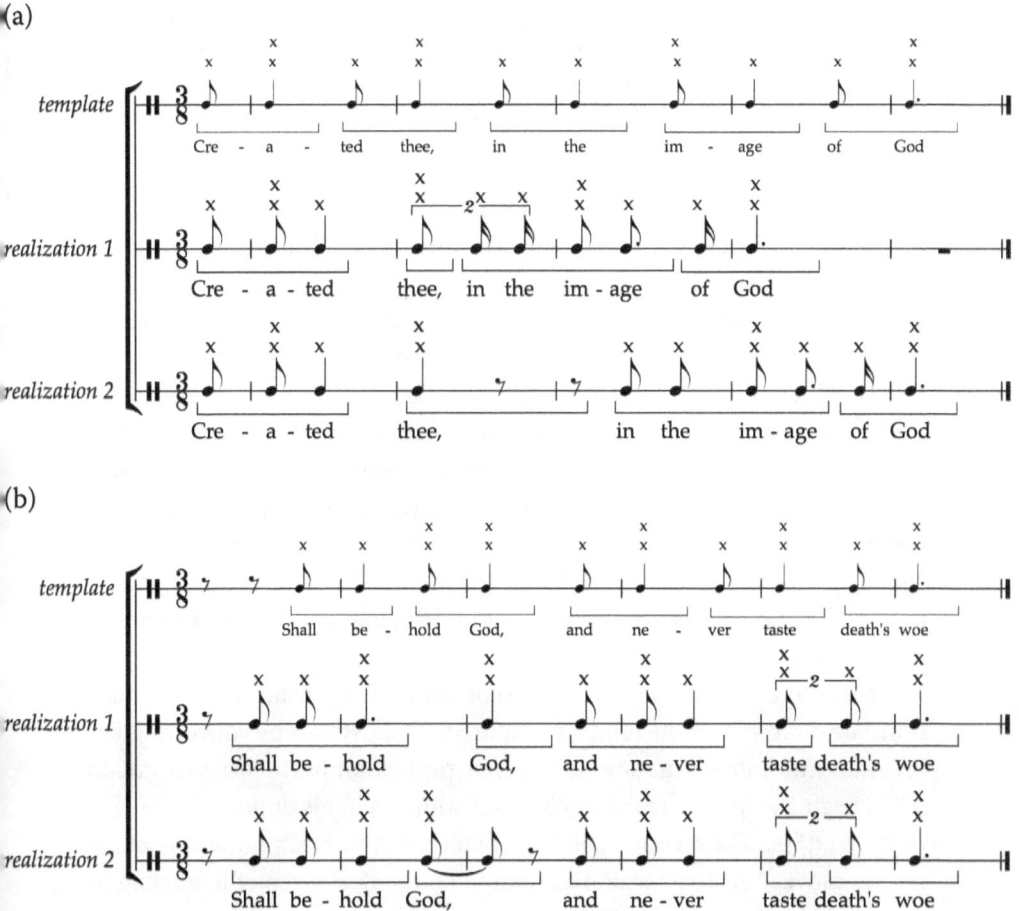

FIGURE 4.25 Figure 4.24 adapted to the present model.

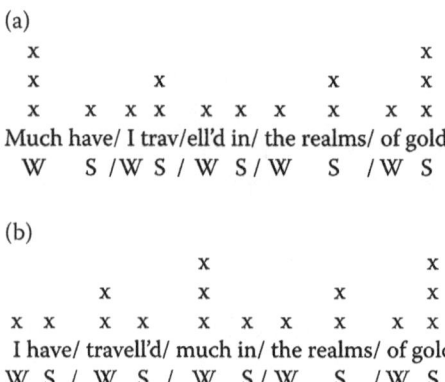

FIGURE 4.26 First line of John Keats's sonnet "On First Looking into Chapman's Homer," shown with stresses over iambic feet: (a) the original, (b) the line in syntactically noninverted form.

stresses match but at the cost of an unacceptably long duration (within a phonological phrase) on "-hold." The second realization rectifies this defect but at the cost of tying "God" across a bar line. These results illuminate the widespread judgment that Donne takes prosodic liberties that most poets in the iambic-pentameter tradition would not countenance.

A third generalization is that a common function of syntactic inversions—that is, non-normative word order, as often happens in poetry—is to approximate the iambic prototype, thereby lessening the degree of a line's complexity (Youmans, 1983). Consider the inverted syntax in figure 4.26a compared to the line's noninverted form in 4.26b. Keats's original is prosodically unexceptional, but at "travell'd" the noninverted version violates both Halle and Keyser's stress maximum principle and Kiparsky's monosyllabic word constraint.

This difference emerges in the present model in a greater metrical-durational deviation from the template. Figure 4.27 illustrates by converting figure 4.26 into musical notation. The first realization of the original line in 4.27a begins with a standard trochaic substitution but is unnaturally long at unstressed "in." The second realization (which is more easily notated in duple meter) moves "in" to a weak beat, and in so doing shortens the reading to four bars in coordination with the line's four main stresses. This realization is complex but acceptable. The line's noninverted form in 4.27b presents a

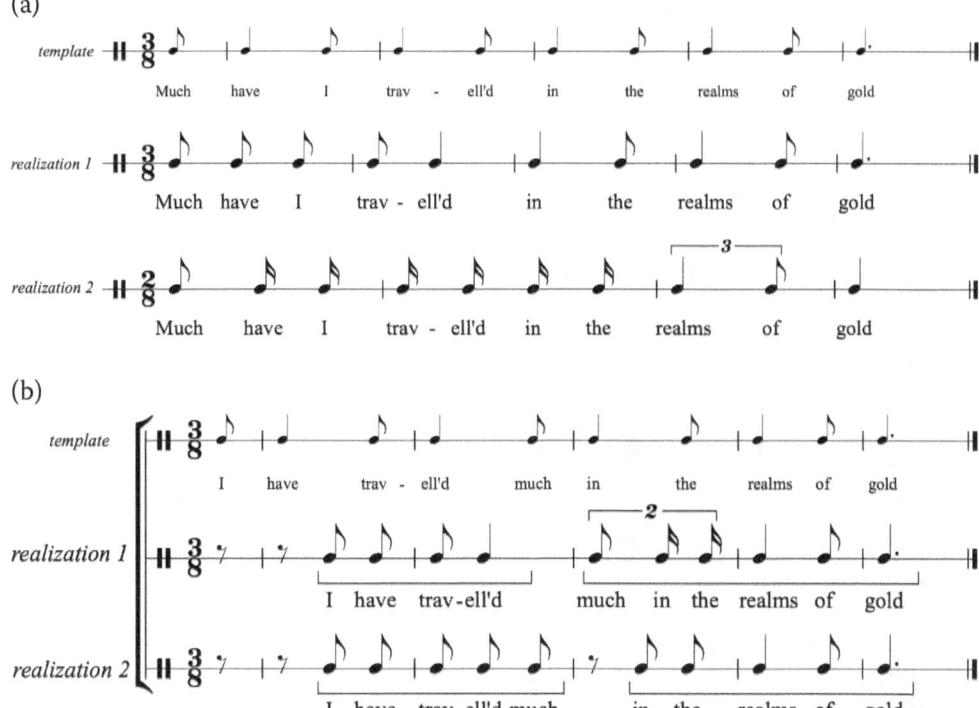

FIGURE 4.27 Figure 4.26 adapted to the present model.

contrasting picture. Its first realization results in two nonpreferred structures: there is a double anacrusis at the line's beginning, and, as shown by the brackets, "much" groups with the second instead of the first phonological group, contrary to the sense of the original. The second realization in 4.26b rectifies the latter problem by moving "much" back an eighth note, but in so doing this stressed word arrives awkwardly on a weak beat.

Another example from Youmans (1983): "void immense" in figure 4.28a accommodates his iambic prototype, whereas in 4.28b the normal word order "immense void" violates the monosyllabic word constraint (but not the stress maximum principle). The present model, not having poetic feet and the rules associated with them, does not generate this analysis. Nevertheless, the metrical-durational realization in 4.28c shows that Milton's original line perfectly fits the iambic template of figure 4.13a, whereas

(a)
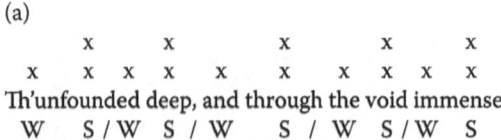

(b)
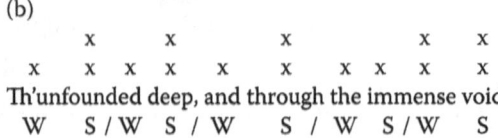

(c)
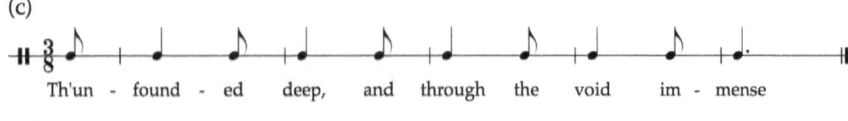

(d)
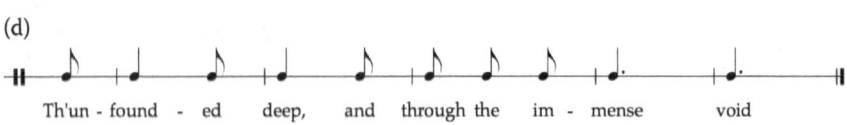

FIGURE 4.28 *Paradise Lost*, 2.829: (a) the original line, analyzed with poetic feet; (b) the same line but with the last two words inverted to normal ordering; (c) metrical-durational realization of (a); (d) metrical-durational realization of (b).

the noninverted ordering of 4.28d creates a problematic rhythm, the long duration on "-mense" within a phonological phrase. One might argue that this appropriately lends focus to "immense," but the inverted order in Milton's line accomplishes the same goal in a less anomalous way by placing "immense" in a position of maximal nuclear stress.

From my perspective, Milton manipulates word order not to circumvent an impermissible foot construction; rather, he strives for smoothly undulating rhythms and hence avoids noninverted orderings if they jar the rhythmic flow. This very different explanation depends on musical metrical-durational analysis, a resource beyond the purview of traditional scansion or its generative-prosodic refinements.

5

Contour

5.1 GOALS AND ASSUMPTIONS

The metrical-durational realizations in chapters 2–4 are monotonal, but actual speech rises and falls in pitch. This chapter develops a method for assigning intonational contour to poetic lines.[1] Changes in contour are a source of semantic and affective nuance, and a given phrase can be spoken in a variety of contour patterns. This variability makes contour more resistant than prosodic rhythm to systematic treatment. My limited goal is to assign a normative contour that sounds natural and that can serve as a point of departure for further analysis from a musical point of view. As in the exposition of prosodic rhythm, references to other intonational theories are deferred until after the model is presented.

I begin with four postulates that set the stage for the model. First, contour is not just a continuous rise and fall in pitch but anchors on central vowels of discrete syllables in sequence. Figure 5.1 illustrates with an abstract intonational phrase. The phrase's contour is continuous in (a), but in (b) it breaks up into syllables, represented by "S" with connecting contour lines. The model assumes that (b) is the case. This view meshes with chapter 2's rhythmic components, which similarly take syllables to be the basic units of analysis, and it facilitates the use of musical notation.

FIGURE 5.1 Abstract representation of contour: (a) contour over continuous sound, (b) contour over a sequence of discrete syllables.

A second postulate is that the sound of a syllable does not fully resolve perceptually into a stable pitch but is nevertheless relatively low or high in relation to other syllables. Pitch fuzziness results from the continuous rise and fall of the sound stream. The degree of fuzziness varies according to context. Some languages sound more melodious than others because their pitch resolution is clearer. At the other extreme, the pitch/nonpitch boundary itself can be uncertain. Certain genres of speech singing—as in religious chanting, sprechstimme, some cabaret, and rap—overtly exploit pitch/nonpitch ambiguity.

These two postulates seek a balance between continuous sound and discrete units of sound. A sound stream is continuous yet has moments that are sufficiently stable to be identified as events that are relatively low or high.

A third postulate is that there are four tiers of pitch height, shown in figure 5.2 on a musical staff of two lines. Tier 1 is on the lower line, tier 2 between the two lines, tier 3 on the upper line, and tier 4 above the upper line. The seemingly arbitrary choice of four tiers is based on my experience of hearing and transcribing the contour of spoken phrases. Three tiers do not offer enough distinctions, and five are too fine-grained to resolve reliably.[2] These pitch heights are not absolute but are relative to one another. One person's voice may be higher or lower than another's; a person may speak with an exaggerated contour or a comparatively flat one. The tier

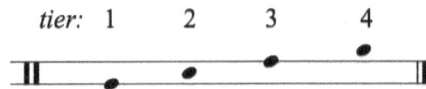

FIGURE 5.2 Four tiers of pitch height.

relationships do not change under these conditions. There is a general tendency across languages for the pitch level to decline within an intonational phrase or utterance because of the diaphragm's exhalation of air. Imagine figure 5.2 as tilted downward to the right about 15 degrees; the relationships on the tiers remain constant. These considerations hold for tone languages as well (Ladd, 2008).

A fourth postulate concerns not the elements of contour analysis but the way in which contour is assigned. One possibility is that a speaker generates contour from left to right, syllable by syllable, with no memory or expectation. Contrary to this sequential view, a hierarchical approach assigns the tier position of a given syllable in relation to past and future more prominent syllables. The model takes the hierarchical view. It derives contour from global to local levels because otherwise the tier position of subordinate syllables cannot be determined.

5.2 THE CONTOUR MODEL

The contour model will be introduced in stages. For the moment, assume that each syllable has a single pitch height. This is an oversimplification; long syllables often glide between two pitch levels. This feature will be addressed in section 5.3.

We begin with a distinction between syllabic height and syllabic prominence.[3] A syllable's pitch height corresponds to its position on the four tiers. Its prominence is the intonational equivalent of rhythmic stress. As with stress, height is a strong acoustic contributor to prominence. A strict mapping between height and prominence, however, would be mistaken. Other factors that project prominence are syllabic length and adjacency to a major prosodic boundary.[4]

Contour prominence depends on stress in relation to the prosodic hierarchy. As discussed in chapter 2, the most stressed syllable receives four x's at the intonational level, three at the phonological level, and two at the clitic level; clitic syllables and weak syllables in polysyllabic words receive one x. To show the prominence hierarchy, a notation adapted from musical reduction theory represents note values as standing not for duration but for hierarchical domination. In figure 5.3, a quarter note signifies prominence for a syllable with a stress of four x's, an eighth note for a syllable with three x's, a sixteenth note for a syllable with two x's, and a stemless notehead for a syllable with one x.

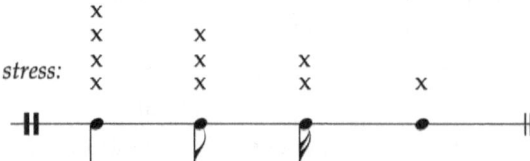

FIGURE 5.3 A musical notation for syllabic prominence. Durational values represent degrees of prominence and correspond to degrees of syllabic stress.

Figure 5.4 shows the hierarchically derived contour for the first couplet of Frost's "Nothing Gold Can Stay" if prominence were incorrectly to map directly to pitch height. The analysis begins at level figure 5.4a by assigning the two four-x words, "gold" and "hold," to tier 4. At level 5.4b, "green" and "hard-" have three x's and are placed on tier 3.[5] At level 5.4c, "Na-," "first," and "hue" have two x's and are on tier 2. At level 5.4d, the syllables "-ture's," "is," "Her," "-est," and "to" have one x and appear on tier 1.

This mapping is unsatisfactory. There are awkward leaps of unstressed syllables—"is," "Her," "-est," and "to"—to the more prominent syllables with which they group in the prosodic hierarchy. Such leaps are particularly

FIGURE 5.4 Hierarchical derivation of the contour of the first couplet of Robert Frost's "Nothing Gold Can Stay," assuming a direct mapping of pitch prominence to pitch height.

disruptive because unstressed syllables are usually short in duration. Therefore, to promote a smooth curve, an unstressed syllable will be assigned to one tier below the stressed syllable with which it groups in the prosodic hierarchy. But if its dominating syllable is on tier 1, the unstressed syllable cannot be one tier lower, so it is assigned one step higher to tier 2.

A second problem with figure 5.4 is that "hold" is much too high. Declarative utterances in English generally end low, so utterance-ending syllables with four x's will be assigned not to tier 4 but to tier 1. They project prominence not by height but by being at the right edge of a major prosodic boundary and by being relatively long in duration. Lowness and length combine to project closure. Even "gold," the other four-x syllable in the couplet, is too high unless it is meant to receive special emphasis. But such syllables at the ends of intonational phrases must not be relocated on tier 1 because that would signal premature closure. They are better placed on tier 2, where they project the moderate lowness appropriate to the right edge of a major prosodic boundary yet signal that the utterance has not concluded.

Figure 5.5 reanalyzes the contour of the Frost couplet by these criteria: "gold," which terminates an intonational phrase, is on tier 2, and "hold," which terminates the utterance, is on tier 1. In the first line, the unstressed syllables "-ture's" and "is" are on tier 1 because they are one tier lower than "Na-" and "gold," respectively. In the second line, "Her" and "-est" are one tier below "hard-," but "to" is one tier above "hold" because the latter is on tier 1.

FIGURE 5.5 An improved contour analysis of the first couplet of "Nothing Gold Can Stay."

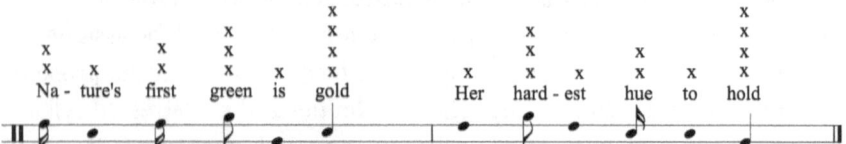

FIGURE 5.6 Optional analysis that fills out the tier space (compare to figure 5.5d).

A consequence of moving "gold" to tier 2, however, is that tier 4 is now vacant, leaving only three active tier levels. Moving "green" up a step from tier 3 to tier 4 will fill out the tier space. Because "green" dominates (or is head of) the phonological phrase "Nature's first green," the other syllables in the phrase also move up a step. The same reasoning applies to "Her hardest." Figure 5.6 gives the result.

Figure 5.7 inserts the contour from figure 5.6 into the couplet's metrical-durational realization in figure 2.17b, with a silent tactus beat added between the two lines. Contained within this seemingly transparent representation are the structures of the prosodic hierarchy, phonological stress, meter, duration, and contour.

Figure 5.8 applies the same procedure to the opening lines of Shakespeare's Sonnet 29. Again, each line is an intonational phrase, and the two together form an utterance (ignoring the appended subordinate phrases that continue to the sonnet's eighth line). The stress grid duplicates the one in figure 2.5. The most prominent syllables, those with four x's, appear in figure 5.8a, with "eyes," which terminates an intonational phrase, on tier 2, and "state," which terminates the utterance, on tier 1. In 5.8b, the syllables with three x's, "-grace" and "-lone," are on tier 4. In 5.8c, the syllables with two x's that belong in phonological phrases with "-grace" and "-lone" are on tier 3, but those that are not stay on tier 2. In 5.8d, the remaining unstressed syllables are a tier below the dominating syllables in their disyllabic words or clitic groups.

FIGURE 5.7 Combined contour and metrical-durational analysis for the first couplet of "Nothing Gold Can Stay." The metrical-durational realization is taken from figure 2.17b.

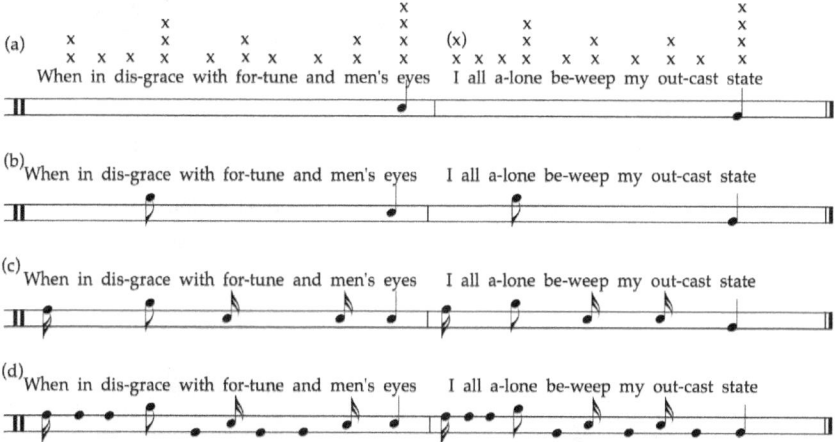

FIGURE 5.8 Hierarchical derivation of the contour of the first two lines of William Shakespeare's Sonnet 29.

Figure 5.9 plugs the contour in figure 5.8 into the couplet's metrical-durational realization taken from figure 2.20.

Unlike declarative utterances, many interrogatives rise at the end. Consider the first line of Shakespeare's Sonnet 18, "Shall I compare thee to a summer's day?" Figure 5.10 shows its prosodic hierarchy and stress analysis. The metrical-durational realization in figure 5.11a approximates the standard iambic template, clumsily assigning a strong beat and long duration to the unstressed syllable "to." Figure 5.11b instead highlights the phonological phrase boundary with an eighth rest after "thee" and assigns "to" to the subsequent weak beat. This better matches the stress grid. Figure 5.11b adds the option of duple rhythm for "-pare thee."

Figure 5.12 derives the contour for figure 5.11b. Let us temporarily assign tier 3 for a stressed syllable at the right boundary of an interrogative that can be answered by yes or no. Thus, four-x "day" appears on tier 3 in

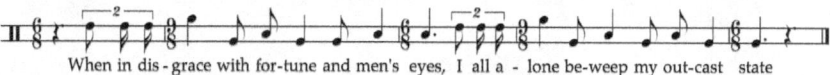

FIGURE 5.9 Combined contour and metrical-durational analysis for lines 1 and 2 of Sonnet 29.

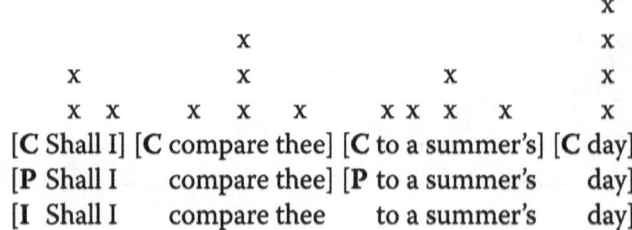

FIGURE 5.10 The prosodic hierarchy and stress grid for the first line of Shakespeare's Sonnet 18.

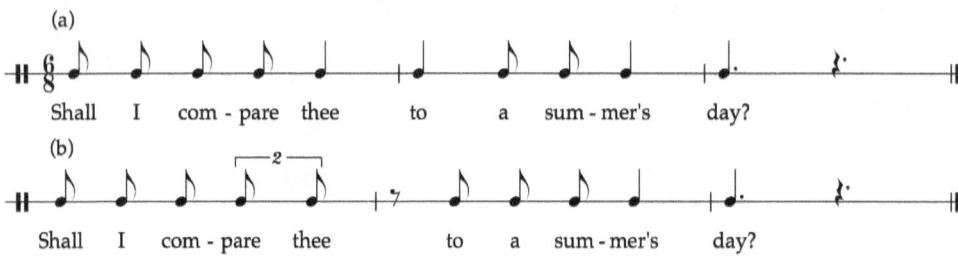

FIGURE 5.11 Two metrical-durational realizations of the first line of Sonnet 18.

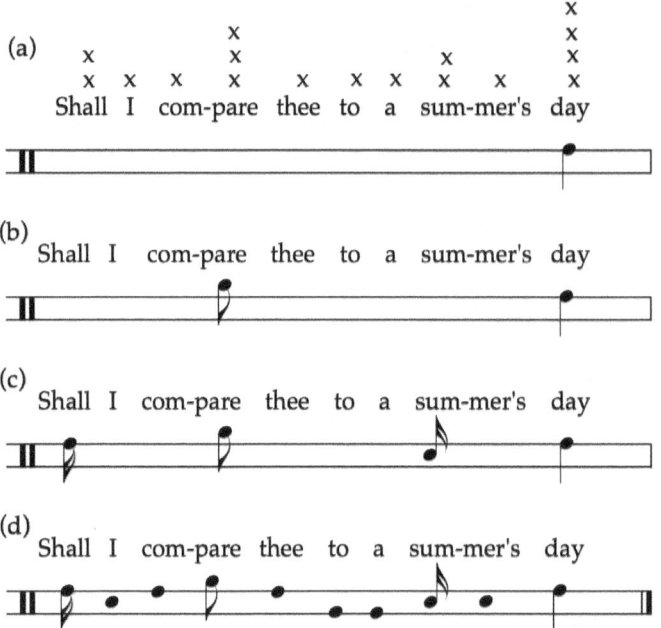

FIGURE 5.12 Contour analysis of the first line of Sonnet 18.

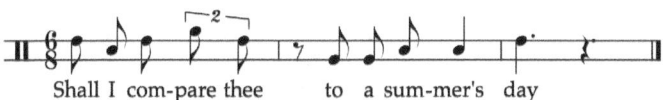

FIGURE 5.13 Combined contour and metrical-durational analysis for the first line of Sonnet 18.

figure 5.12a. The rest of the analysis proceeds as before: three-x "-pare" is on tier 4, bringing "Shall" to tier 3. In the second phonological phrase, "sum-" remains on tier 2. All but one of the unstressed syllables are one tier below the more prominent syllables they elaborate. The exception is "-mer's," which is optionally raised from tier 1 to tier 2 so that it smooths out the curve to "day" within the phonological phrase "to a summer's day."

Figure 5.13 completes the analysis by inserting the contour in figure 5.12 into the rhythm of figure 5.11b.

5.3 ADDITION OF BITONAL SYLLABLES

Up to this point, the model assigns a single pitch to each syllable. Not infrequently, a syllable is better understood as moving between two pitches, its focal center and its embellishment. Such a syllable is bitonal. Usually it is relatively long, affording time for elaboration. In figure 5.14, it is represented by a standard notehead for its focal pitch and a grace note for its embellishment, with the two connected by a slur (as in the notation of a musical melisma). The embellishing pitch can be either after the focal pitch, as in 5.14a and b, or before it, as in 5.14c and d; and it can be lower than the focal pitch, as in 5.14a and c, or higher, as in 5.14b and d.

This derivational stage takes place in the context of metrical-durational realizations rather than of the hierarchical format for tier assignments

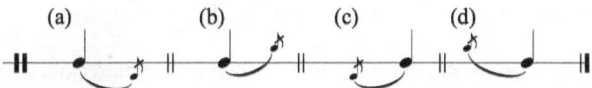

FIGURE 5.14 Repertory of bitonal pitch representations.

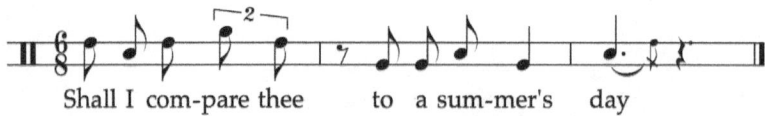

FIGURE 5.15 Bitonal treatment of "day" in the first line of Sonnet 18.

because of the essential role of syllabic duration in bitonal assignments. The embellishing pitch is generally either one tier above or below its focal companion in declaratives, but in the final syllable of a yes-no interrogative, a postfocal embellishment is exclusively one tier above its focal pitch. Because of the space taken by the obligatory final rise, the focal pitch is preferably on tier 2 instead of tier 3. Figure 5.15 illustrates with a bitonal treatment of "day" in the first line of Sonnet 18. The focal point of "day" is on tier 2, and the grace note appended to "day" is on tier 3.

In the first couplet of "Nothing Gold Can Stay" in figure 5.16, the postfocal embellishment of "green" eases the leap from "green" to "is." The focal pitch "gold" on tier 2 is followed by an embellishing slide downward. For "hold," in contrast, the embellishment precedes the descent to its focal pitch. That is, "gold" and "hold" cover the same tier space, but the emphasis of "gold" remains on tier 2 and that of "hold" on tier 1. The descending motion on "hold" reinforces its closing function. Finally, "hue" is optionally treated as bitonal to avoid tier repetition for "hue to;" there is a slight rise between the two syllables.

Figure 5.17 offers a similar treatment for the opening of Sonnet 29. The embellishments of "-grace" and "-lone" smooth out the turn downward to their succeeding syllables. The embellishing rise after the focal point of "eyes" launches the first line into the second, and the embellishment of "state" gives a downward motion appropriate to the utterance's closure (although if the continuation to the third line were brought into

FIGURE 5.16 Bitonal treatment of the first couplet of "Nothing Gold Can Stay." The metrical-durational realization is taken from figures 2.17b and 5.7.

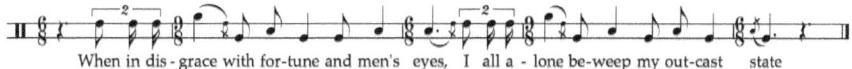

FIGURE 5.17 Bitonal treatment of the opening lines of Sonnet 29. The metrical-durational realization is taken from figure 2.20.

consideration, "state" would have an ensuing embellishment like that of "eyes"). Long syllables in a stepwise relation to—that is, one tier above or below—preceding or succeeding syllables in their clitic group do not receive bitonal treatment, for example, "-tune" and "-weep."

The bitonal analyses in figures 5.15–17 are an improvement over their monotonal counterparts, and they stand as the contour model's final output for these lines. Chapter 6 will review how these and other analyses stack up against actual readings.

The following statement summarizes the derivation of pitch contour.

Procedure for contour assignment:

Well-formedness condition: Assign every syllable a focal position on one of four tiers of pitch height.

Derivational procedure: Assign syllabic prominence from global to local levels of stressed syllables within the framework of the prosodic hierarchy,[6] as follows:

(1) Match syllables with four x's within a U to a global contour schema, such that:
   (a) If U is a declarative, place the terminating stressed syllable with four x's on tier 1.
   (b) If U is a yes-no interrogative, place the terminating stressed syllable with four x's on tier 2.
(2) In I, place the terminating syllable with four x's on tier 2.
(3) In P in which there is not a four-x syllable, place a syllable with three x's on tier 4; otherwise, place it on tier 3.
(4) In C, place a syllable with two x's on tier 3 if C is contained within a P or I in which a three-x syllable is on tier 4; otherwise, place a syllable with two x's on tier 2.

(5) Place a syllable with one x:
   (a) On a tier below the position of the dominating syllable within its **C** if the dominating syllable is not on tier 1; an option is to place it one tier equal to or above the position of the dominating syllable if doing so achieves stepwise motion within its **P**.
   (b) On tier 2 if the dominating syllable is on tier 1.
(6) If a syllable that does not terminate **U** or **I** is long and is not in a stepwise relation to the preceding or succeeding syllable, treat it as a bitonal syllable with a focal pitch and an embellishing pitch, such that the embellishing pitch:
   (a) Is one tier above or below the focal pitch, or
   (b) Fills in a tier gap between the preceding or succeeding syllable.
(7) If a syllable terminates **U** or **I** and is long:
   (a) For a declarative, the embellishing pitch is either before and one tier above the focal pitch, or it is after and one tier below the focal pitch.
   (b) For a yes-no interrogative, the embellishing pitch is after and one tier above the focal pitch.

5.4 CONNECTIONS TO OTHER APPROACHES

The topic of melodic contour has been peripheral in music theory. Theorists of tonal music have concentrated on the pitch structures of harmony, counterpoint, voice leading, and tonal space. Melodic contour in atonal music, however, has received attention in recent decades (Friedmann, 1985; Marvin and Laprade, 1987; Polansky and Bassein, 1992; Quinn, 1997). Notably, Morris (1993) develops a formal hierarchical approach, based on prominence by height and phrase edge and carried out from level to level, that broadly resembles the contour model proposed in this chapter.

In contrast to the relative neglect of contour in the musical literature, the phonological literature on contour is vast, often at levels of detail far beyond what is attempted in this book. It is concerned not with poetry but with speech in general, and much of it has little bearing on the present project, which is to assign normative, intuitively viable contours to poetic lines. There are nevertheless points of intersection with the phonological literature that are worth reviewing, beginning with the foundational issue of the basic unit of analysis. In the mid-twentieth century, phonologists debated whether intonational patterns are better described as rising and falling waves or as sequences of events at different levels of height (Bolinger, 1965). The issue is whether a contour wave, which tracks the rise and fall of an utterance, is perceptually primary, or if instead it is understood as organized into events and groups of events. My first postulate (see section 5.1) asserts the second view: the basic unit of analysis is the syllable, and syllables group according to levels of the prosodic hierarchy. Each syllable centers on a particular pitch tier. The next issue is how fine-grained the representation of pitch height of successive syllables ought to be. Pike (1945), Trager and Smith (1951), and Liberman (1975) posit four tiers, as does the present model.

The British school of intonation, in contrast, focuses on rising and falling contour patterns, not by placing syllables on tiers but by situating them in an undivided space between two parallel lines (Crystal, 1969; Cruttenden, 1997). To illustrate, figure 5.18 employs a version of the British representation to replicate, in part, the present theory's analysis of the first couplet of "Nothing Gold Can Stay" (compare it to figures 5.6 and 5.16). In their attractive quasi-musical notation, large noteheads stand for nuclear and prenuclear tones, which in present terms are syllables having stress with four x's and three x's, respectively. The tadpole tags that appear only after nuclear tones indicate downward slides comparable to embellishments in my bitonal syllables. The small noteheads apply to syllables of lesser stress—in present terms, syllables with one or two x's.

Most of the research done by the British school preceded the development of the prosodic hierarchy and stress grids. Thus, the school's parsing of utterances into tone groups is less precise than in later work done in the generative tradition. Only two levels of stress are represented, nuclear and non-nuclear tones. Meter and duration do not play a role. The goal is not to derive intonational structure but to describe it, primarily with the

FIGURE 5.18 Contour of the first couplet of "Nothing Gold Can Stay," as represented by the British school of intonation. Compare to figure 5.16.

purpose of identifying rise-and-fall patterns that convey nonverbal meaning. This fascinating topic is beyond theoretical treatment in this book, although it will arise anecdotally in chapter 6 in connection with spoken readings of poetic lines that the theory analyzes.

Pierrehumbert (1980) advances an intonational theory that finesses the wave-versus-event debate and that has become the frame of reference for much recent work in the field. She argues that four levels overspecify the data and posits only two levels, high (H) and low (L), for features that are prominent either by stress or by being at the edges of major syntactic units. These features are only partly coextensive with syllables and groups of syllables. She relegates other spans in a contour wave to the category of intonationally unspecified—that is, as variables that do not affect the overall shape of an intonational phrase. This is insufficient for the present project, which requires a contour position for each syllable in an intonational phrase or utterance. Just as there are no extra-metrical syllables in this model (see chapter 4.2), so are there no extra-contour syllables.

Two levels do not offer sufficient contrast if all syllables are assigned contour positions. In this connection, Hayes (2009b, p. 294) invokes a third, middle level. It is possible to adjust the rules of the present model to squeeze syllable height into three tiers instead of four. My sense is that meaningful distinctions would thereby be lost, however, so the model continues with four tiers.

Pierrehumbert develops subcategories within the binary H-L framework. If an H is at a wave peak and is stressed, it is marked H*; similarly, if an L is at a wave trough and is stressed, it is marked L*. H, L, H*, and L* combine for bitonal syllables so that the part of the syllable that aligns with stress receives "*" and the other part does not. My musically notated representation for bitonal syllables in figure 5.14 is an adaptation of her classification, as shown in figure 5.19. (The other logical possibilities for

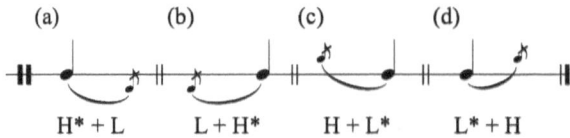

FIGURE 5.19 Bitonal syllabic representations from figure 5.14 matched to Pierrehumbert's notation.

bitonal syllables, a combination of H with H* and of L with L*, are not used.) Unlike Pierrehumbert's notation, the bitonal representation in figure 5.19 accommodates not only up-or-down sliding within a syllable but also four possible tier locations for the height of the syllable's focal point. These multiple possibilities permit greater specificity in contour mapping than does Pierrehumbert's theory.[7]

A second subcategory in Pierrehumbert's theory is the boundary tone, symbolized by H% or L%. It marks the left or right edge of a major syntactic category. In practice, the main interest is the right edge because speakers and listeners are highly attentive to how an intonational phrase or utterance ends. A third subcategory is the phrase accent, which occurs between the last pitch accent and the boundary tone. A phrase accent can cover the span of several syllables.

Pierrehumbert and Hirschberg (1990) define the contour of an intonational phrase as "a sequence of pitch accent(s), phrase accent(s), and boundary tone" (p. 277). Pitch accents offer the greatest variation. Depending on the shape of the contour curve, they can be H*, L*, L* + H, L + H*, H* + L, or H + L*. Phrase accents and boundary tones offer two possibilities each, H or L for phrase accents and H% or L% for boundary tones. This taxonomy fits the present model as follows. A pitch accent is a syllable with three or four x's in the stress grid. A right-edge boundary tone is the last syllable of an intonational phrase, or the last part of the syllable, represented by either a quarter note or a grace note, according to the four cases in figure 5.19. The model does not acknowledge phrase accents.

Pierrehumbert's types of H and L and the concepts "pitch accent," "phrase accent," and "boundary tone" suggest a kind of intonational quasi-syntax. For example, a standard declarative utterance takes the minimal form of H* L L%, and a standard interrogative takes the minimal form of L* H H%. The order of accent types is fixed. I am skeptical of the status of these concepts and symbols. In the present model, there is no such apparatus. There are only syllables having locations in time and space—that is, having metrical-durational realizations and tier positions.

Pierrehumbert's derivations are linear from left to right, whereas in the present model, they are hierarchical. This factor is key to how my model's analyses relate to hers: hierarchically dominant syllables mark some version of H*or L*. Figure 5.20 illustrates with the first couplet of "Nothing Gold Can Stay." Only syllables with three or four x's, represented by eighth and quarter notes, receive H* or L* designations. In the first line, "green" is

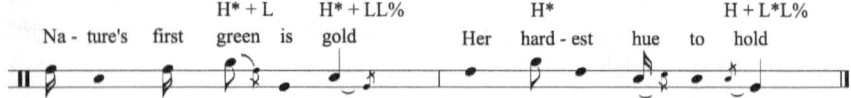

FIGURE 5.20 Superimposition of Pierrehumbert's notation on a hierarchical analysis, amalgamated from figures 5.6 and 5.16, of the first couplet of "Nothing Gold Can Stay."

bitonal H* + L, and "gold" is bitonal H* + L in which L also functions as L%. In the second line, "hard-" is H*, and "hold" is bitonal H +L* in which L* doubles as L%. Both lines express the declarative minimal form of H*L L%.

Figure 5.21 illustrates the same procedure with the interrogative opening line of Sonnet 18. H* is assigned to "-pare" and L* + H to bitonal "day," with H% a tail on "day." All the action in achieving the typical interrogative pattern L*HH% takes place on this last word.

The broad contour shapes of these examples—a mid-phrase stress peak and closing descent in figure 5.20 and a mid-phrase stress peak, dip, and closing rise in figure 5.21—are typical of declaratives and yes-no interrogatives, respectively. In the present theory, they are normative outputs, so it is not surprising that the theory yields these shapes again and again. But there are many ways of intoning an utterance. A recurring theme in intonational phonology, shared by the British and Pierrehumbert schools as well as others (e.g., Bolinger, 1986; Cruttenden, 1997; Hayes, 2009b; Pierrehumbert and Hirschberg, 1990), concerns how different contour shapes of phonological and intonational phrases convey different meanings. As mentioned, this topic lies beyond the scope of this book.

Intonational phonologists have codified Pierrehumbert's accent types in a labeling system called Tones and Break Indices (ToBI). Its methodology contrasts with that of the contour model proposed in this chapter. It starts with empirical data by tracking the fundamental frequency of an utterance

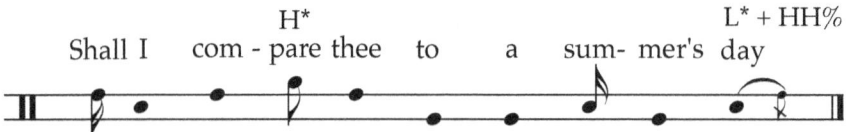

FIGURE 5.21 Pierrehumbert's notation paired with a hierarchical analysis, from figures 5.12d and 5.15, of the first line of Sonnet 18.

and anchors Pierrehumbert's symbols to time points on the waveform (Ladd, 2008, pp. 104–107).[8] Details of accent classification are often subject to debate. The present model begins instead with a string of syllables and, in the context of their metrical-durational derivation, assigns pitch height to each of them on one of four tiers. Only then does it engage with and respond to empirical data.

Dilley (2005) critiques the Pierrehumbert model and proposes an intonational theory that, in several respects, resembles that of the present approach. Inspired in part by musical analogies and theories, she aligns syllabic contour with syllabic assignments in the stress grid (which, following linguistic practice since Liberman [1975], she calls the metrical grid). Tone levels are assigned hierarchically according to three relations—higher, lower, or the same—so that adjacencies take place not just at the sequential surface but also at underlying levels. Pitch height is specified relationally without the scaffolding of tiers. She adapts a simplified H-L notation to represent derived contours, but most of her figures could be recast in musical notation as presented in this book. Neither she nor Pierrehumbert incorporates duration as a key factor in intonational analysis.

5.5 SUMMARY

The contour component of the theory assumes the syllable as the unit of analysis, just as in the rhythmic component, and it postulates four tiers of pitch height. The model assigns contour from global to local levels according to degrees of syllabic prominence. Syllabic prominence corresponds to syllabic stress as assigned in the rhythmic component, and it is projected by pitch height, duration, or right-edge adjacency to an intonational phrase boundary. All syllables receive a tier position. A heavily stressed syllable at the right edge of an intonational phrase or utterance is on a low tier in declarative statements, and in interrogatives it is on a middle tier. A next less stressed syllable within an intonational phrase goes to the highest tier, and the next less stressed syllable after that goes to the next highest tier, continuing cyclically through levels of the prosodic hierarchy. An unstressed syllable appears one tier below or above the stressed syllable with which it is grouped. A long syllable can be bitonal, with a focal pitch and its embellishment on an adjacent tier.

My model treats intonational contour not as an isolated phonological component but as existing in the context of an utterance's prosodic hierarchy, stress grid, and metrical-durational structure. The derivational procedure for contour assignment depends on these rhythmic features.

Much recent research in intonational phonology takes a linear rather than hierarchical approach to syllabic contour. It assumes only two tiers, but it supplements this shrinkage by positing several contour categories. My model avoids this quasi-syntactic approach in favor of an exhaustive assignment of syllables on four tier positions without further categorization. Ostensible contour categories can be mapped onto hierarchically dominating syllables assigned by my model.

6

Transcriptions and Analyses

6.1 INTRODUCTION

The methods proposed in chapters 2 and 5 predict normative rhythms and contours for poetic lines. This chapter will evaluate these predictions by comparing them with recorded spoken readings. Because recitations of any given line vary according to the reader, choices must be made which to consider. I prefer to take readings by the poets themselves, where possible. An author's interpretation is not uniquely authoritative—Igor Stravinsky's recording of *Le sacre du printemps* may not be its best recording—but it does provide evidence of authorial intent. For poets who precede the era of recordings, I turn to readings by accomplished actors.

The derivation of contour is more uncertain than that of meter and duration because contour depends in part on focus and its effect on stress. Stress assignments can be ambiguous in complex sentences in which alternative groupings of the prosodic hierarchy are possible. But once groupings and a stress hierarchy are assigned, the contour rules apply in a straightforward way.

I begin with two Robert Frost poems and continue to lines by William Shakespeare and John Milton. The final section engages excerpts recorded by William Butler Yeats, T. S. Eliot, Wallace Stevens, Langston Hughes, and Elizabeth Bishop.[1]

6.2 TWO ROBERT FROST READINGS

Chapter 2 analyzed the first couplet of Robert Frost's "Nothing Gold Can Stay." Figure 6.1 continues in slightly abbreviated form for the entire poem. The brackets beneath the text show the phonological phrases, and the lines, separated by rests, are all intonational phrases. The stress grid appears above. The realization is in 6/8 meter to neutralize the metrical-phase conflict discussed in connection with figure 2.19c–d, which is notated in 12/8.

The rhythmic derivation is straightforward except for the fourth line, "But only so an hour." Figure 6.2a gives a simple realization, but "only so" feels too slow. The sequence of unstressed syllables "-ly so an" can be compressed as in figure 6.2b, shortening the line by a tactus beat. The metrical grid is included to show that, at different metrical levels, the pattern of strong and weak beats is essentially the same. This interpretation matches the meaning of the line, and it creates an extra silent beat before the next line, delineating the division between the two quatrains. Figure 6.1 takes option 6.2b.

The contour for the first couplet was derived in figures 5.5, 5.6, and 5.16. The upper staff of figure 6.3 completes the process in accordance with the rules for contour assignment stated in chapter 5. This is the predicted normative realization of the poem.

The lower staff in figure 6.3 is a transcription of Frost's reading of the poem, coordinated bar by bar with the predicted version. The two interpretations are close in both rhythm and contour. Consider rhythm first. Frost observes a silent beat at the end of each line, turning the poem's trimeter

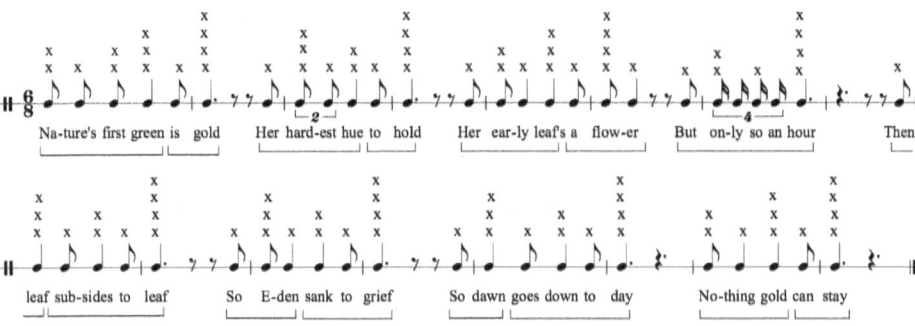

FIGURE 6.1 Metrical-durational realization of Robert Frost's "Nothing Gold Can Stay," with phonological phrase bracketing and stress grid.

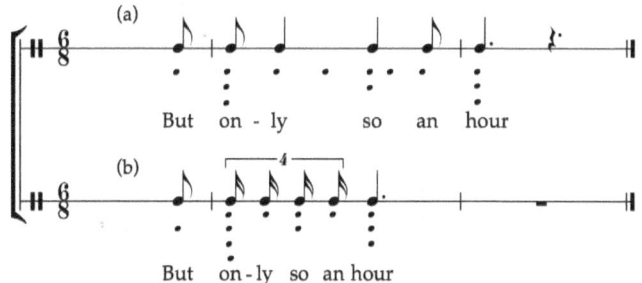

FIGURE 6.2 Two rhythmic versions of the fourth line: (a) a simple realization, (b) a rhythmically contracted version.

FIGURE 6.3 The predicted realization of "Nothing Gold Can Stay" and a transcription of Frost's reading of the poem.

into a tetrameter setting. Even when he speeds up or slows down slightly at the dotted-quarter tactus level, he immediately makes up the difference to achieve metronomic regularity at the level of the dotted-half note. The only place where the dotted-half level is somewhat free is at the beginning, where he starts a little slowly, as if groping for the right tempo. These deviations act as nuances rather than as changes in metrical structure.

Beyond the similarities, there are a few conspicuous rhythmic divergences between the two versions. In bar 5 of Frost's reading, "leaf's" arrives an eighth note early, creating a syncopation and lengthening that syllable by an eighth note before resuming "a flower" in tempo. He does likewise with "gold" in bar 15. The effect is to emphasize "leaf's" and "gold" both by length and by the perceptual prominence of the syncopations. These details are significant because "leaf" and "gold" are the nouns that uniquely repeat in the poem and that are its central images.

A second noteworthy divergence takes place in bar 7. Frost says "only so an" in a rhythm like the predicted version but at a slower speed, achieved by changing the bar's time signature effectively from 6/8 into 3/4—that is, not two dotted-quarter-note tactus beats but three quarter-note tactus beats, as in a hemiola. The metrical grid beneath bars 6 and 7 in figure 6.3 spells out the difference. Notice that the eighth-note and measure levels of the grid remain unaltered; only the tactus level changes. As with the syncopations on "leaf's" and "gold," Frost resumes the continuation in tempo.

These two instances—an anticipatory syncopation and a shift between triple and duple metrical subdivisions—also occur in music. Anticipatory syncopations are widespread in jazz and rock (Temperley, 1999), and hemiolas are common in many kinds of music, for instance, at cadences in baroque music. These rhythmic possibilities enlarge the repertory of durational patterns listed in figure 2.14.[2]

Some instances of divergence in contour are worth remarking. In bar 2, Frost's "gold" is higher than predicted, underscoring the word's importance. The relative height of "sank" in bar 11 has a similar effect. In bar 9, Frost's "sub-" is one tier above rather than below "-sides," but its relative height does not produce stress because its vowel is spoken without full resonance; the unstressed vowel is reduced.[3]

Taking a broader view, the peak syllables in Frost's recitation vary more than they do in the predicted version. In bar 3, Frost's "hard-" is on tier 3 instead of tier 4, lending the line lower tension than its neighboring lines. In the second quatrain, the predicted version has one syllable per phrase

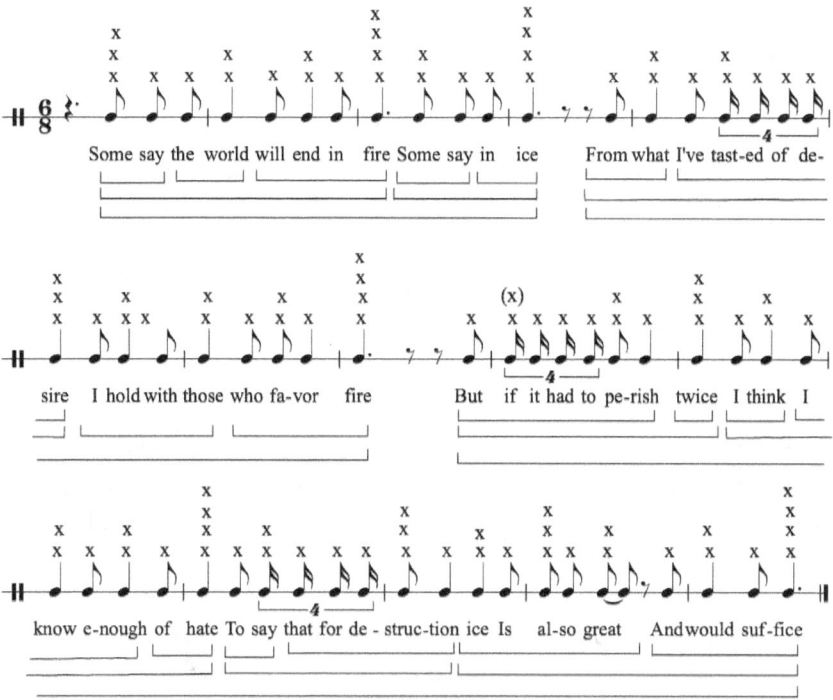

FIGURE 6.4 Metrical-durational realization of Frost's "Fire and Ice," with phonological and intonational phrase bracketing and the stress grid.

on tier 4, but Frost treats bar 9 in a subdued manner and reserves the tension of pitch height for bar 11 at the point where "Eden" enlarges the scope of the poem's meaning. Bar 13 continues the tension at "dawn," after which the final line conveys resignation with "gold" lowered to tier 3. These larger shapes give a narrative arc to the whole.

Figure 6.4 presents a metrical-durational realization of "Fire and Ice." In two places, focus overrides nuclear stress in the assignment of three x's: at "Some" instead of "world" in the first line, and at "al-" instead of "great" in the penultimate line. In addition, "if" in the fifth line optionally receives focus.

Figure 6.5 displays two kinds of rhythmic variation. Figure 6.5a offers a straightforward realization of "From what I've tasted of desire." But because the consecutive syllables "-ed of de-" are unstressed, this segment contracts to the rhythm in figure 6.5b. The same transformation applies,

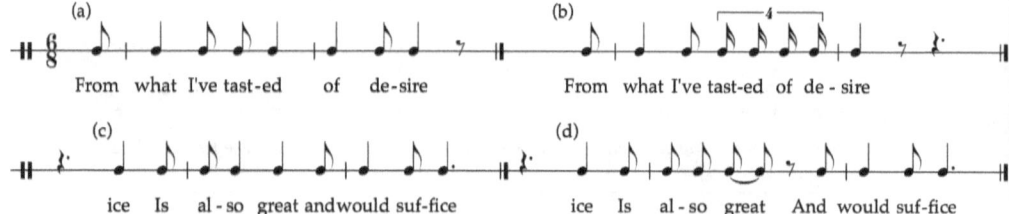

FIGURE 6.5 Rhythmic options for "Fire and Ice": (a) a straightforward realization of the third line; (b) a contracted reading of the third line; (c) a straightforward realization of the last two lines; (d) a syncopated reading at "great," with an eighth rest before the last line.

later in the poem, to "if it had to" and "that for de-." Second, the enjambed intonational phrase "ice Is also great and would suffice" receives a standard derivation in 6.5c. But it may be desirable to convey Frost's layout on the page, in which "Is also great" and "And would suffice" are on separate lines (see figure 3.9a). One way to do this is to give an anticipatory syncopation to "great," as in figure 6.5d. This step permits an eighth rest between "great" and "And," projecting the line division. Figure 6.4 follows figure 6.5b and d.

The top staff in figure 6.6 adds contour to the predicted analysis in figure 6.4. A transcription of Frost's and Richard Burton's readings are on the second and third staves, respectively. The intricate syntax of the sentences yields rather complex rhythms that could be notated by changes in meter, but a change in time signature in one reading would not coordinate with the metrical context of another reading. Hence the expedient of maintaining 6/8 throughout. The fermatas over eighth rests in bar 2 stand for silent tactus beats; the alternative of notating the pause with dotted-quarter rests would create unwieldy misalignments of their readings compared to the predicted version.

Metrical changes from 6/8 to 3/4 occur in three places: at "hold with those who favor" in Frost's reading, and at "think I know enough of" and "And would suf-" in Burton's reading. To illustrate, figure 6.7a shows the metrical grid for Frost's "hold with those who favor." Figure 6.7b represents the grid instead by beaming pairs of eighth notes, indicating that the first notes in each pair are metrically stronger. Figure 6.6 adopts this second representation.

Some rhythmic details in figure 6.6 deserve special attention. Frost and Burton both begin with a pause after "Some say," and both inject a pause

FIGURE 6.6 Comparison of the predicted realization of "Fire and Ice" to Robert Frost's and Richard Burton's readings.

in the transition from the third to the fourth line, most likely in response to the expressed emotion. Burton does so by pausing naturally between the two lines: "From what I've tasted of desire / I hold with those who favor fire." Frost oddly makes the break after "I": "From what I've tasted

FIGURE 6.7 Metrical representations in 3/4: (a) by a metrical grid, (b) by beaming pairs of eighth notes.

of desire I / hold with those who favor fire." He does not observe the line break at "Is also great / And would suffice" but accelerates to the end, as if the mixture of wit and pain that these lines express were beyond spoken conveyance. Burton, in contrast, dramatizes the break by a long pause and a quick, quiet close.

In all these respects, the predicted reading is merely normative. It does not pause after "Some say," or between the first two lines, or at the transition between the third and fourth lines. Although there is a pause before "And would suffice," it is brief. Except for a few line compressions, sub-tactus rhythms are all triple. In the Frost and Burton readings, triple and duple rhythms intermix, creating a modulated rhythmic flow. Notice how they both emphasize the line "I know enough of hate" by speaking its syllables in equal duple eighth notes (although at different speeds).

The contours of the three readings in figure 6.6 are similar except for a few notable details. Frost speaks "ice" in bar 4 and "fire" in bar 8 rather high followed by a bitonal drop, unlike the predicted and Burton's versions, which both place these words at a low pitch. Frost's intention is presumably to emphasize the two nouns that govern the imagery of the entire poem. In bar 14, he emphasizes "great" not by duration, as in the predicted and Burton's versions, but by a slight rise in pitch, the only resource available given his choice of rhythm.

6.3 LINES FROM SHAKESPEARE AND MILTON

Figure 6.8 compares a predicted version of the first quatrain of Shakespeare's Sonnet 29 to readings by Ian McKellen and Matthew Macfadyen. In contrast to figure 5.17, the predicted version in figure 6.8 opts for a silent tactus beat between lines. The resulting rhythmic similarity of the three versions permits them to be notated with the same time signatures. The predicted version also treats the contour at "state" at the end of the second line differently than in figure 5.17. There, the context is the first couplet, and "state" is assumed to terminate the utterance. Here, the context is the quatrain and its continuation to the second quatrain, and the bitonal rise in the last syllable of each line carries the argument forward into the next clause. McKellen and Macfadyen's readings conform to the predicted contraction of the third and fourth lines into four instead of five tactus beats.

The rhythms of the recorded readings are almost identical to those of the predicted version, but the contours of the recorded readings often differ

TRANSCRIPTIONS AND ANALYSES | 109

FIGURE 6.8 The predicted realization paired with Ian McKellen's and Matthew Macfadyen's readings of the first quatrain of Shakespeare's Sonnet 29.

in their details from the predicted contour. McKellen utters unstressed syllables on reduced vowels at pitches above rather than below the focal pitches with which they group. In the first phrase, "dis-" is higher than "-grace," and "with" and "-tune" are higher than "for-." His unusual rendition, which has a tentative and probing expression, is as the Earl of Southampton addressing Shakespeare in the movie *All Is True*, and perhaps it cannot be evaluated outside that context. Another difference takes place in the fourth line: McKellen and Macfadyen both stress the emotionally charged word "curse" instead of "-self." This is not a departure from the theory but a focused reaction to the word's emotional force.

Figure 6.9 compares the predicted version of the first line of Sonnet 18, taken from figure 5.15, to Helen Mirren's and John Gielgud's readings. The rhythm of the predicted version corresponds to Mirren's, but Gielgud takes a quicker rhythm, ending in an anticipatory syncopation on "day." He resumes the next line, "Thou art more lovely and more temperate," on the downbeat of the next measure.

Again, the predicted contour differs from the actors' interpretations. They both—surprisingly and playfully—give non-normative focus, hence

FIGURE 6.9 The predicted realization of the first line of Shakespeare's Sonnet 18 to Helen Mirren's and John Gielgud's readings of the line.

higher pitch and stress, to "Shall" instead of "com-." Gielgud speaks the line not as a question but as a proposition. Unlike the predicted and Gielgud's versions, Mirren's adds emphasis to "thee," intimately singling out the recipient of the verse. Her contour rises at the line's close, as expected of an interrogative, but Gielgud's does not. These realizations are options interpretable within the framework of my theory.

Difficulties in transcription and analysis multiply when turning from Shakespeare's sonnets to Milton's *Paradise Lost*, with its long, embedded sentences and frequent enjambment. It is often uncertain how to parse an extended utterance into intonational phrases. Figure 6.10 attempts to do so for the opening lines and assigns them a stress grid. The commas divide most of the phonological phrases, and the brackets mark intonational phrases.

The upper staff of figure 6.11 gives the metrical-durational and contour analysis of the passage. Bars 1 and 9 are marked 3/4 in parentheses to show that these measures divide tactus beats into 2 + 2 + 2 eighth notes instead of 3 + 3. This interpretation responds to the adjacent stresses on "Man's first" and "one great-," putting them both at the tactus level within the 3/4 bar. In bar 2, "-dience" is assumed to be pronounced as one syllable; if it were two, the line would have eleven instead of ten syllables. (Milton is strict in counting ten syllables per line.) A rhythmic contraction occurs in bar 6, a result of the three adjacent unstressed syllables "into the." Special focus is assigned to "death" in bar 6, "all" in bar 7, "one" in bar 9, and "Sing" in bar 13. Not focusing on these syllables would alter the contour of these phrases accordingly.

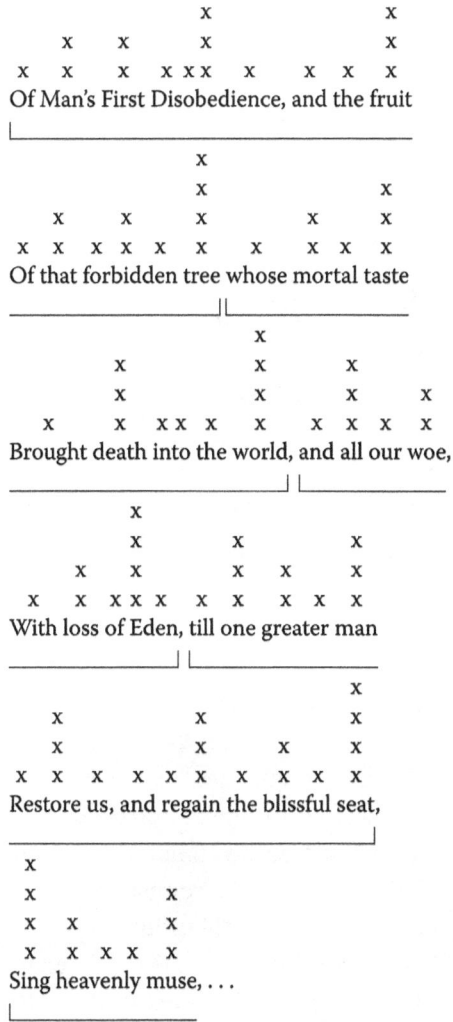

FIGURE 6.10 Intonational grouping and stress grid for the first five and a half lines of John Milton's *Paradise Lost*.

The lower staff of figure 6.11 is a transcription of Ian Richardson's reading of these lines. He places the most stressed syllables on regularly timed tactus beats, as the theory does. Within this rhythmic framework, several deviations from the predicted rhythm take place. In bar 2, he pronounces "-dience" as two syllables, and he pauses after "disobedience," as indicated

FIGURE 6.11 The predicted realization of the opening lines of *Paradise Lost* and Ian Richardson's recitation of them.

by the fermata. He agrees with the predicted rhythmic contraction in bar 6. The greatest deviation takes place in bars 9–11: after a clear pause, he speaks "till one greater" quickly and compresses "restore us and regain" by a tactus beat, ignoring the comma after "us;" he also stresses the first instead of second syllable of "regain." These features combine to accelerate this phrase, so that "seat" arrives a beat early in bar 12 compared to the predicted version. He then pauses markedly, after which "Sing heavenly muse" resumes in metrical alignment with the predicted rhythm. His treatment of bars 9–11 lends a dramatic shape to the excerpt that is absent from the predicted version.

Richardson's contour corresponds rather well to the predicted contour, but there are differences worth noting, all of them resulting from choices of focus. He lowers the pitch at "disobedience" in bar 2, thereby highlighting the preceding "man's first," and raises the pitch at "forbidden" in bar 4. In bar 5, he drops down at "taste Brought" in order to leap dramatically to "death" in bar 6. He sustains a high range at "all our woe, With loss" in bars 7–8 and at "blissful seat" in bars 11–12. Finally, in bar 13 he gives similar emphasis to "Sing" and "heavenly."

In a broader view, both the predicted version and Richardson maintain a steady tactus that is anchored on evenly distributed stressed syllables. However, the readings only intermittently project regular sub-tactus patterns or, crucially, line boundaries. Thus, the iambic-pentameter aspect of this poetry is imaginary as an audible experience. Yet when reading the text on the page, it is rewarding to pay attention to the ten-syllable lines against the rhythmic ebb and flow of the phrases. In this connection, Hopkins (1995) refers (with specific reference to Milton) to "counterpoint rhythm": a heard rhythm against a posited, imagined rhythm. The term is suggestive if the purported counterpoint is not between two melodic lines, as in music, but between the heard rhythm and the written line with its ten syllables and four or five regular stresses.

6.4 LINES FROM TWENTIETH-CENTURY POETS

Yeats's early poem "The Lake Isle of Innisfree" is in three quatrains, each comprising three long lines (usually 13 syllables) and a shorter fourth line. Figure 6.12 offers a stress analysis of the first quatrain. Each line is an intonational phrase, and the commas mark phonological phrases. At "small cabin," focus on "small" overrides nuclear stress on "cab-." At "bee-loud," bee is the more stressed, but "loud" is nonetheless lightly stressed by virtue of its long diphthong vowel.

Figure 6.13a realizes the first two lines in 6/8 meter, but the setting is awkward. "I" is unstressed and should not take place on a tactus beat, and the long pauses in bars 2 and 5 are unmotivated. Figure 6.13b instead casts the lines in 2/2, with the tactus at the half-note level. It begins with a three-note anacrusis, locating "I" on a metrically weak position. There are no inappropriate mid-line pauses. This is the preferred metrical-durational realization.

Figure 6.13b extends the analysis to the third and fourth lines. The first three lines all have four tactus beats grouped in pairs, with a string of eighth notes leading to their last syllables. The fourth line is shorter by a tactus beat in response to its shorter poetic line. Bar 4 expands by a quarter note to a 5/4 time signature to make room for a quarter-note value on "Nine" with its two x's and diphthong vowel. The unstressed syllables "will I," "for the," and "in the" contract to sixteenth notes to fit within the stressed syllables and tactus beats surrounding them.

The top staff of figure 6.14 adds contour to the metrical-durational analysis in figure 6.13b, and the bottom staff is a transcription of Yeats's mannered recorded reading of the quatrain. His rhythms generally match the predicted rhythms, although sometimes he shortens unstressed syllables. Before reciting the poem, he says that he will speak it "with great emphasis

```
                                        x
                        x        x      x
            x           x    x x x
x x x x    x x x    x  x x x x x
I will arise and go now, and go to Innisfree,
```

```
                                                        x
                    x           x                       x
        x  (x)  x           x       x                   x
x x x   x x     x       x x x   x x x                   x
And a small cabin build there, of clay and wattles made;
```

```
                                                            x
            x                           x                   x
x   x   x       x                   x               x       x
x   x   x       x x x       x   x x    x   x       x x x
Nine bean-rows will I have there, a hive for the honey-bee,
```

```
                                x
                x               x
        x   x           x  (x)  x
x   x x x   x x     x           x   x
And live alone in the bee-loud glade.
```

FIGURE 6.12 Stress grid for the first quatrain of William Butler Yeats's "The Lake Isle of Innisfree."

upon the rhythm" because it is not prose but poetry. He magnifies the stress on each tactus beat so that even when the pace varies, the tactus beats remain firm.

Yeats's intonation has a narrow compass, notated here on just three tiers. He finishes the lines almost identically, on rising syllables that land at the

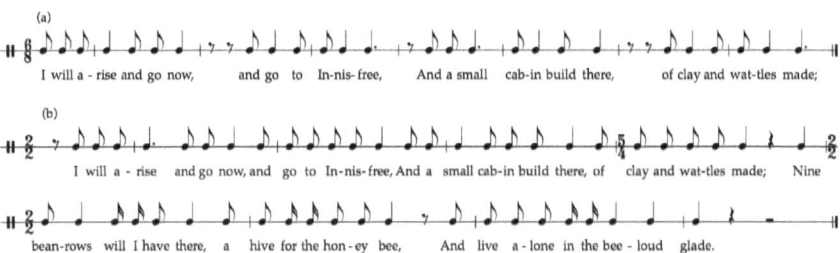

FIGURE 6.13 Metrical-durational realization of the beginning of Yeats's "The Lake Isle of Innisfree": (a) the first two lines in triple meter, (b) the quatrain in duple meter.

FIGURE 6.14 The predicted realization and a transcription of Yeats's reading of the first quatrain of "The Lake Isle of Innisfree."

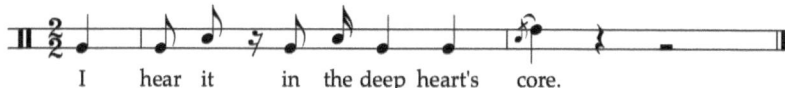

FIGURE 6.15 Transcription of Yeats's reading of the last line of "The Lake Isle of Innisfree."

same high pitch level. This choice gives his contour a very different shape from the predicted contour. Rather than articulating closure, his endings propel the text forward. Even the last line of the poem—"I hear it in the deep heart's core"—receives this treatment, as shown in figure 6.15. Notice the similarity to how he speaks "in the bee-loud glade," notated in figure 6.14: two sixteenth notes and two quarter notes, all very low, followed by a rise at the final word. More generally, the rhythms and contours of Yeats's reading are quite repetitive. He incants these lines, like a priest or mythical bard.[4]

Figure 6.16 shows the stress grid and phonological groupings of the opening lines of "Burnt Norton," the first poem of Eliot's *Four Quartets*. Lines 1–2, 3, 4, and 5 are each intonational phrases, and lines 1–3 and 4–5 are utterances. Nuclear stress governs the number of x's except for focus on "all" instead of "time" in the fourth and fifth lines and, in the fifth line, the optional contrastive emphasis on "un-" instead of lexically stressed "deem-."

The metrical-durational realization of this passage in ostensibly free verse yields the familiar rhythms of figure 6.17a.[5] This unadorned setting is made less monotonous in figure 6.17b by halving unstressed syllables that are naturally spoken quickly: "and" in bar 1, "per-" in bar 3, and "con-" in bar 5. The second half of bar 8 is in duple rhythm to give the long syllable

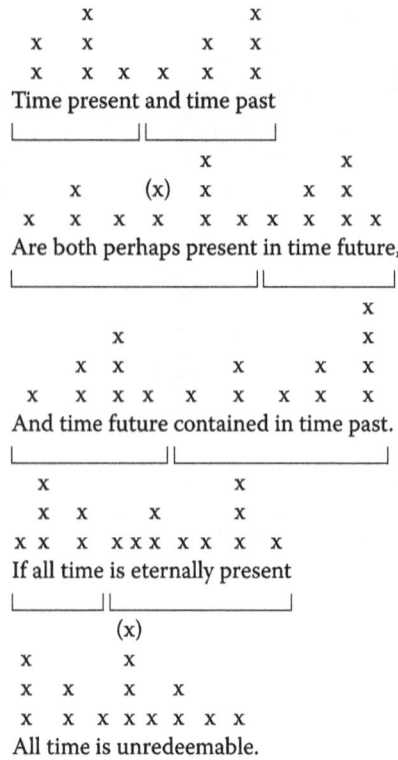

FIGURE 6.16 Stress grid for the opening lines of T. S. Eliot's "Burnt Norton."

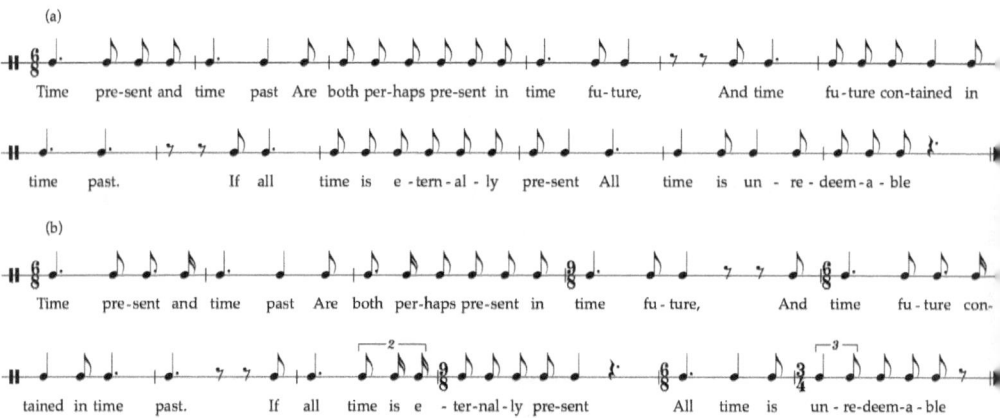

FIGURE 6.17 Metrical-durational realization of the opening lines of "Burnt Norton": (a) an unadorned version, (b) an elaborated version.

TRANSCRIPTIONS AND ANALYSES | 117

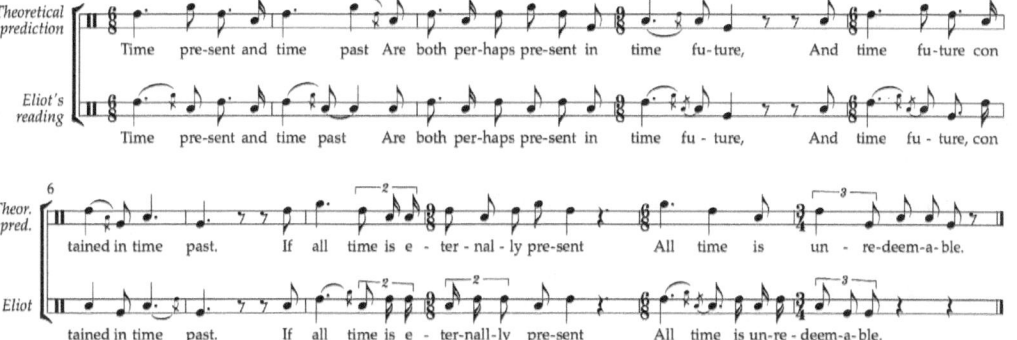

FIGURE 6.18 The predicted analysis and Eliot's reading of "Burnt Norton." The top staff adds contour to figure 6.16b, and the bottom staff transcribes Eliot's reading.

"time" more space. The option of inserting a silent tactus beat between lines is taken in bars 4 and 9. In bar 11, "unredeemable" is in 3/4 instead of 6/8 so that "-deem-" takes place on a stronger beat than "-re-" and "-a-." Finally, "un-" is slightly elongated to bring out the focus on that syllable.

The top staff of figure 6.18 shows the derived contour over the rhythms of figure 6.17b, and the bottom staff transcribes Eliot's recorded reading. The two versions mostly correspond rhythmically, including observance of silent tactus beats after intonational-phrase boundaries, but there are differences. Although Eliot sometimes gives full tactus value—a dotted quarter note—to "time" in bars 1, 6, and 8, he reduces it almost to a quarter note in bar 2 and to lengths between a quarter and a dotted quarter in bars 4, 5, and 10. In bar 9, he continues a duple division at "eternally." In bars 10 and 11, he compresses the rhythm of "unredeemable" and puts the lexically stressed "-deem-" instead of contrastive "un-" on the downbeat.

The contour of Eliot's delivery differs markedly from the predicted version in its treatment of "time." The predicted version stresses the ensuing adjective, on grounds of both nuclear stress and contrastive emphasis— "time présent," time pást," "time fúture"—whereas he places the greater stress on "time," in each case with a bitonal rise over its diphthong vowel. In the fourth and fifth lines, however, he contrastively emphasizes "all" instead of "time," as in the predicted version.

Granted that the predicted version places the greater stress on the adjectives following "time," it would achieve a better metrical-durational

118 | TRANSCRIPTIONS AND ANALYSES

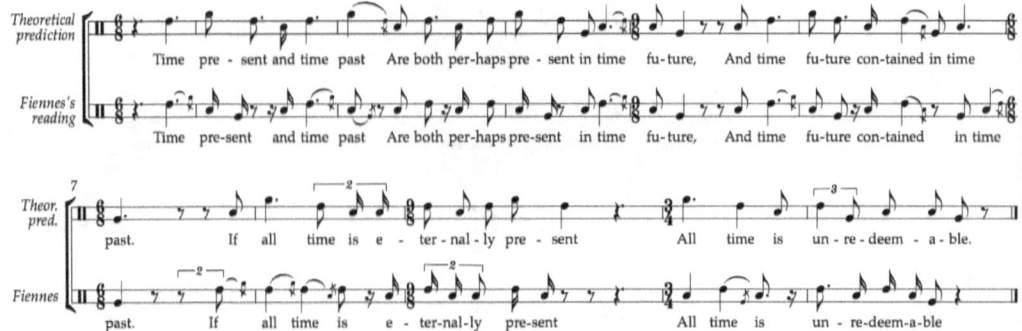

FIGURE 6.19 Comparison of the predicted realization and Ralph Fiennes's reading of "Burnt Norton."

realization in bars 1–5 if "time" were notated on an upbeat and the adjective on the ensuing downbeat. Figure 6.18 does not do this because of my goal to align, as much as possible, the predicted analysis with Eliot's reading. The top staff of figure 6.19 rectifies the matter by shifting the notes and rhythms in bars 1–5 by a tactus beat. Nothing else is changed in the predicted analysis.

The lower staff of figure 6.19 transcribes Ralph Fiennes's recitation of these lines. He places greater stress on the ensuing adjectives than on "time," and he puts contrastive emphasis on "un-" in "unredeemable." In these respects, his interpretation agrees with the predicted version. In small details, however, they diverge. He speaks "all time is" in a hemiola rhythm, and he reduces durations at "eternally present" and "unredeemable." Like Eliot, he always says "time" at a high range with a bitonal swoop upward, after which "present," "past," and "future" are low, always on tiers 2 to 1. These pitch-rhythm recurrences act like a repeating musical motive.

Figure 6.20 supplies the major prosodic boundaries and stress grid for the opening lines of Wallace Stevens's "The Idea of Order at Key West." The first line is an intonational phrase and utterance. The second line is an intonational phrase, as is the third line plus the beginning of the fourth; together these two intonational phrases form an utterance. The first syllable of "never" would typically be stressed in isolation, but in the context of "The water never formed" it is not; hence, the parenthesized x there. Nuclear stress puts greater stress on the second "body" in "Like a body wholly body," but the second "body" can just as well be viewed as a repetition of the first; hence, the parenthesized x over the first "body."

Figure 6.21a assigns to these lines a metrical-durational realization in triple meter. The adjacent unstressed syllables "-ius of the," "-ter ne-ver,"

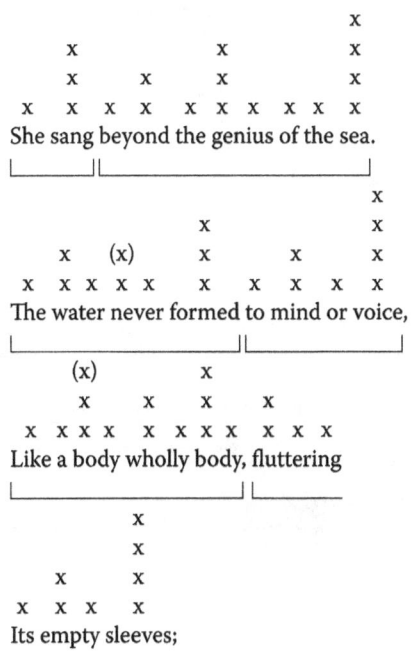

FIGURE 6.20 Stress grid for the opening lines of Wallace Stevens's "The Idea of Order at Key West."

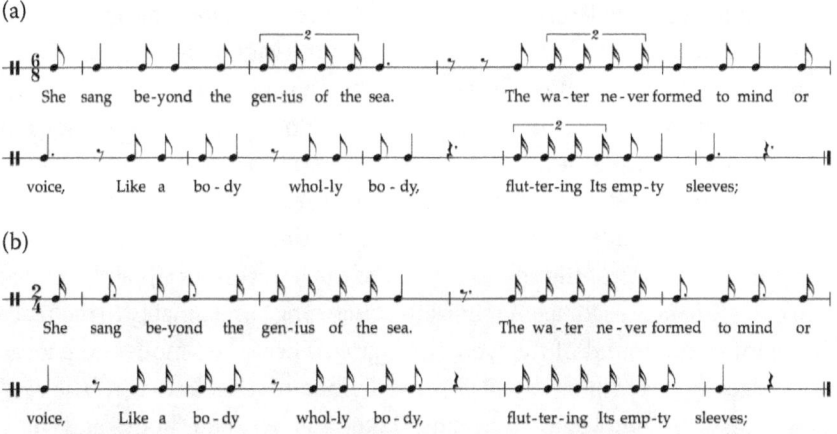

FIGURE 6.21 Metrical-durational realizations of the opening lines of "The Idea of Order at Key West": (a) in 6/8, (b) in 2/4.

FIGURE 6.22 Rhythmic and contour analysis of the opening lines of "The Idea of Order at Key West": (a) the contour derived from figure 6.21b, (b) a transcription of Stevens's reading.

and "-ter-ing its" trigger rhythmic contractions in these places. The rests mark the commas in the text. (I assume an implicit comma after the first "body"—"Like a body, wholly body"—even though Stevens did not write it.) Figure 6.21b offers an alternative analysis in duple meter. Here the iambic short-long stretches from a 1:2 ratio (eighth note plus quarter note) to a 1:3 ratio (sixteenth note plus dotted eighth note).

Stevens's recorded reading more closely approximates the rhythms of figure 6.21b, so the theory's predicted contour assignment in figure 6.22a is built over that realization. It is not feasible, however, to align his reading directly beneath the predicted version, as was done in previous analyses in this chapter, because—even though the poem is written in blank verse—he speaks in bursts separated by pauses of various lengths. Figure 6.22b transcribes the reading, employing changing time signatures to approximate the durations of the silences. Each of the bursts is a snippet from figure 6.22a. He pauses for a long time after "She sang," presumably to recollect in memory the sound of the woman singing. Thereafter, moderate pauses take place between phonological prosodic boundaries: between "the sea" and "The water," between "voice" and "Like," and between "body" and "fluttering." Short pauses correspond to clitic boundaries: between "genius" and "of the sea," between "formed" and "to mind" and "or voice," and between "body" and "wholly body." The pauses and their varying lengths subvert the sense of meter—of a tactus—and bring out instead the groupings of the prosodic hierarchy. The location and length of the pauses are structural.

The contour of Stevens's reading diverges from the predicted version in several places. His pause after "formed" projects its 3-x stress by duration rather than pitch height. In "body," he speaks "bo-" a tier lower than "-dy," rather than a tier higher, likewise with "-ty" in "empty." He closes the utterance at "sleeves" not on tier 1 but with a bitonal rise, much as Yeats does in "The Lake Isle of Innisfree."

Like "The Idea of Order at Key West," Langston Hughes's "The Weary Blues" responds to a musical performance. Figure 6.23 provides the main groupings and stress grid of the poem's opening section. The parenthesized x's mark syllables at the 2-x level that are less stressed than their neighbors. In line 3, "Ne-" receives focus and therefore has four x's instead of "play," which would normally have nuclear stress, likewise with "la-" instead of "sway" in line 6.

The form imitates the music it describes. The standard phrase schema for a 12-bar blues is a four-bar phrase followed by a parallel four-bar phrase, with a concluding four-bar phrase that cadences on the tonic in its third bar. Hughes imitates this form with groupings of three lines comprised of two parallel intonational phrases, each with four tactus beats, and a concluding phrase that completes the utterance on its third tactus beat. Lines 4–6 repeat the pattern. In a musical gesture, line 7 repeats line 6 (literal repetitions are common in music). Line 8 is an extension or codetta.

Figure 6.24 gives a metrical-durational realization based on figure 6.23. In line 1, "Droning a" could be cast in triplet eighth notes, but the long syllable "Dron-" needs the slightly extra length provided by assigning it an eighth followed by two sixteenths. The syllables "back" in line 2 and "Le-" in line 4 are treated as unstressed. In "other night," "night" is given an anticipatory syncopation so that it has a longer duration and "-ther" a shorter duration (much as Frost does at "early leaf's" and "Nothing gold" in "Nothing Gold Can Stay;" see figure 6.3). This solution reinforces the stress grid. The rests after "sway" after lines 6 and 7 reflect Hughes's notated ellipsis.

Figure 6.25 adds contour to figure 6.24 and juxtaposes the result against a transcription of Hughes's reading. The fermatas over sixteenth rests in his reading mark slight pauses between phrases. In contrast, the parenthesized eighth rest in bar 8 signals a rhythmic elision; Hughes rushes through lines 4 and 5 without a phrase break. The biggest rhythmic difference from

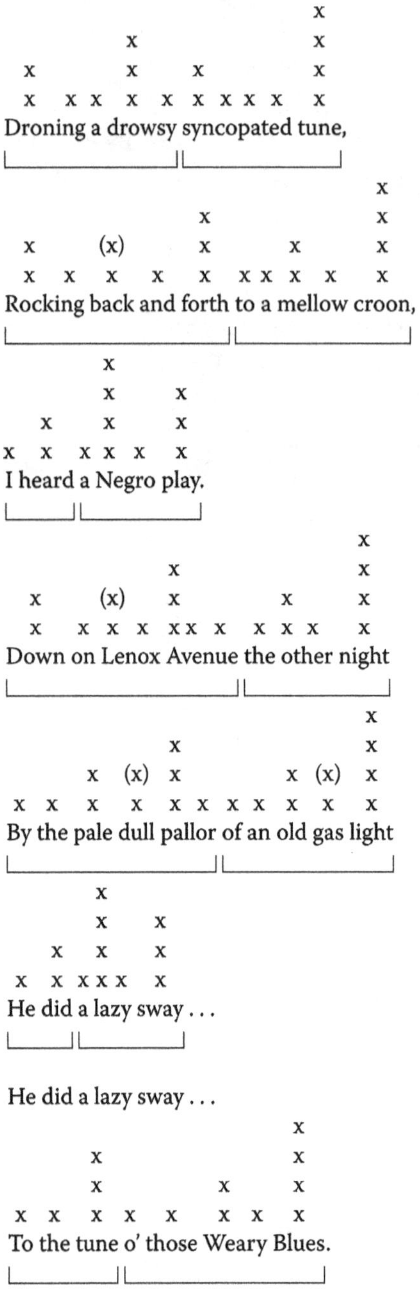

```
                        x
            x           x
x           x    x      x
x  x x  x   x  x x x x  x
Droning a drowsy syncopated tune,
└─────────────┘└──────────────┘

                              x
                  x           x
x      (x)        x      x    x
x  x   x     x    x   x x x   x
Rocking back and forth to a mellow croon,
└──────────────────┘└──────────────┘

      x
      x   x
x     x   x
x  x  x x x  x
I heard a Negro play.
└────┘└─────┘

                              x
                  x           x
x    (x)    x           x     x
x   x x x   x x  x   x x x    x
Down on Lenox Avenue the other night
└──────────────────┘└────────────┘

                                    x
                  x                 x
x    (x)  x              x  (x)  x
x x  x    x   x x x x x  x  x    x
By the pale dull pallor of an old gas light
└──────────────────┘└──────────────┘

      x
      x   x
x     x   x
x  x x x x   x
He did a lazy sway . . .
└────┘└─────┘

He did a lazy sway . . .
                                x
         x                      x
         x             x        x
x  x  x  x   x    x  x    x
To the tune o' those Weary Blues.
└──────────┘└────────────────┘
```

FIGURE 6.23 Stress grid for the first eight lines of Langston Hughes's "The Weary Blues."

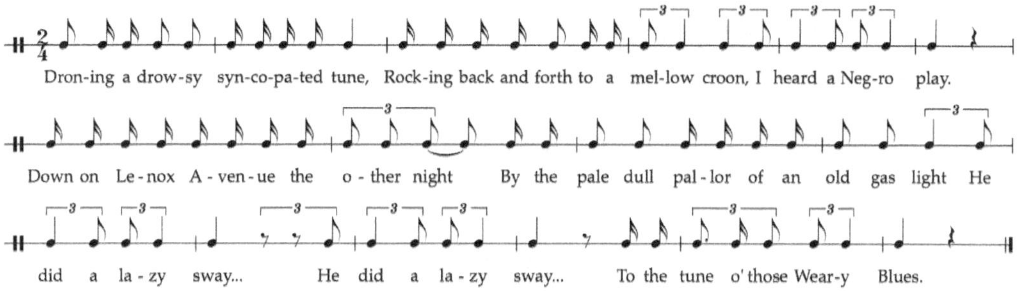

TRANSCRIPTIONS AND ANALYSES | 123

FIGURE 6.24 Metrical-durational realization of the opening lines of "The Weary Blues."

FIGURE 6.25 Comparative analysis of "The Weary Blues." The top staff adds contour to figure 6.24, and the bottom staff transcribes Hughes's reading.

the derived version is in his reading of lines 3 and 6. He treats "heard" in line 3 and "did" in line 6 as unstressed function words, and this in turn causes rhythmic contractions at "I heard a" and "He did a." This interpretation supports the stress grid and allows for longer durations ending the previous lines at "croon" and "light."

Hughes's rhythmic contraction in line 6 and the line's repetition cause the two instances of "la-" to be three tactus beats apart. On the principle that repeated phrases ought to receive parallel metrical analyses, his

[musical notation: 3/4 time signature with notes]

old gas light   He did a   la - zy sway...   He did a   la - zy sway...To the tune o' those Wear-y Blues.

FIGURE 6.26 A rewriting in 3/4 of Hughes's reading of lines 6–8.

reading of lines 6–8 could be rewritten in 3/4 meter, shown in figure 6.26. The shift to 3/4 embodies the line's "lazy sway."

There are discrepancies in contour between the derived and transcribed versions of "The Weary Blues." The derived contour generally moves by step from one syllable to the next, but Hughes often sits on pitches for successive syllables. As a result, one hears actual rather than approximate pitches in much of his recitation. It would be possible to transcribe many of his syllables as recurring microtonal pitches. This lends his recitation a particularly musical quality.

Elizabeth Bishop's "The Fish" is in free verse often with three stresses (syllables with two or more x's) per line. But the uneven count of syllables per line, the irregular distribution of stresses, the use of enjambment, and the absence of rhyme combine to make the poetic line perceptually marginal. Its existence depends on seeing it on the page.

Figure 6.27 presents the stress grid for the poem's opening lines, with the brackets marking intonational phrases. There is an enjambment in the third line. Adjacent stresses straddle line boundaries between lines 3–4 ("boat half") and 4–5 ("hook fast"). The x's over "did-" and "had-" are in parentheses because, even though these syllables are slightly stressed within their contractions, they are function words and typically behave as clitics.

Figure 6.28a gives a preliminary metrical-durational realization based on figure 6.27. Beats are irregular above the dotted-quarter tactus level; the meter oscillates between 6/8 and 9/8 so that syllables with three and four x's can align with downbeats. The sequence of three unstressed syllables in "corner of his mouth" induces the fast duple rhythm there. The analysis observes the parenthesized x's at "didn't" and "hadn't."

The long durations on "boat" and "hook" in figure 6.28a, both in the middle of their intonational phrases, is disconcerting, as is their contrast in length compared to their adjacent two-x syllables, "half" and "fast." Figure 6.28b alleviates these difficulties by evening their durations to two quarter notes. Another imperfect solution in 6.28a is the ponderous rhythm at "He

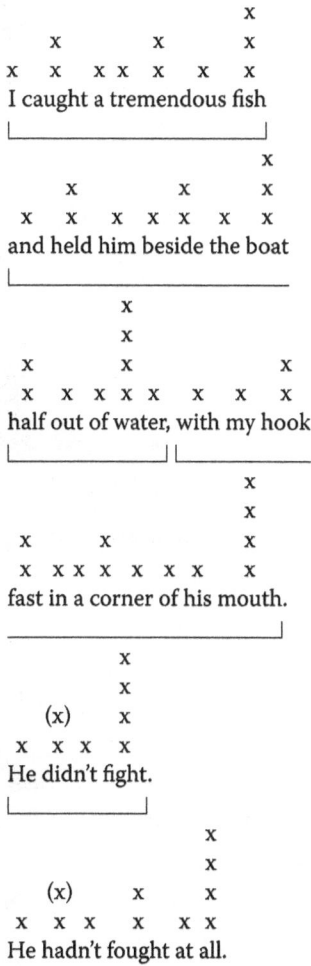

FIGURE 6.27 Stress grid for the opening lines of Elizabeth Bishop's "The Fish."

didn't fight/He didn't fight at all." If the parenthesized x's in figure 6.27 are not observed, the sequence of adjacent nonstresses condenses "He didn't" and "He hadn't" to the sixteenth notes shown in figure 6.28b. Finally, 6.28b casts the second and third syllables of "tremendous" in duple rhythm. With these changes, 6.28b is the preferred metrical-durational realization.

The top staff in figure 6.29 builds a contour analysis over the rhythms of figure 6.28b, and the bottom staff transcribes Bishop's recitation. Adjusting for tempo fluctuations, the predicted rhythms mostly correspond to Bishop's reading. She accelerates in bars 2 and 3 and pauses after "mouth" in bar 6. The sense of meter weakens at these moments. She projects

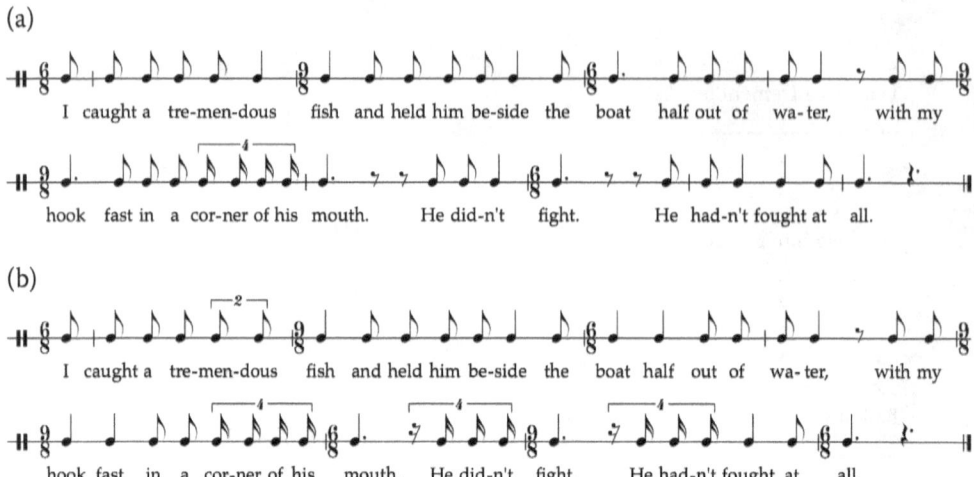

FIGURE 6.28 The opening lines of "The Fish": (a) preliminary metrical-durational realization, (b) revised realization.

intonational phrases but runs through many of the phonological phrase boundaries. She ignores line breaks unless they are supported by punctuation or by major phrase boundaries.

The predicted phrasal shapes generally rise and then fall, whereas Bishop's, after initial anacruses, generally descend. In the first line, she places focus on "tremendous" instead of "fish," which would ordinarily receive

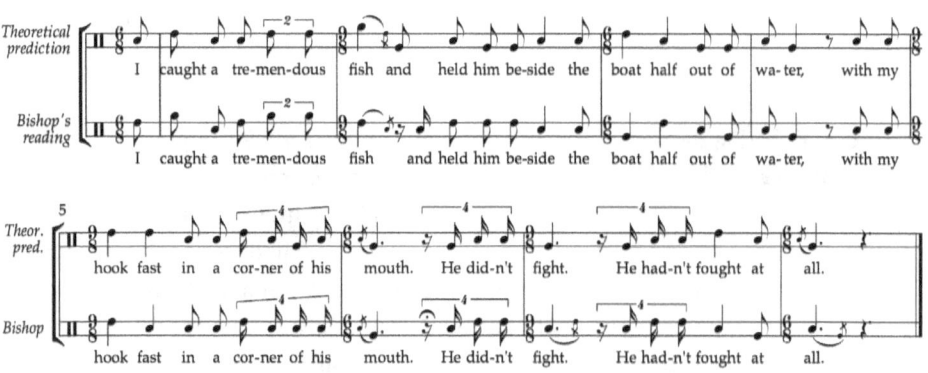

FIGURE 6.29 Comparative analysis of "The Fish." The top staff adds contour to figure 6.28b, and the bottom staff transcribes Bishop's recitation.

nuclear stress, and her tessitura is high, indeed higher than in the rest of the excerpt. After that, she speaks most of the strongly stressed syllables in a low range. The bitonal syllable "fight," however, rises, preventing closure; she treats "He didn't fight/He hadn't fought at all" not as two utterances but as two intonational phrases joined in a single utterance. Her slight rise-fall at "all" conveys wonderment at the fish's stoic resilience.

Prosodic details aside, Bishop recounts an intense experience at a brisk tempo and in an understated tone, a far cry from Eliot's elevated rhetoric or Stevens's resonant silences.

6.5 CONCLUDING REMARKS

The transcriptions and analyses in this chapter suggest a few broad conclusions. First, the theory's rhythmic predictions are mostly compatible with readings by poets and actors. Sometimes a small discrepancy leads to a refinement of the metrical-durational rules. The one large discrepancy, Stevens's striking pauses in "The Idea of Order at Key West," reveals an emphasis on his part on a parallel component within the theory rather than on a poetic or structural feature outside the theory.

Second, the theory's contour predictions often diverge more from the readings than do the rhythmic predictions. This result is expected because there is substantial variation in how speakers intone, and the goal of this part of the theory is only to derive a normative contour. Nevertheless, the contour component needs refinement. Factors appear to influence contour beyond those that have been discussed, for instance, phonetic features, a topic that my model barely touches on. Most important is that contour conveys meaning, and therefore it depends on the speaker's intent, an aspect beyond the scope of this book.

Despite its limitations, the theory as it stands provides a detailed representation and exegesis of the rhythms and contours of poetic lines. Even where—especially where—its predictions are at variance with recorded readings, it offers means to explain the differences.

7

Sound Color

7.1 SOUND ASSOCIATIONS AND PATTERNS

A major aspect of any poem is the sound color of its syllables and words, their degree of similarity, and the patterns they make. At one pole of similarity is word identity. In rhyme, two words are not identical, but their final stressed syllables are, beginning with their vowels. A second kind of similarity is assonance, in which syllables share the same vowel but not the same consonants. A third kind is alliteration, in which words begin with the same consonant. Fourth, there is contrast between syllables, defined for present purposes as syllables without identity, rhyme, assonance, or alliteration.

Although these degrees of similarity and dissimilarity are central to the perception and appreciation of poetry, they have only a marginal effect on how poetic lines are spoken. To take examples from chapter 6, William Butler Yeats's unusual contour at line-end rhyming words in "The Lake Isle of Innisfree" gives them further prominence. T. S. Eliot leans into his pronunciation of "Time" in precisely the same way in its first four occurrences in "Burnt Norton," giving the word additional prominence, as befits the poem's theme. But these details are points of emphasis and do not fundamentally alter the spoken rhythm or contour.

Books on poetry typically discuss rhyme schemes and point out cases of assonance and alliteration. Figure 7.1 illustrates this kind of analysis in

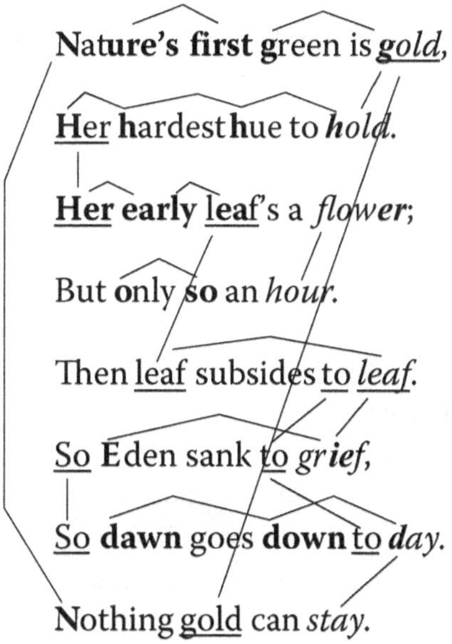

> Nature's first green is *gold*,
> Her hardest hue to *hold*.
> Her early leaf's a *flower*;
> But only so an *hour*.
> Then leaf subsides to *leaf*.
> So Eden sank to *grief*,
> So dawn goes down to *day*.
> Nothing gold can *stay*.

FIGURE 7.1 A network of sound associations in Robert Frost's "Nothing Gold Can Stay." Key: underlining = identity, italic = rhyme, and bold = assonance or alliteration.

some detail for Robert Frost's "Nothing Gold Can Stay," a poem that is rich in sound associations. Words that repeat are underlined and connected by lines. Rhyming words are italicized and connected by lines. Words, syllables, or phonemes that manifest assonance or alliteration are in bold and connected by lines. The result is a tangled network of associations from which various patterns can be gleaned. The rhyme scheme is aabb/ccdd. The second and seventh lines both have three alliterative words. The repetition of "Her" beginning the second and third lines is echoed symmetrically by the repetition of "So" in the sixth and seventh lines. The fifth, sixth, and seventh lines all repeat "to" between a verb and a noun. The first and eighth lines, already associated by the repetition of "gold," both begin with an alliterative "N" on a stressed syllable.

This kind of analysis, however, lacks methodology and structure. The next section offers a hierarchical approach to poetic sound color.[1]

7.2 A HIERARCHICAL MODEL

The combination of the prosodic hierarchy and stress grid formed a basis for assigning meter and duration in chapter 2 and contour in chapter 5. Here, it serves the further purpose of providing a hierarchical framework for the analysis of syllabic sound color. The prosodic hierarchy determines the nested temporal units within which words or syllables reside, and the stress grid establishes the perceptual importance of words or syllables within these units.

It is convenient to divide degrees of similarity into three categories: strong repetition, which encompasses word identity and rhyme; weak repetition, which comprises assonance and alliteration; and nonrepetition or contrast, in which there is neither strong nor weak repetition. These classifications are rough; the reality is more continuous. For instance, syllables related by alliteration are perceptually more salient than those by assonance and could be classified as strong repetition along with rhyme. The primacy of alliteration in Old English poetry would support this reclassification. However, alliteration, like assonance, usually depends on a single repetition, in this case, the opening consonant of a syllable, whereas rhyme usually depends on two, the vowel and the closing consonant. Thus, as an approximation, let alliteration stand with assonance as weak repetition.

These tripartite relations take place at multiple levels and can be represented by a tree structure or its equivalent. Here, I dispense with trees and employ the notation from chapter 5 in which note values stand not for duration but for relative prominence. A larger note value connected by a slur to a smaller note value specifies domination of the former over the latter. To illustrate, in the top staff of figure 7.2, the first word or syllable, represented by a quarter note, dominates the second, represented by an eighth note. Conversely, in the bottom staff, the second word or syllable dominates the first. Figure 7.2a shows strong repetition, connected by a dashed slur, 7.2b weak repetition by a dotted slur, and 7.2c nonrepetition by a solid slur.

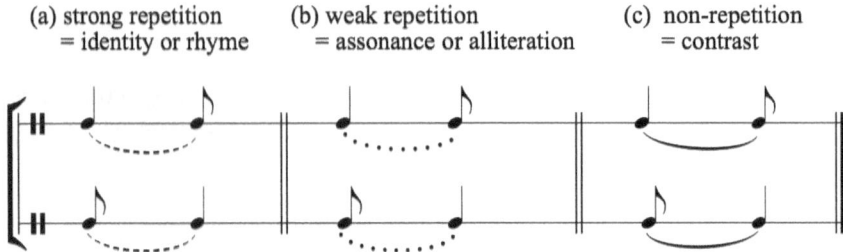

FIGURE 7.2 Three categories of hierarchical connection. Dashed slur = strong repetition (identity or rhyme), dotted slur = weak repetition (assonance or alliteration), solid slur = nonrepetition (contrast). Larger note values dominate smaller note values.

```
(a) 4-x level:  [                         gold] [                      hold]
(b) 3-x level:  [              green][    gold] [   hard-       ][     hold]
(c) 2-x level:  [Na-    ][first][green][  gold] [   hard-    ][hue][  hold]
(d) 1-x level:  [Na-][ture's][first][green][is][gold]  [Her hard-][est][hue][to][hold]
```

FIGURE 7.3 Prosodic hierarchy and stress grid of the first couplet of "Nothing Gold Can Stay," shown in the layered format of figure 4.7c.

Figure 7.3 resumes the layered format from figure 4.7c to display the prosodic grouping and stress grid for the first couplet of "Nothing Gold Can Stay." The brackets mark the prosodic grouping. Words or syllables that are assigned four x's appear at level (a), three x's at level (b), two x's at level (c), and one x at level (d).

The next step, shown in figure 7.4, is to connect words or syllables at each level by strong repetition, weak repetition, or contrast and to designate them as dominant or subordinate in accordance with the number of x's. At any given level, a subordinate word or syllable attaches to the adjacent left or right superordinate word or syllable by degree of similarity rather than by grouping in the prosodic hierarchy (although the two often coincide).

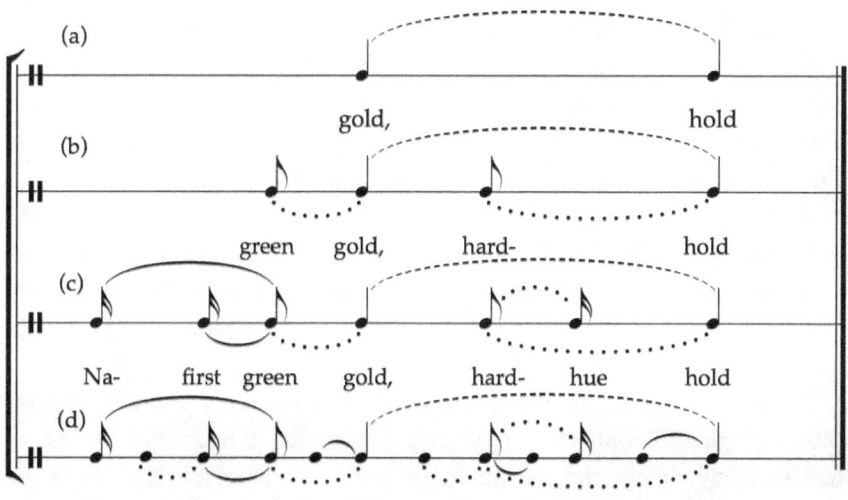

FIGURE 7.4 Hierarchical sound-color analysis of the first couplet of "Nothing Gold Can Stay." Dashed slur = strong repetition (identity or rhyme), dotted slur = weak repetition (assonance or alliteration), solid slur = nonrepetition (contrast).

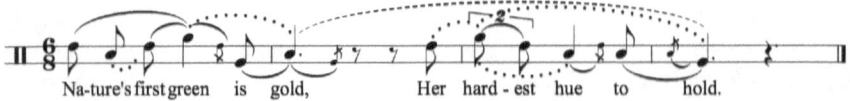

FIGURE 7.5 Hierarchical sound-color analysis from figure 7.4d combined with the rhythmic and contour analysis in figures 5.16 and 6.3.

The most global connections appear at the top of the figure, and successive levels fill in connective details. At level (a) in figure 7.4, "gold" connects as a strong repetition to "hold." At level (b), "green" connects alliteratively to "gold" and, in parallel, "hard-" to "hold." At level (c), "Na-" attaches contrastively to "green," within which "first" also attaches to "green," and "hard-" connects alliteratively to "hue." The alliterative connection of "hue" to "hold" is indirect through its hierarchically prior connection to "hard-."[2] At level (d), "-ture's" attaches to "first" assonantly rather than to the contrasting syllable "Na-." This is an example of attachment by similarity overriding attachment by prosodic parsing. For the other unstressed syllables, there is no disparity between similarity and parsing.

Notice that each successive level inherits connections from its predecessor. Level (d) retains all the information from levels (a–c).

Figure 7.5 adds the slurs from figure 7.4d to the predicted metrical-durational and contour analysis from figures 5.16 and 6.3, creating a combined representation. But the hierarchy of domination and subordination is obscured in this format (although it is traceable through the pattern of slurs) because note values now stand for duration rather than hierarchical rank. For instance, "hard-" dominates "hue," but its duration is an eighth note and that of "hue" is a quarter note. To avoid confusion and keep the focus on sound-color patterns, let us continue with the format employed in figure 7.4, in which the sound-color analysis is separate from analyses in the other components.

Figures 7.6 and 7.7 continue the sound-color analysis, couplet by couplet. In figure 7.7, only the equivalents of level (d) in figure 7.4 are shown because they include the hierarchical connections from levels (a–c). In the second couplet, "flower" is treated as disyllabic yet rhymed with "hour." There are two instances in figure 7.7 of similarity overriding the parsing in figure 7.6: "-ly" to "leaf's" (instead of to "ear-") and "down" to "dawn" (instead of to "day"). The rest of the analysis is straightforward.

```
(a) 4-x level: [                    flow-                       hour]
(b) 3-x level: [         leaf's     flow-   ] [  on-             hour]
(c) 2-x level: [  ear-  ][leaf's][  flow-   ] [  on-     so][    hour]
(d) 1-x level: [Her][ear-][ly][leaf's][a][flow-][er] [But][on-][ly][so][an][hour]
```

```
(a) 4-x level: [                    leaf                        grief]
(b) 3-x level: [         leaf                leaf] [  E-         grief]
(c) 2-x level: [         leaf][  -sides][   leaf] [  E-   ][sank  grief]
(d) 1-x level: [Then][leaf][sub-][sides][to][leaf] [So][E-][den][sank][to][grief]
```

```
(a) 4-x level: [                    day                         stay]
(b) 3-x level: [  dawn               day] [               gold   stay]
(c) 2-x level: [  dawn][   down      day] [No-       gold][      stay]
(d) 1-x level: [So][dawn][goes][down][to][day] [No-][thing][gold][can][stay]
```

FIGURE 7.6 Prosodic hierarchy and stress grid of the second, third, and fourth couplets of "Nothing Gold Can Stay." The pattern of x's corresponds to the stress grid in figure 6.1.

Some might object that figure 7.7 gives inadequate structural value to "Eden," the most striking word in the poem's most striking line. But the analysis is concerned with sound color rather than meaning. It matters not to the sound itself that the Fall of all falls is invoked. In music as well as in poetry, it often happens that the most powerful moments are structurally

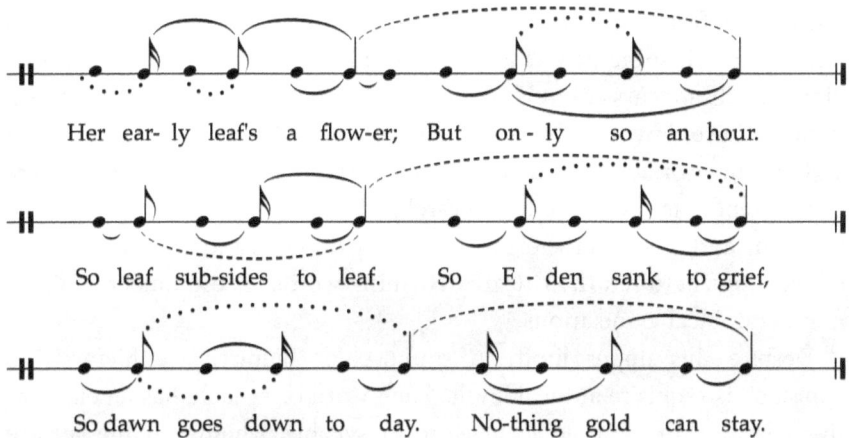

FIGURE 7.7 Hierarchical sound-color analysis of the second, third, and fourth couplets of "Nothing Gold Can Stay."

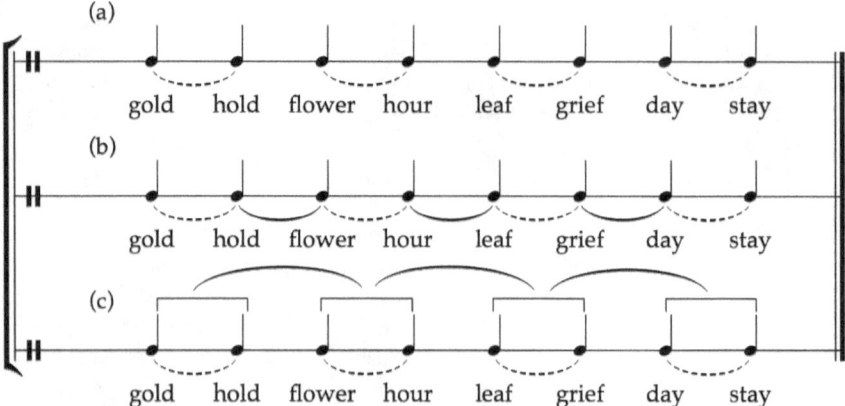

FIGURE 7.8 Sound-color connections for rhyming words in "Nothing Gold Can Stay."

embedded. "Eden" appears unceremoniously, as if it were no more extraordinary than the other words in the poem.

Distinctions in stress become perceptually meaningless above four tier levels. As a result, intuitions of a hierarchy of sound colors dissolve at global levels. To illustrate, figure 7.8a preserves from figures 7.4d and 7.7 just their 4-x words, represented by quarter notes. Dashed slurs are drawn between couplet rhymes. They are not in a dominating-subordinating relationship but form equal pairs. Another possibility, shown in figure 7.8b, is to draw linear links from word to word without hierarchy. Another, in 7.8c, is to regard each rhyming pair as a unit that links to the next pair. Either way, hierarchy disappears at levels larger than the couplet. Distant connections, such as those drawn in figure 7.1 between "leaf's" and "leaf" in the third and fifth lines or between "gold" and "gold" in the first and eighth lines, are consequently not available for hierarchical analysis because "leaf's" in the third line and "gold" in the eighth have only three x's and are subsumed by connections between their nearby rhyming words. These links remain as nonhierarchical associations.

Despite this upper limit on sound-color hierarchy, a hierarchical approach is requisite at local levels. Each word or syllable has an elaborative relationship to an adjacent word or syllable, whether at the surface or at an underlying level. Those that form strong or weak repetitions are salient if stressed but unobtrusive if unstressed. For instance, the rhyme

(a) *4-x level:*
(b) *3-x level:* [death]
(c) *2-x level:* [Rocks][caves][lakes][fens][bogs][dens][shades][death]
(d) *1-x level:* [Rocks,][caves,][lakes,][fens,][bogs,][dens,][and shades][of death]

FIGURE 7.9 Prosodic hierarchy and stress grid of John Milton's *Paradise Lost*, line 2.621 (see figure 3.20a).

of "gold" and "hold" is conspicuous, whereas the repetition of "Her" in the second and third lines is not.

The string of rhyming words of undifferentiated stress in figure 7.8 is at a level beneath the poem's surface, but this feature can also occur at a poetic surface, as in the following line from Milton's *Paradise Lost* (discussed in chapter 3.6):

Rocks, caves, lakes, fens, bogs, dens, and shades of death;

Figure 7.9 casts its prosodic hierarchy and stress grid in the layered format. The first seven nouns all have two x's. The only word with three x's is "death," by virtue of nuclear stress.

Figure 7.10 shows the line's hierarchical sound analysis. The first four nouns connect sequentially, but "fens" rhymes with "dens," causing it to link not to "bogs" but to "dens" with a dashed slur. Similarly, "dens" and "death" are alliterative and assonantal, causing "dens" to link not to "shades" but to

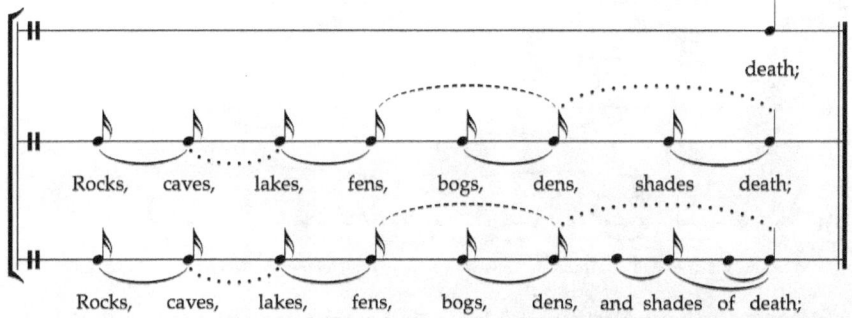

FIGURE 7.10 Hierarchical sound-color analysis of *Paradise Lost*, line 2.621.

```
(a) 4-x level:  [                                      eyes] [                                    state]
(b) 3-x level:  [                grace][                eyes] [      -lone                         state]
(c) 2-x level:  [When            grace][     for-    ][ men's][eyes] [  -lone][ -weep      out-    state]
(d) 1-x level:  [When][in][dis-][grace][with][for-][tune][and][men's][eyes] [I all alone][beweep][my outcast][state]
```

FIGURE 7.11 Prosodic hierarchy and stress grid of the first couplet of William Shakespeare's Sonnet 29. The analysis duplicates that of figure 2.5.

"death" with a dotted slur. These instances express a principle of sound-color analysis: in sequences of equal stress, where possible assign strong or weak repetitions even if there is an intervening word or syllable at that level. This precept reflects the perceptual force of repetition. The assonance between "lakes" and "shades," however, is beyond the reach of a hierarchical description because "shades" is contained within the span connecting "dens" and "death." In addition, the sheer distance between "lakes" and "shades" weakens the association. The preference to connect repetitions is constrained not only by the stress configuration but also by distance. Rhymes, assonances, and alliterations matter less if they are far apart.[3]

Figure 7.11 gives the prosodic hierarchy and stress grid of the first couplet of Shakespeare's Sonnet 29 (adapted from figure 2.5), and figure 7.12 displays its sound-color analysis. In contrast to the Frost poem, the syntax

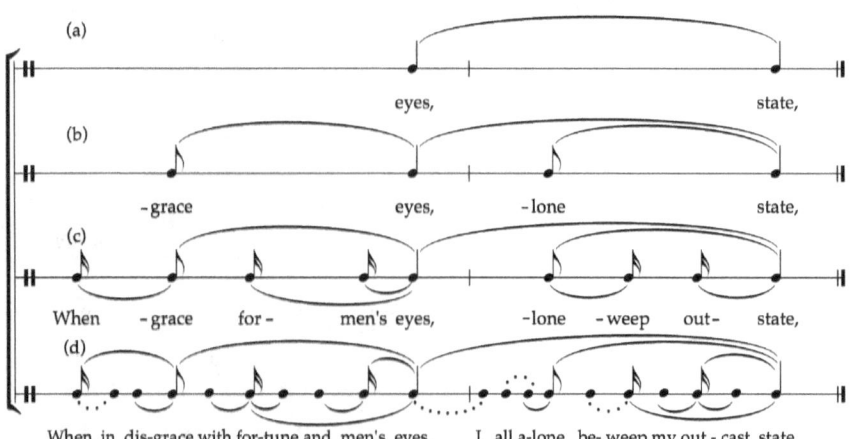

FIGURE 7.12 Hierarchical sound-color analysis of the first couplet of Sonnet 29.

SOUND COLOR | 137

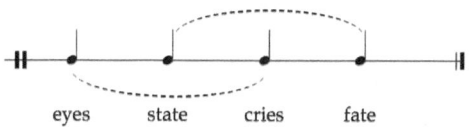

FIGURE 7.13 Connections for rhyming words in the first quatrain of Sonnet 29.

and rhythm of the sonnet are complex, but its sound structure has few strong or weak repetitions. The most marked is the assonantal connection of "eyes" to "I" crossing a line boundary. Frost maximizes sound repetition; Shakespeare maximizes sound variety.

Hierarchical description breaks down above level (a) in figure 7.12. Figure 7.13 retains just the 4-x rhyming words from the first quatrain and illustrates the rhymes "eyes/cries" and "state/fate" as a nonhierarchical interleaved pattern. The same pattern continues in the second and third quatrains before the concluding rhymed couplet. (This rhyme scheme is standard for an Elizabethan sonnet.) Long-distance repetitions such as the return of "state" at the end of the tenth line and internally in the fourteenth line are associative but not hierarchical.

Figure 7.14 displays one interpretation of the prosodic hierarchy and stress grid of T. S. Eliot's "Burnt Norton" (adapted from figure 6.16), and figure 7.15 shows the resultant hierarchical sound-color analysis.

The slurs in figure 7.15 aptly convey the give and take of "present," "past," "future," and their repetitions, but at the price of suppressing the strong

```
(a) 4-x level:  [                                                                              fu-    ]
(b) 3-x level:  [       pre-    ][        past]  [                      pre-    ][        fu-    ]
(c) 2-x level:  [Time][pre-     ][   time][past]  [    both][           pre-    ][  time][fu-   ]
(d) 1-x level:  [Time][present][and time][past]  [Are both][perhaps present][in time][future]

(a) 4-x level:  [                                     past]
(b) 3-x level:  [           fu-    ][                 past]
(c) 2-x level:  [      time][fu-   ][  -tained][ time][past]
(d) 1-x level:  [And time][future][contained][in time][past]
```

FIGURE 7.14 Prosodic hierarchy and stress grid of the first three lines of T. S. Eliot's "Burnt Norton": first version.

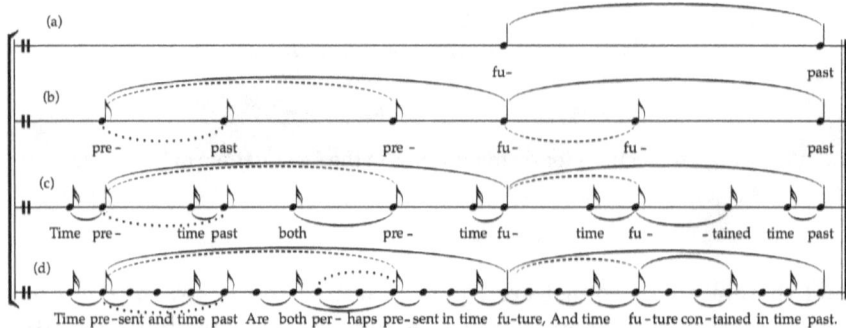

FIGURE 7.15 Hierarchical sound-color analysis of the first three lines of "Burnt Norton": first version.

repetitions of "time." An alternative analysis in figure 7.16 places greater stress on "time," in accordance with Eliot's reading (see the discussion of figure 6.18 in chapter 6). This change leads to the sound-color analysis in figure 7.17, in which instances of "time" connect as strong repetitions at three levels. Again, there is a cost: the lack of interconnections for "present," "past," and "future."

These lines are poised between the two sound-color interpretations in figures 7.15 and 7.17. Some insight can be gained by inverting, in the spirit of Youmans (1983), noun-adjective pairings to their normal ordering: "Present time and past time / Are both perhaps present in future time." This leads to the prosodic hierarchy and stress grid in figure 7.18a and to the metrical-durational realization in figure 7.18b. Here contrastive stress

(a) *4-x level:* [time   ]
(b) *3-x level:* [Time   ][time   ] [pre-][time   ]
(c) *2-x level:* [Time][pre-][time][past] [both][pre-][time][fu-   ]
(d) *1-x level:* [Time][present][and time][past] [Are both][perhaps present][in time][future]

(a) *4-x level:* [time   ]
(b) *3-x level:* [fu-   ][time   ]
(c) *2-x level:* [time][fu-   ][-tained][time][past]
(d) *1-x level:* [And time][future][contained][in time][past]

FIGURE 7.16 Prosodic hierarchy and stress grid of the first three lines of "Burnt Norton": second version.

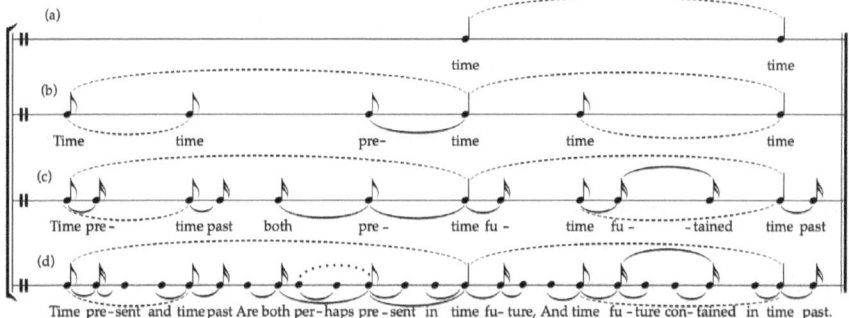

FIGURE 7.17 Hierarchical sound-color analysis of the first three lines of "Burnt Norton": second version.

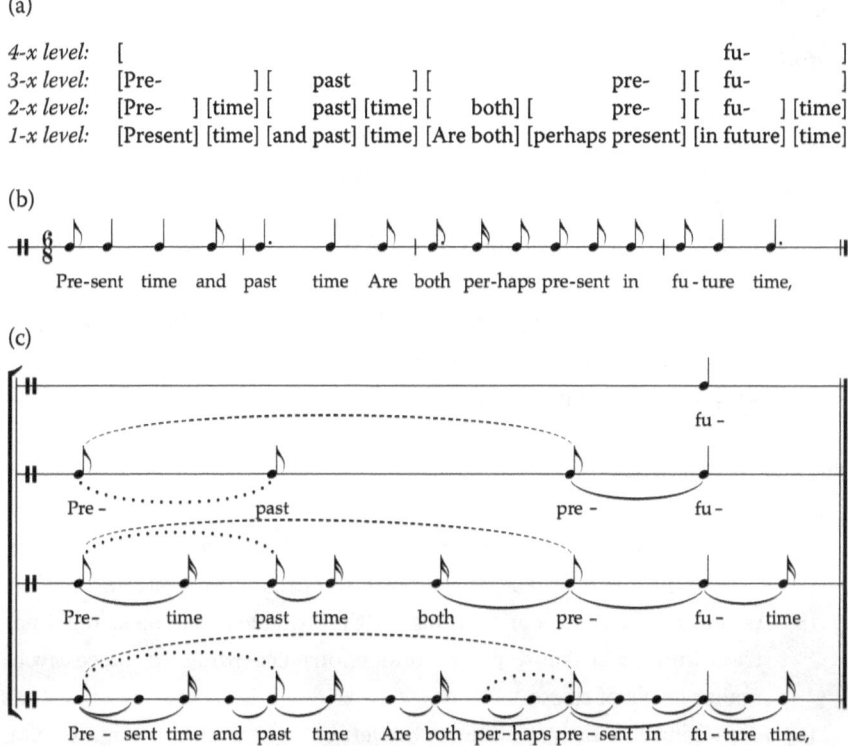

FIGURE 7.18 The first two lines of "Burnt Norton" with inverted adjectives rearranged to normal ordering: (a) prosodic hierarchy and stress grid, (b) metrical-durational realization of (a), (c) sound-color analysis.

on the adjectives seems obligatory: Présent time, pást time, fúture time. Consequently, "time" is perceptually subjugated to its adjectives, as shown in the sound-color analysis in figure 7.18c. This analysis is nearly identical to figure 7.15.

By inverting the word order, Eliot brings "time" into perceptual balance with its adjectives. Unlike the normal ordering, "time" is always adjacent to stressed syllables—tíme présent, tíme pást, tíme fúture. As a result, "time" and the stressed adjectival syllables must occur on tactus beats, causing "time" to have a relatively long duration. Eliot's inversions trigger duration as well as sound-color prominence to support the centrality of time to the poem.

The following statement summarizes the hierarchical sound-color model.

Procedure for sound-color assignment:

Definitions and stipulations

(1) There are three kinds of sound-color connection:
   (a) Strong repetition for word identity or syllabic rhyme.
   (b) Weak repetition for syllables related by assonance or alliteration.
   (c) Nonrepetition, or contrast, for syllables not related by (a) or (b).
(2) At any given time-span level, a sound-color region is the span between the immediately superordinate syllable to the left and the immediately superordinate syllable to the right.
(3) Every syllable in a poem has a sound-color connection.

Derivational procedure

(4) Assign sound-color prominence level by level, according to the number of x's in the stress grid as derived over the prosodic hierarchy.
(5) Assign sound-color connections to the syllables that have maximal stress and make subsequent connections according to successively smaller levels of stress.[4]
(6) At each level, attach syllables to the left or right within its sound-color region, in this order of priority: strong repetitions, then weak repetitions, then nonrepetitions.

(7) If, at a given level, there is a string of syllables having equal stress, give preference, where possible, to attaching strong or weak repetitions but over distances of no more than one intervening syllable at that level.

(8) All else being equal, give preference to sound-color connections that are congruent with the groupings of the prosodic hierarchy.

7.3 TIME-SPAN REDUCTION

As far as I am aware, no other prosodic study has attempted a hierarchical model of syllabic sound color. The present approach proceeds from my music-theoretic work with Ray Jackendoff (Lerdahl and Jackendoff [1983]) and subsequent work of my own. The rest of this chapter discusses these musical connections.

A key component in *A Generative Theory of Tonal Music* is time-span reduction, which, as mentioned in chapter 4.2, organizes pitch events into hierarchically organized rhythmic units from the smallest to the largest levels of a piece. At subgroup levels, time spans are from beat to beat in the metrical grid. At larger levels, from a musical motive to phrases and sections, grouping boundaries demarcate time spans. Each event has a time-span address.

In the reduction process, given two (or sometimes three) events in the same span, the less stable event reduces out and the more stable event advances to the next larger level to compete against another event that dominates its own span. Figure 7.19 illustrates with the opening bars of "God Save the King." The brackets beneath the music at level (c) mark the first phrase and the beginning of the second. Within this grouping, the time spans are between quarter notes at level (c) and dotted-half notes at level (b). In the first phrase, the most stable events at level (c) are the C major chord in bar 1 and the G major chord in bar 2. The other, less stable events in bars 1–2 reduce out, leaving these two chords at level (b). The C major chord is more stable than the G major chord, so at level (a) the latter reduces out, leaving only the C major chord to represent bars 1–2. The second phrase, which groups with the first phrase, begins with another C major chord that also appears at level (a).

The concept of time-span reduction stems from contrapuntal practice going back to the sixteenth century. It was partially systematized in the

FIGURE 7.19 Time-span reduction of the initial bars of "God Save the King."

pedagogy of species counterpoint (Fux, 1725/1965), which remains widely taught in harmony and counterpoint courses, and was extended to larger levels of structure by twentieth-century theorists (e.g., Schenker, 1921–1924; Lewin, 1974/2013; Schachter, 1980). Its perceptual force is especially palpable in classical variations, in which a melody or harmonic progression is progressively elaborated, and in jazz improvisations based on song standards. It also plays a role in music from other cultures, for instance, North Indian raga.

It was observed in chapter 4 that Liberman and Prince's (1977) phonological trees are a form of time-span reduction, as is Hayes's (1989) combination of prosodic hierarchy and stress grid. All the poetic analyses in this book that assign prosodic bracketing and stress levels are versions of time-span reduction. In this chapter, I have displayed prosodic-hierarchic and stress analyses in time-span reductional format to emphasize the connection.

There are two differences, one minor and one major, worth noting. The minor difference is that, in music, the metrical grid specifies time spans at subgroup levels, whereas in language, the prosodic hierarchy and word morphology determine spans all the way down to the syllable. The major difference is that, in tonal music, the chief criterion for selecting the event that dominates a span is its contextual stability. Prominence criteria (registral extreme, relative loudness, relative duration, etc.) play a marginal role. In language, in contrast, stability is not a factor, and the relevant criterion is perceptual prominence, codified as stress. Tonal stability is a powerful

SOUND COLOR | 143

factor that extends the musical reduction process to comparatively large levels of structure (although how far is a matter of debate). Distinctions in linguistic stress, however, are inherently limited, and phonological time-span reduction is a local phenomenon.[5]

7.4 LINEAR CONNECTIONS

GTTM's time-span reduction establishes a hierarchy of events within a rhythmic framework, but it does not assign connections among them. For this, the additional step of linear analysis—a hierarchical set of connections among events—is needed.[6] A *GTTM* linear analysis is done top-down so that a subordinate event at any level can be evaluated in the context of its immediate region. Events connect in one of three ways: strong repetition, notated by a dashed slur, represents the return of a pitch or chord; weak repetition, notated by a dotted slur, represents the recurrence of a chord but with an arpeggiated melodic or bass note; and progression or nonrepetition, notated by a solid slur, represents a connection to a different pitch or chord.

Figure 7.20 offers a linear analysis derived from figure 7.19. Only the soprano and bass lines are shown. Labeled levels and the events they contain correlate between the two figures. Events that appear at level (a) in figure 7.20 are notated as quarter notes, those at level (b) as eighth notes,

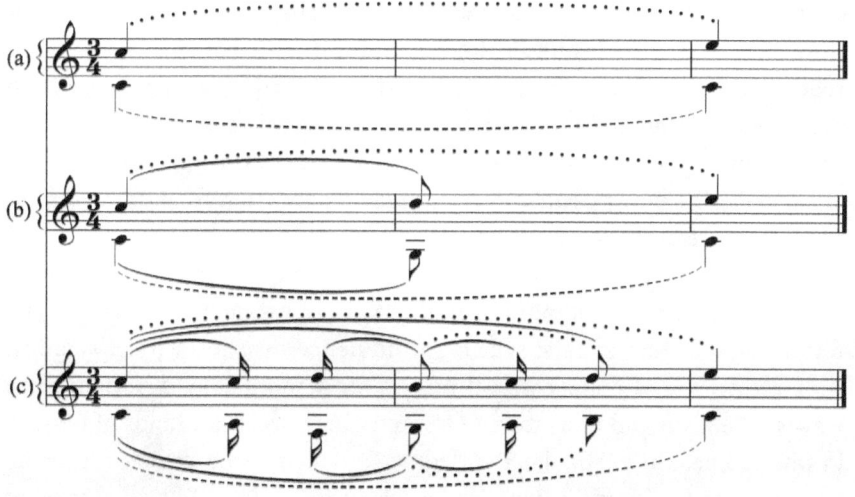

FIGURE 7.20 Linear analysis derived from figure 7.19.

and those at level (c) as sixteenth notes. The derivation begins with level (a). The bass note C in bar 1 repeats in bar 3, so the slur between them is dashed. In the soprano, however, C arpeggiates to E so there, the slur is dotted. At level (b), the dominant chord in bar 2 connects as a progression from the preceding C major chord, hence, the solid slur. At level (c), the remaining events in bar 1 connect as progressions, and in bar 2, they connect as an arpeggiation of the G major chord enclosing a progression.

This analysis can also be interpreted as representing waves of tonal tension and relaxation, with slurs to subsequent subordinate events signifying increasing tension, and slurs to subsequent superordinate events signifying decreasing tension. A strong repetition does not alter tension, a weak repetition alters it slightly, and a progression does so markedly. Thus, in bar 1 there is a wave of tension and relaxation going into the G major chord in bar 2, which is slightly more tense than the initial C major chord. Within bar 2, the passing notes A and C mark a bump in tension. The surrounding C major chords in bars 1 and 3 are relaxed.

Most of the points covered in this short summary of *GTTM*'s component of linear analysis transfer to the hierarchical sound-color model proposed in section 7.2. A sound-color region corresponds to a comparable analytic region in the music theory. The types of syllabic connection in figure 7.2 are based on *GTTM*'s tripartite classification of linear connections. The favoring of repetition over contrast in assigning sound-color connections (conditions 6 and 7 of the sound-color rule) follows from *GTTM*'s preference rules.[7] However, *GTTM*'s top-down derivation of linear connections from corresponding levels in the associated time-span reduction is not requisite in the present model. Rather, there is a two-step process within the stress-grid/prosodic-hierarchy complex: first establish the hierarchical prominence of syllables; then, for any subordinate syllable at any given level, make the best possible (most similar) connection to an immediately superordinate event to its left or right.[8]

The place where the treatment of sound-color connections diverges most markedly from its musical counterpart is, as mentioned, in the criterion for selecting events: syllabic prominence instead of tonal stability. As a result, sound-color connections are only marginally experienced as waves of tension and relaxation.[9] Granted, there are other kinds of tension in poetic lines, in particular the degree to which a line deviates from its prototype or template, as discussed in chapters 3 and 4. But tonal tension and the waves it engenders are properties that belong chiefly to music.

7.5 LINEAR FUNCTIONS

Chapter 5 of *Tonal Pitch Space* (Lerdahl, 2001b) explores the idea of functions issuing from linear connections.[10] It does this in the context of tonal music and employs the linear functions (slightly modified) listed in figure 7.21. Less stable events are represented by smaller note values. Figure 7.21a shows the configuration for a repetition function, marked by *rpt*; the repetition can be strong or weak. Figure 7.21b shows a neighbor function, or *N*: a less stable event enclosed by a strong repetition. It can attach either to left or to the right, as indicated by the slurs. Figure 7.21c shows the less stable event in a passing function, or *P*, within a weak repetition. The dominating event can be in the first or third position. Figure 7.2d shows a departure function, or *dep*: an event leading away from a more stable event. It is often paired with a return function, or *ret*, shown in figure 7.21e, signifying a return to a more stable event. Figure 7.21f shows closure, or *clos*, realized by a cadence at the end of a phrase.[11]

Figure 7.22 adds function labels to the linear analysis of "God Save the King" in figure 7.20. Lower levels inherit functions from higher ones. At level (b), the G major chord takes a passing function between repetitions of the C major chord. At level (c), there is a departure in bar 1 followed by a return toward stability, and in bar 2, the arpeggiated G major chord encloses passing notes. Thus, passing functions occur at two levels in this passage.

As this example implies, a functional description does not add structure to a linear analysis; rather, it annotates it. In this view, function is a property of an event's connective context.

Only the first three cases in figure 7.21—*rpt*, *N*, and *P*—transfer convincingly from music to poetry. A word or syllable can repeat; within a strong repetition, there can be a contrasting neighbor; within a weak repetition, there can be a contrasting passing word or syllable. *N* and *P* take

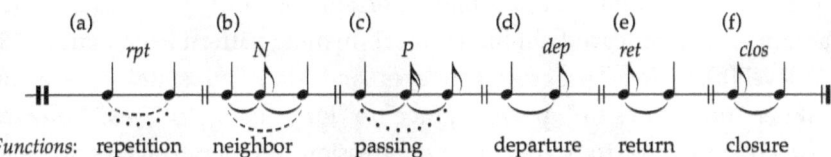

FIGURE 7.21 Basic linear functions for tonal music: (a) *rpt* = repetition; (b) *N* = neighbor; (c) *P* = passing; (d) *dep* = departure; (e) *ret* = return; (f) *clos* = closure.

FIGURE 7.22 Function labels added to the linear analysis of "God Save the King" in figure 7.20.

place within the boundaries of an intonational phrase. But the last three cases—*Dep, ret,* and *clos*—lose meaning in the absence of tonal stability as a reference. Besides, language lacks a syntactic equivalent to a musical cadence. In place of these last three functions, let us posit instead a general progression function, or *prog*, signifying movement to or from a more prominent syllable that is adjacent at the level in question.

To illustrate, figure 7.23 repeats from figure 7.4 the hierarchical sound-color analysis of the first couplet of "Nothing Gold Can Stay" and adds function labels to it. Each syllable is assigned a function, starting with a strong repetition at level (a). At level (b), "gold" weakly repeats "green" and, in parallel, "hold" weakly repeats "hard-." At level (c), "Na-" and "first" both progress to "green," and "hue" both weakly repeats and passes between "hard-" and "hold." At level (d), "-ture's" and "first" link as a weak repetition, as do "Her" and "hard-." Finally, "is," "-est," and "to" take passing functions.

Figure 7.24 similarly performs a function analysis of the first two lines of Sonnet 29, based on the sound-color analysis in figure 7.12. Level (a) assumes the interleaved nonhierarchical rhyming pattern from figure 7.13. At level (b), "-grace" progresses to "eyes" and "-lone" to "state." At level (c), "When" progresses to "-grace," "-grace" to "for-," "men's to "eyes," "lone" to "-weep," and "out-" to "state." More progressions proliferate at level (d), and "I" functions as a weak repetition of "eyes."

Function analyses can bring out similarities in lines that are dissimilar on the surface. In figure 7.25a, lines 2 and 7 of "Nothing Gold Can

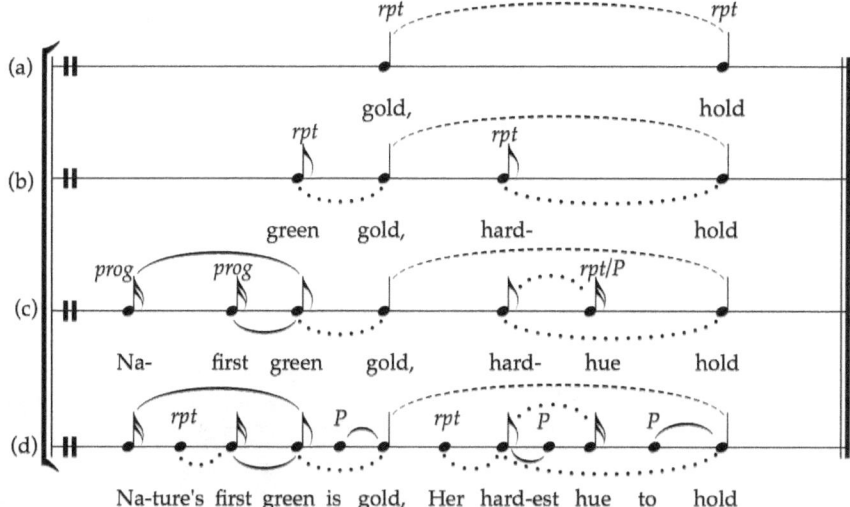

FIGURE 7.23 Functions for the first couplet of "Nothing Gold Can Stay," based on the sound-color analysis in figure 7.4.

Stay" share only one word, but they have almost identical function structures. The same holds for lines 5 and 6 in 7.25b. In addition, the single functional difference between 7.25a and b is that the midpoint stresses in 7.25a—"hue" and "down"—are weak repetitions, whereas in 7.25b—"-sides" and "sank"—they are neighboring or passing.

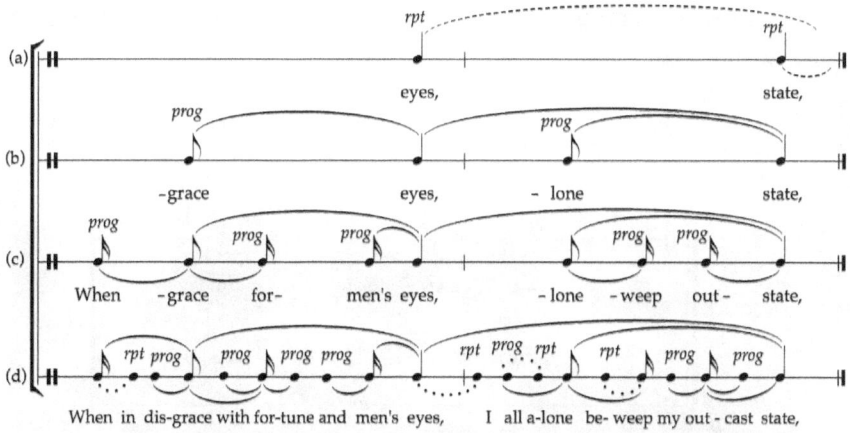

FIGURE 7.24 Functions for the first couplet of Sonnet 29, based on the sound-color analysis in figure 7.12.

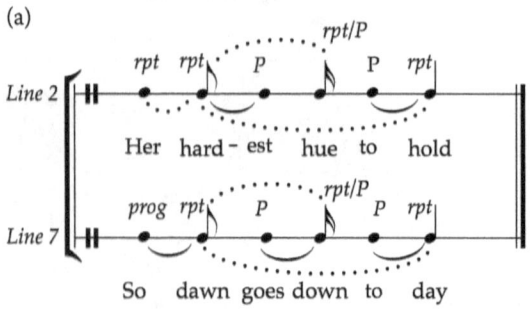
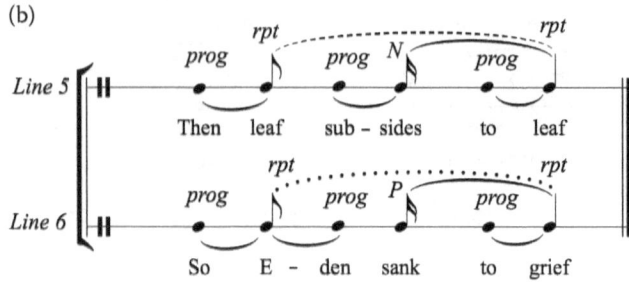

FIGURE 7.25 Comparison of functions in "Nothing Gold Can Stay": (a) lines 2 and 7, (b) lines 5 and 6.

Figure 7.26 compares, by contrast, sound-color functions in lines 7 and 8. Weak repetitions dominate line 7, but progressions prevail everywhere in line 8 until the rhymed word "stay." Line 8 breaks the closely related function patterns of the previous lines to declare the poem's conclusion.

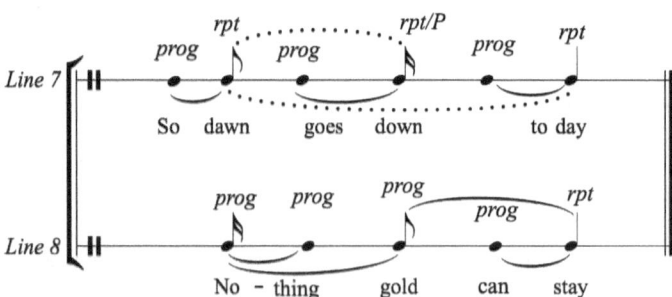

FIGURE 7.26 Comparison of functions in lines 7 and 8 in "Nothing Gold Can Stay."

7.6 REMARKS ON TONAL AND SYLLABLE SPACES

Both *GTTM* and the hierarchical sound-color model rely on a three-way distinction: the same, partly the same, and different. It is a useful but rough classification. To improve this part of the music theory, *Tonal Pitch Space* (Lerdahl, 2001b) develops *GTTM*'s underspecified stability conditions, including this classification, into a quantified model that is representable in geometric format. It builds on historical music-theoretic key charts (Weber, 1821–1824; Schoenberg, 1954/1969) and on recent multidimensional scaling models of perceived pitch relations in cognitive music psychology (Balzano, 1982; Shepard, 1982; Krumhansl, 1983). In all this literature, the more similar or related two pitches or chords or keys are, the closer they are in the space. *Tonal Pitch Space* unifies distances between pitches, chords, and keys into a single model whose distances correlate with the relevant empirical data (Krumhansl, 1990; Lerdahl and Krumhansl, 2007).[12]

It is reasonable to ask, given this development in music theory, if a spatial approach might apply to syllabic sound color—that is, if a syllable space could be constructed so that it accurately represents and measures degrees of similarity and dissimilarity among syllables. This goal is not easily achieved.[13] Distances between pitches, chords, and keys take place in a uniform multidimensional space, but vowels and consonants have contrasting kinds of organization. The International Phonetic Alphabet's (IPA's) vowel chart locates vowels in a continuous two-dimensional space, whereas consonants are organized by a set of binary distinctive features that resist geometric display. Syllabic sound color does not possess an equivalent to the musical octave, which makes possible the group-theoretic treatment of pitch in terms of pitch classes (the class of all C's, the class of all C#'s, etc.).

Figure 7.27 sketches a path in a hypothetical sound-color space, which loosely mimics locations in the IPA chart, for the syllables of the first line of Sonnet 29. "When" and "in" are close in the space; their vowels are similar, and they both end with the consonant "n." With its fresh consonants, "dis-" is a little farther away. There is a jump to the contrasting syllable "-grace," followed by further distant moves to "with" and "for-." A partial return takes place at "-tune." The words "and" and "men's" are close, again because their vowels are similar and followed by "n." They are in the same spatial region as "When in." The line closes with a second jump at "eyes." In short, the spatial pattern is of proximate syllables followed by a jump, then a

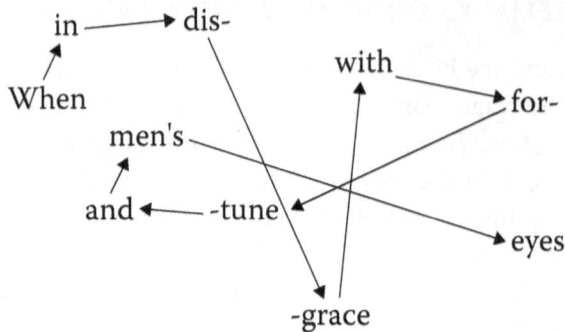

FIGURE 7.27 Mock-up of a spatial representation of sound-color relatedness for the first line of Sonnet 29.

return to the original region and another jump. Such a sound-color pattern, reflecting the effect of combined vowels and consonants, promises to offer a more fine-grained picture than do the broad categories of rhyme, assonance, alliteration, and contrast. Another goal would be to integrate this presumed spatial path with the linear and functional analysis in figure 7.24.

This book will not attempt to go further in constructing a syllabic sound-color space. Even if it did, the space would likely not be capable of conveying robust intuitions of stability and instability or waves of tension and relaxation. The capacity of tonal space to transmit these intuitions ultimately depends on its grounding in strong yet subtle gradations of psychoacoustic consonance and dissonance, a central attribute of music but not of language.

Tonal space exists in varied yet related forms in most cultures, and it reached its apex of complexity in the harmonic and contrapuntal idioms of classical Western music. By the early twentieth century, accelerating innovations brought the tonal system to a state of collapse. Arnold Schoenberg and other composers began to write atonal music—in present terms, music with a nonhierarchical, flat space. In the absence of stability conditions, listeners to atonal music compensate in part by constructing local hierarchies based on the surface salience of events (Lerdahl, 1989; Lerdahl, 2001b, chap. 8). In this sense, atonal music is organized like the sounds of poetry. This statement may seem surprising; atonal music is often compared not to metrical, rhymed verse but to abstract art and free verse. After all, the three types of art undertook these revolutionary changes at about the same time.[14] But the claim is not cultural or historical. Rather, it is a nontrivial formal point: atonal music, like language, depends on prominence instead of stability as the driver of structural selection within a temporal span.

7.7 SUMMARY

The sound-color component of the theory addresses the relatedness of syllabic sounds and how they are organized in a poetic line. Rather than settle for a jumbled network of associations, it proposes a rule-based, hierarchical model. The model posits three categories of similarity or dissimilarity: strong repetition (identity or rhyme), weak repetition (assonance or alliteration), and nonrepetition (contrast). It builds structure on two cornerstones, the prosodic hierarchy for parsing the stream of syllables and the stress grid for determining syllabic prominence. Because distinctions in stress are limited, the model operates only at local levels of form. It establishes syllabic connections within sound-color regions at each level, with a preference to connect strong repetitions, then weak repetitions, then nonrepetitions. Every syllable has a sound-color connection.

Unlike the rhythmic and contour components of the theory, there is no precedent for sound-color analysis except in music theory. The model arises from the musical component of time-span reduction and linear analysis. A few functions transferred from music theory annotate the analysis. The chief difference between the sound-color model and its musical counterpart is that the latter (except for atonal music) assigns hierarchy based on tonal stability instead of perceptual prominence.

Tonal stability is representable in a multidimensional geometric format in which spatial distance correlates with cognitive distance. This raises the possibility of casting syllabic relatedness in a space that integrates vowels and consonants in a quantitative way.

8

Coda

8.1 ARCHITECTURE OF THE THEORY

The chart in figure 8.1 summarizes the architecture of the theory as set forth in chapters 2, 5, and 7. Criteria for grouping (word morphology and the categories of the prosodic hierarchy) and criteria for stress (lexical stress, content and function words, the nuclear-stress principle, focus, and evenness) are inputs to the stress-grid/prosodic-hierarchy complex, which, from a musical perspective, corresponds to nonmetrical, nondurational time-span reduction. This core component is an input to the metrical grid and consequent syllable durations, as well as to the derivation of contour

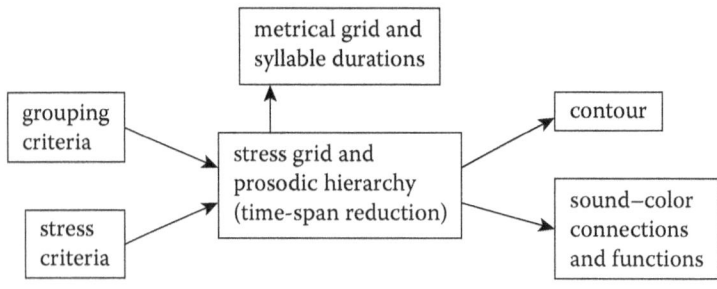

FIGURE 8.1 Flowchart of the components of the theory.

CODA | 153

and of sound-color analysis with its associated functions. If the theory had a coherent model of syllable space, it too would be an input to the analysis of sound-color connections. The diagram highlights the centrality of the stress-grid/prosodic-hierarchy complex for the entire theory.

8.2 PROSPECTS

As it stands, the theory suggests several avenues to explore. First, this study has sought only to specify the factors involved in generating an analysis and to offer procedures for deriving it. A fully formal implementation would reveal errors and omissions and give a more complete account. It would also be useful to automate transcriptions of spoken readings.

The theory could assist speech synthesis, assigning normative rhythms and contours to texts. Current research in this area is widely done by means of statistical learning over large datasets. That approach may successfully imitate human speech, but it does not elucidate how or why. The model presented in this book provides relevant structures and explanations.

An additional area to consider is the relationship between a poetic text and its musical setting, a topic barely touched on in this book. In brief, the rhythmic rules in chapter 2 provide a foundation for normative principles of text setting. (Contour is a relatively free variable in setting words to music.) Composers and analysts have long pursued parallels between poetic form and its musical realization. The musical and phonological correspondences developed in the theory offer means for exploring such parallels in depth. The theory can also serve as a compositional platform for new text setting: first, analyze a poem's rhythm, contour, and sound color; then create music that grows out of the poem's sound structure.

Another route comes from the sound-color component of the theory. Syllabic sound color is an aspect of timbre. Timbral effects have assumed ever greater importance in both art and pop music, especially in the last half century. Yet timbre is difficult to organize structurally beyond a simple classification of sound types. It bears an aesthetic weight that it cannot sustain formally. The sound-color model makes modest headway toward the goal of a timbral syntax. This topic requires further investigation.

A different route to explore is the theory's analytic tools in service of literary interpretation. This book mostly avoids relating the sounds of poetry to meaning. Dealing with poetic sound itself in all its ramifications is, for the present, challenge enough. But the theory promises to build bridges to interpretation that are far more illuminating than is possible with the blunt instrument of traditional scansion.

Yet another area is to apply the theory to poetry in languages other than English. The rhythmic component readily adapts to accentual verse in other languages, but quantitative verse would require more extensive changes.

A more distant area turns from human language to animal aural communication. The songs of whales and songbirds, for example, call for treatment beyond an acoustic level of representation. They form patterns of grouping, duration, stress, contour, and timbre; in some cases, they also project metrical structure. The components of the theory could be adapted to provide structural descriptions of such utterances.

Behind this point lies the perennial issue of the evolutionary origins of music and language and their anatomical, neural, and cognitive underpinnings.[1] I shall not engage with this vast topic except to say that this entire book indicates a convergence in rhythm, contour, and sound color but not in pitch relations, syntax, or semantics. It suggests that the sound structures of music and language coevolved from proto-musical, proto-linguistic expressive utterances, an idea that goes back to Charles Darwin (1871) and even to the pre-evolutionary speculations of Jean-Jacques Rousseau (1760).[2]

Appendix A

Cited Poems

Single lines and very short excerpts cited in the main text are not included.

SONNET 29

When in disgrace with fortune and men's eyes,
I all alone beweep my outcast state,
And trouble deaf heaven with my bootless cries,
And look upon myself and curse my fate,
Wishing me like to one more rich in hope,
Featured like him, like him with friends possessed,
Desiring this man's art, and that man's scope,
With what I most enjoy contented least;
Yet in these thoughts myself almost despising,
Haply I think on thee, and then my state,
Like to the lark at break of day arising
From sullen earth, sings hymns at heaven's gate;
For thy sweet love remembered such wealth brings,
That then I scorn to change my state with kings.
—WILLIAM SHAKESPEARE

PARADISE LOST

Of Mans First Disobedience, and the Fruit
Of that forbidden tree whose mortal taste
Brought death into the World, and all our woe,
With loss of Eden, till one greater Man

Restore us, and regain the blissful Seat,
Sing heav'nly muse. . . .

—JOHN MILTON, BOOK I, LINES 1–6

NOTHING GOLD CAN STAY

Nature's first green is gold,
Her hardest hue to hold.
Her early leaf's a flower;
But only so an hour.
Then leaf subsides to leaf.
So Eden sank to grief,
So dawn goes down to day.
Nothing gold can stay.

—ROBERT FROST

FIRE AND ICE

Some say the world will end in fire,
Some say in ice.
From what I've tasted of desire
I hold with those who favor fire.
But if it had to perish twice,
I think I know enough of hate
To say that for destruction ice
Is also great
And would suffice.

—ROBERT FROST

THE LAKE ISLE OF INNISFREE

I will arise and go now, and go to Innisfree,
And a small cabin build there, of clay and wattles made;

Nine bean-rows will I have there, a hive for the honey-bee,
And live alone in the bee-loud glade.

—WILLIAM BUTLER YEATS,
FIRST STANZA

BURNT NORTON

Time present and time past
Are both perhaps present in time future,
And time future contained in time past.
If all time is eternally present
All time is unredeemable.

—T. S. ELIOT, LINES 1–5

THE IDEA OF ORDER AT KEY WEST

She sang beyond the genius of the sea.
The water never formed to mind or voice,
Like a body wholly body, fluttering
Its empty sleeves; . . . .

—WALLACE STEVENS, LINES 1–4

THE WEARY BLUES

Droning a drowsy syncopated tune,
Rocking back and forth to a mellow croon,
I heard a Negro play.
Down on Lenox Avenue the other night
By the pale dull pallor of an old gas light
He did a lazy sway . . .
He did a lazy sway . . .
To the tune o' those Weary Blues.

—LANGSTON HUGHES, LINES 1–8

THE FISH

I caught a tremendous fish
and held him beside the boat
half out of water, with my hook
fast in a corner of his mouth.
He didn't fight.
He hadn't fought at all.

—ELIZABETH BISHOP, LINES 1–6

Appendix B

Metrical Grids and Time Signatures

FIGURE B.1 Metrical grids for four basic time signatures. Values could be halved, for example, 2/4 to 2/8.

FIGURE B.2 Example of hemiola: 3/2 over two bars of 3/4.

Appendix C

Rule Index

Procedure for assigning the prosodic hierarchy:

Let **S** = syllable, **W** = word, **C** = clitic group, **P** = phonological group, **I** = intonational phrase, and **U** = utterance. Then,

(1) Assign **S** and **W** lexically.
(2) Categorize **W**'s as either content or function words.
(3) Group function words with adjacent content words in their syntactic unit.
(4) Assign **C** to content words and to clitic groupings of function and content words.
(5) Assign **P** to a grouping of adjacent **C**'s that form a syntactic unit.
(6) Assign **I** to a grouping of adjacent **P**'s that form a syntactic unit.
(7) Assign **U** to a grouping of adjacent **I**'s that form a sentence.
(8) The grouping of **C**, **P**, or **I** can repeat at the next larger level.

Procedure for assigning syllabic stress:

Let the number of x's assigned to a syllable represent the syllable's relative stress. There are no more than four stress levels. To build a stress grid:

(1) Assign an x to each syllable.
(2) Add an x (or more, as required) to the lexically stressed syllable(s) in a polysyllabic word.
(3) Nuclear stress:
   (a) Add an x to a monosyllabic word if it is the rightmost content word in **C**.
   (b) Add a third x to the syllable with the most x's in the rightmost content word in **P**.
   (c) Add a fourth x to the syllable with the most x's in the rightmost content word in **I**.

(4) Nuclear stress can optionally be overridden by:
   (a) Focus: stress a normally unstressed syllable to convey a nuance or contrastive emphasis.
   (b) Evenness: distribute stresses to approximate periodicity.

Metrical well-formedness conditions:

Definition: A beat is strong at any level L if it is also a beat at L + 1; if it is not a beat at L + 1, it is a weak beat at level L.

(1) Every syllable receives a beat.
(2) A beat at any level L is also a beat at L − 1 (except at the terminal level).
(3) At the tactus level, time spans between beats are equal.
(4) At sub-tactus level L, beats are equally spaced between beats at L + 1.
(5) Strong beats are spaced two or three beats apart within a level.

Procedure for metrical and durational assignment:

(1) Establish the tactus by finding the pattern of equidistant beats that causes the fewest mismatches with stressed syllables, preferably:
   (a) At a tempo between seventy and one hundred beats per minute.
   (b) With one or two unstressed syllables between adjacent tactus syllables.
(2) An option is to insert a silent tactus beat at the end of an intonational phrase.
(3) Assign sub- and supra-tactus layers, observing the metrical well-formedness conditions.
(4) Of the available metrical grids, the preferred grid is one that yields the fewest syllabic mismatches with the associated stress grid.
(5) Congruence principle (corollary to [4]): Strongly avoid stress-meter mismatches within polysyllabic words and clitic groups.
(6) Proximity principle: Assign durations so that longer durations are between rather than within the constituents of the prosodic hierarchy.
(7) Length principle: Assign greater length to syllables with stronger stress, unless doing so violates (6).
(8) Avoid long, tactus-length syllables within phonological phrases.
(9) An option is to move between duple and triple metrical subdivisions at a sub-tactus level in order better to satisfy (6).
(10) An option is to assign greater duration to phonetically long syllables.
(11) Eliminate a tactus beat if there are three consecutive unstressed syllables.

(12) Avoid double anacruses (two weak beats before a tactus beat at the beginning of an intonational phrase).

Procedure for contour assignment:

Well-formedness condition: Assign every syllable a focal position on one of four tiers of pitch height.

Derivational procedure: Assign syllabic prominence from global to local levels of stressed syllables within the framework of the prosodic hierarchy, as follows:

(1) Match syllables with four x's within a **U** to a global contour schema, such that:
  (a) If **U** is a declarative, place the terminating stressed syllable with four x's on tier 1.
  (b) If **U** is a yes-no interrogative, place the terminating stressed syllable with four x's on tier 2.
(2) In **I**, place the terminating syllable with four x's on tier 2.
(3) In **P** in which there is not a four-x syllable, place a syllable with three x's on tier 4; otherwise, place it on tier 3.
(4) In **C**, place a syllable with two x's on tier 3 if **C** is contained within a **P** or **I** in which a three-x syllable is on tier 4; otherwise, place a syllable with two x's on tier 2.
(5) Place a syllable with one x:
  (a) On a tier below the position of the dominating syllable within its **C** if the dominating syllable is not on tier 1; an option is to place it one tier equal to or above the position of the dominating syllable if doing so achieves stepwise motion within its **P**.
  (b) On tier 2 if the dominating syllable is on tier 1.
(6) If a syllable that does not terminate **U** or **I** is long and is not in a stepwise relation to the preceding or succeeding syllable, treat it as a bitonal syllable with a focal pitch and an embellishing pitch, such that:
  (a) The embellishing pitch is one tier above or below the focal pitch, or
  (b) The embellishing pitch fills in a tier gap between the preceding or succeeding syllable.
(7) If a syllable terminates **U** or **I** and is long:
  (a) For a declarative, the embellishing pitch is either before and one tier above the focal pitch, or it is after and one tier below the focal pitch.
  (b) For a yes-no interrogative, the embellishing pitch is after and one tier above the focal pitch.

Procedure for sound-color assignment:

Definitions and stipulations

(1) There are three kinds of sound-color connection:
    (a) Strong repetition for word identity or syllabic rhyme.
    (b) Weak repetition for syllables related by assonance or alliteration.
    (c) Nonrepetition, or contrast, for syllables not related by (a) or (b).
(2) At any given time-span level, a sound-color region is the span between the immediately superordinate syllable to the left and the immediately superordinate syllable to the right.
(3) Every syllable in a poem has a sound-color connection.

Derivational procedure

(4) Assign sound-color prominence level by level, according to the number of x's in the stress grid as derived over the prosodic hierarchy.
(5) Assign sound-color connections to the syllables that have maximal stress and make subsequent connections according to successively smaller levels of stress.
(6) At each level, attach syllables to the left or right within its sound-color region, in this order of priority: strong repetitions, then weak repetitions, then nonrepetitions.
(7) At a given level, if there is a string of syllables having equal stress, give preference, where possible, to attaching strong or weak repetitions but over distances of no more than one intervening syllable at that level.
(8) All else being equal, give preference to sound-color connections that are congruent with the groupings of the prosodic hierarchy.

Appendix D

Links to Recordings

The following links are to readings discussed in chapter 6. Some of the readings are also available on CD in Paschen and Mosby (2001).

Robert Frost, "Nothing Gold Can Stay," read by the poet:
https://www.youtube.com/watch?v=sDPUdK2tcdA
Also available on CD in Paschen and Mosby (2001).

Robert Frost, "Fire and Ice," read by Richard Burton:
https://www.youtube.com/watch?v=PaaAn8B1Wsk

William Shakespeare, Sonnet 18, read by John Gielgud:
https://www.youtube.com/watch?v=GVtObfiCXVA

William Shakespeare, Sonnet 18, read by Hellen Mirren:
https://www.youtube.com/shorts/x6AxTVNPvuE

William Shakespeare, Sonnet 29, read by Mathew Macfadyen:
https://www.youtube.com/watch?v=XOCL_NEgf0g&t=13s

William Shakespeare, Sonnet 29, read by Ian McKellen:
https://www.youtube.com/watch?v=qdhqUI1tU5Q

John Milton, *Paradise Lost*, beginning, read by Ian Richardson:
https://www.youtube.com/watch?v=aw6adXO2RLQ

William Butler Yeats, "The Lake Isle of Innisfree," read by the poet:
https://www.youtube.com/watch?v=QLlcvQg9i6c
Also available on CD in Paschen and Mosby (2001).

T. S. Eliot, "Burnt Norton," read by the poet:
https://www.youtube.com/watch?v=3BKUfk1amb4&t=87s

T. S. Eliot, "Burnt Norton," read by Ralph Fiennes:
https://www.youtube.com/watch?v=z4clm7xUzPU&t=2s

Wallace Stevens, "The Idea of Order at Key West," read by the poet:
https://www.youtube.com/watch?v=CLUNw6w4ynI

Langston Hughes, "The Weary Blues," read by the poet:
https://www.youtube.com/watch?v=PPjo4903UpU
Also available on CD in Paschen and Mosby (2001).

Elizabeth Bishop, "The Fish," read by the poet:
https://www.youtube.com/watch?v=bnkD_m3rhn8&t=11s
Also available on CD in Paschen and Mosby (2001).

Notes

1. PRELUDE

1. Philippe Schlenker (2017) undertakes an exploratory referentialist approach to musical semantics.
2. See Jackendoff (2009) for related discussion of the parallels and non-parallels between music and language.
3. The term "generative" refers in a narrow sense to a system that produces a potentially infinite set of outputs from a finite set of inputs. In a broad sense, generative linguistics refers to some version of linguistic theory stemming from Noam Chomsky's rule-based, cognitive approach to linguistics (Chomsky 1957, 1965). The varieties of syntactic and semantic theories within generative linguistics are beyond the purview of this study.
4. Chapters 2–4 of *GTTM* treat these components in detail.
5. Other notations for meter worth mentioning are Christopher Hasty's (1997) employment of arrows to emphasize the projective, processive nature of meter, Justin London's (2012) embedded circles to bring out meter's cyclic aspect, and John Paul Ito's (2021) gestural representations. The grid notation is both standard and practical, however, and it has the advantage of corresponding to notations used in generative phonology.
6. The term "tactus" originated in Renaissance music theory and has been adapted in *GTTM* and other current music theories (e.g., Mirka 2009, London 2012) to indicate the perceptually most prominent metrical level, the level at which conductors wave their batons and listeners tap their feet.
7. *GTTM*'s term for event salience is "phenomenal accent."
8. Americans will recognize this tune as "My Country 'Tis of Thee."

2. PROSODIC RHYTHM

1. The material in this chapter was first sketched in Lerdahl and Halle (1991) and Lerdahl (2001a).
2. The complete sonnet is cited in appendix A.
3. One could insert an intermediate **P** level that contains repetitions from the **C** level:

[**P** When in disgrace] [**P** with fortune] [**P** and men's eyes] [**P** I all alone] [**P** beweep] [**P** my outcast state]

But I have found in practice that the resulting added level does not enhance the analysis once levels of stress are derived from it.

4. This grid notation for stress is an adaptation of representations in generative phonology such as Prince (1983), Halle and Vergnaud (1987), and Hayes (1989). The latter's combination of prosodic hierarchy and stress grid influenced the present approach.
5. Alfred Corn (2008), in a notation borrowed from structural linguistics, represents degrees of stress in a poetic line by numbers from 1 to 4. These numbers map onto the levels of x's in the stress grids employed here. His intuitive stress analyses generally agree with what my rule-based methodology would assign.
6. The limitation to four levels may be related to the general psychological inability to distinguish instantly more than four items in a set. See Dehaene (1997), and Hauser and Spelke (2004). I discuss this phenomenon with respect to musical processing in Lerdahl (2020, pp. 54–56).
7. The complete poem is cited in appendix A.
8. In the first line, **P** bifurcates into two phonological sub-levels, "first green" and then "Nature's first green." To keep the analysis within the bounds of four stress levels, the figure merges the two into one phonological level, with "Na-" retaining two x's instead of adding a third.
9. The evenness principle is called the "rhythm rule" in the phonological literature. See Kiparsky 1975; Liberman and Prince 1977. I prefer not to use this phrase because "rhythm" is a broad term in music, encompassing multiple temporal structures (grouping, meter, durations, patterns of repetition, etc.) beyond what is meant in this case. The term "evenness" appears in music theory as part of the theory of scales (Clough & Douthett 1991) and, by extension, to duration and meter (Lerdahl 2001b, pp. 286–87). Its use in this book is compatible with that practice.
10. Certain metrical idioms in music permit unequal tactus beats in 2:3 proportions (figure 1.7 is an example). I set this exception aside.
11. In the second line, three x's are given to "hard-" instead of "hue," in an application of the evenness principle (see the discussion surrounding figure 2.6).
12. Chapter 6 introduces a few more rhythmic patterns in response to readings. These additions do not weaken the picture drawn here.
13. Kevin M. Ryan (2022) provides evidence for a variety of phonetic and phonological factors such as this that contribute to syllable lengthening in text setting.

3. HISTORICAL APPROACHES TO PROSODIC RHYTHM

1. Many writers have expressed reservations about or ignored the poetic foot. See, for example, Attridge (1982, pp. 6–17). (Incidentally, he uses lines from Sonnet 29 to illustrate some of his points.) Adams (1997) charts a middle course, taking the foot as a "useful fiction" (p. 10). Jespersen (1900/1933) calls

the foot a "paper idea." As for poets, Eliot (1942) writes, "I have never been able to retain the names of feet and metres, or to pay the proper respect to the accepted rules of scansion." Milton, defending his rejection of rhyme in the short preface to *Paradise Lost*, asserts that verse "consists only in apt numbers [appropriate rhythm], fit quantity of syllables, and the sense variously drawn out from one verse to another." In other words, he cares about stress patterns and syllable counts per line, but apparently not poetic feet.

2. Despite my dismissal of the poetic foot, I shall continue to employ the term "iambic pentameter," and likewise for other standard line forms, simply because it is convenient to do so. One can replace "iambic pentameter" with "a ten-syllable line (plus or minus one), usually with five tactus beats," and so on.

3. Mirka (2009, 2021) provides extensive treatment of eighteenth-century metrical and phrasal music theories, both historically and from the perspective of contemporary music theory and cognition.

4. For related discussion, see *A Generative Theory of Tonal Music (GTTM)*, pp. 26–27, 328–329. See also Cohn (2019).

5. It is not uncommon for an eleventh unstressed syllable to conclude a line of iambic pentameter. Sometimes an absent weak syllable at the beginning of a line reduces the count to nine. Such slight variations in syllable count do not compromise the thrust of this discussion.

6. Leithauser (2022, p. 60) compares enjambment to musical syncopation. It is an imprecise analogy because syncopation involves meter—stress on a weak beat—whereas enjambment is a grouping phenomenon. But syncopation and enjambment do share the general feature of projecting structural dislocation, each in its way.

7. This statement applies to accentual-syllabic poetry, which is prevalent from Chaucer to the twentieth century. The accentual meter of medieval English poetry is less concerned with syllable count and relies instead on periodic stresses and beats. The same also holds for many nursery rhymes.

8. This contracting operation applies if there are three consecutive unstressed syllables (syllables with one x). It adds a condition to the rule for metrical and durational assignment in section 2.5. The list of rules in appendix C includes this option.

9. In his film of *Hamlet*, Laurence Olivier delivers this line melodramatically yet in a rhythm close to that in figure 3.14b, except for a longer duration on "is." One wonders if this similarity is a coincidence or if he inherited a performance tradition dating back to Garrick.

10. Kassler (2005) provides historical context for Steele's musically notated analysis of speech.

11. Lanier may have been influenced, presumably indirectly, by eighteenth-century music theories that drew a parallel between the poetic foot and the musical bar (e.g., the article on "Takt" in Schulz [1794]).

12. Lanier's contemporary Gerard Manley Hopkins similarly confounds the foot with the musical bar: ". . . for purposes of scanning it is a great convenience to follow the example of music and take the stress always first, as the accent or

the chief accent always comes first in a musical bar. If this is done there will be in common English verse only two possible feet—the so-called accentual Trochee and Dactyl" (Hopkins, 1995, p. 6). This view denies upbeat-downbeat groupings (iambs and anapests). Fortunately, his poetry does not obey his precept. For example, in the first line of "God's Grandeur"—"The Wórld/is chárged/with the/grándeur/of Gód"—the first, second, and fifth feet are iambic according to standard scansion.

"God's Grandeur" is nominally in iambic pentameter, but other poems by Hopkins, such as "Spring and Fall" and "The Windhover," are in his invented sprung rhythm, in which zero to as many as three unstressed syllables may occur between stressed syllables. How sprung rhythm relates to poetic feet is open to debate. See Kiparsky (1989) for a thorough study of sprung rhythm from the perspective of his own work on prosody.

13. Among Prall's students at Harvard in the 1930s were the composer Arthur Berger, who was one of my teachers, and Leonard Bernstein, who had a lifelong interest in the intersection of music and language, culminating in the book *The Unanswered Question* (Bernstein, 1976).
14. In this connection, Hallmark and Fehn (2010) investigate Schubert's settings of iambic pentameter lines within a musical style for which four-bar phrases are the norm. Sometimes Schubert composes five-bar phrases or extends them to six, but more often he compresses the five main stresses into four bars.
15. Frye's suggestion echoes Hopkins's (1995) concept of sprung rhythm.
16. Leithauser (2022, pp. 73–75) is eloquent on this subject.
17. The topic of prolongational structure resurfaces in chapter 7.4 in the quite different context of sound-color analysis—that is, of hierarchical linear connections between similar and dissimilar syllables.

4. GENERATIVE APPROACHES TO PROSODIC RHYTHM

1. Youmans (1983, 1989), operating within a generative prosodic framework, arrives at the same conclusion through a statistical analysis of a corpus of lines from William Shakespeare and John Milton.
2. Kiparsky (1977) reinstates the poetic foot. This allegiance persists in much of generative prosodic theory.
3. Halle (1997) develops the Halle-Lerdahl approach computationally, and, in a related study, Halle (2004) explores the role of prosodic constituency in text setting. Dell and Halle (2009) apply the approach to a comparative study of text setting in French and English.
4. Jackendoff (1989) briefly reviews this history.
5. See Katz (2022) for related discussion in the context not of poetry but of the music-language connection in general. He describes linguistic metrical structure in Liberman and Prince's sense of "metrical," meaning a syllabic stress hierarchy with a bracketed grid, and he notes its differences from musical

meter. Once the terminologies are disentangled, there are many points of agreement between his account and mine.
6. In music theory, the term "reduction" refers to the process of reducing events out—that is, of removing comparatively ornamental events to reveal structural underpinnings—without reference to other meanings of the word in other disciplines.
7. Liberman and Prince's notation is unclear about the status of W at higher levels. In "a-tion," for example, is the W on "-tion" more stressed than W's on "-con" and "li-" because the former is dominated by S and the latter by W? The time-span tree notation does not raise this ambiguity; all subordinate branches at level d are equally weak.
8. Hayes notates unstressed syllables with a dot instead of an x, thereby enabling two stress levels to appear on a single line. He would write the first two levels of "Nature's" not as

x

x   x   x   .

"Na-ture's" but as "Na-ture's."
9. Notice that figures 4.11 and 4.12 incorporate not two but three orthogonal factors—grouping, prominence (stress), and meter. Wagner's account would be strengthened if it also included metrical (non)alignment as a factor.
10. In this discussion, I usually refer to line "complexity" instead of line "tension." Intuitively, I prefer "complexity" for poetic lines and "tension" for its musical analog. The tension metaphor resonates reliably for listeners of tonal music under a variety of conditions (Lerdahl and Krumhansl 2007). Crucial in the prosodic case is the cognitive distance between a line template and the rhythm of a given poetic line, for which "complexity" seems the apt word.
11. To explain these components, their quantification and their empirical results would require a long technical exposition well beyond the scope of this volume. See Lerdahl (2001b) and Lerdahl and Krumhansl (2007).
12. Smith (1968), in a wide-ranging study of poetic closure, writes: "Metrical regularity at the end of a poem . . . has closural effects. . . . It is a re-establishment of the norm, the most probable and therefore the most stable arrangement of stresses" (p. 160). Her example is the ending of Sonnet 18, but the statement applies equally to the ending of Sonnet 29.
13. The nonpreferred status of double anacruses adds another condition to the rule for metrical and durational assignment (chapter 2.5). See the statement of rules in appendix C.

5. CONTOUR

1. Some ideas in this chapter were sketched in Lerdahl (2001a).
2. The limitation to four tiers, like that of four stress levels, may be another manifestation of general processing constraints. See chapter 2, endnote 6.

3. Phonologists often refer to "pitch accent," but "accent" has several meanings in musical contexts. The term "syllabic prominence" is unambiguous and will be used here.
4. Amplitude, another contributor to prominence, covaries with pitch height; the latter is the stronger variable if the two factors are decoupled (Fry, 1958). Hence amplitude can be disregarded in assigning contour.
5. I am following the option of extra stress on "hard-" instead of "hue." See the discussion of evenness in chapter 2.3.
6. A reminder from chapter 2: **U** = utterance, **I** = intonational phrase, **P** = phonological phrase, and **C** = clitic group.
7. Steele (1775) similarly shows glides within syllables and focal points of relative height. Although he does not posit four tiers as in the present model, some of his graphs imply greater contour variety than is representable by the two levels of Pierrehumbert's approach.
8. It is not certain that the acoustic feature of a fundamental frequency fully conforms to the psychoacoustic perception of pitch height. While transcribing poetic readings for chapter 6, I often sensed that the second and third partials, which can be quite strong, as well as other indeterminate factors influenced my judgment of pitch height. I leave this question open.

6. TRANSCRIPTIONS AND ANALYSES

1. Appendix A reprints the poetic lines examined in this chapter in the order in which they are discussed. Appendix D provides links to audio recordings of the readings. The transcriptions from audio readings were done by ear, monitored by analyses in Praat and Prosogram, freeware programs that analyze acoustic speech signals.
2. Bars 4 and 5 of "God Save the King" in figure 1.8 can also function as a hemiola—strong beats on beats 1 and 3 of bar 4 and on beat 2 of bar 5—especially when reinforced by the usual harmonization.
3. This instance, along with other instances discussed later in this chapter, suggest that condition (4) of the rule for contour assignment might include a third subcondition that allows an unstressed syllable (a syllable with one x) that is spoken with a reduced vowel to be placed one tier above, rather than below, the position of the dominating syllable within its clitic group. I view such instances as non-normative, however, and hence as exceptions to the rules, which are intended to predict normative outcomes.
4. Yeats's reading recalls my witnessing, in 1990, Joseph Brodsky reciting his poetry in Russian. He almost sang the lines, like a cantor. I did not understand the Russian, but I felt intensely the musicality of his expressive vocalization. Brodsky loved music and enjoyed talking about it with my wife, musicologist Louise Litterick, his fellow faculty member at Mount Holyoke College.
5. Gardner's (1949) scansion of these lines (p. 29) is compatible with this analysis, adjusting for differences between her traditional notation and my musical

one. Her discussion of the prosody in *Four Quartets* focuses on the number of main stresses per line, without regard to syllable count or feet (see especially pp. 16–17).

7. SOUND COLOR

1. I take the term "sound color" from Slawson (1981), who uses it in the limited sense of vowel color. I intend it in the broader sense of timbre, defined as the features of a sound that are distinct from the dimensions of pitch, duration, and intensity. In the context of this chapter, it seems natural to refer to poetic timbres as sound colors that are similar or dissimilar in their combinations of vowels and consonants.
2. This indirect alliterative connection is a consequence of a strict hierarchical or tree representation, here shown by slurs. One might rather argue that "hue" is equally subordinate between "hard-" and "hold." This step would require expansion of my theory to include network-like representations. The same issue arises in music theory, in particular with respect to neighboring and passing tones and chords. Yust (2018) develops a network model of pitch-event structures along these lines. In Lerdahl (2001b), I finesse the tree versus network issue through double branching under certain conditions, thereby avoiding unwanted theoretical and representational complications. See also the discussion in Lerdahl (2020, pp. 37–38).
3. Leithauser (2022) discusses this issue at length.
4. This top-down procedure is a convenience, not a formal condition. A derivation could just as well be done bottom-up because what matters at any level is the relative sound-color closeness of adjacent syllables that are also syllables at the next larger time-span level.
5. Hayslett (2019) intriguingly explores the possibility of a hierarchical system for the salience of musical events as a complement to stability criteria and applies it to passages of both tonal and atonal music. He bases his approach on the phonological stress system in Hayes (1995) combined with the method of time-span reduction in *A Generative Theory of Tonal Music* (*GTTM*).
6. For linear analysis, *GTTM* employs the term "prolongational reduction." The term "prolongation" comes from Renaissance music theory and was adapted by Schenker (1935/2001) and his school of analysis to signify the embellishment or elaboration of musical events: a pitch or chord is "prolonged" by its elaboration. *GTTM* adopts this broad meaning. In the present context, it is more direct just to refer to linear connections and analysis.
7. *GTTM* proposes and justifies an interaction principle that allows a strong repetition to be accessed one level below the current stage of analysis. In sound-color analysis, this principle applies in the favoring of repetition over contrast within a given level, as in the analysis of Milton's line in figure 7.10. It appears also to apply to level L – 1, just as in *GTTM*. For example, in the line "To be, or not to be," "not" has three x's and each "be" has two x's (see figure 3.15), but in

the sound-color analysis, the two clitic units "to be" would connect as a strong repetition, overriding the more stressed "not."
8. For readers familiar with *GTTM*, this two-step process suggests a revision of *GTTM*'s reduction components. Instead of deriving prolongational reduction from its parallel time-span reduction, modified where required by application of the interaction principle, there would be a single time-span reduction component within which to make linear connections to adjacent events at any given level (including application of the interaction principle). The resulting prolongational analysis would be the same as before, but its derivation would be more efficient. The top-down method—which in any case is psychologically questionable—of prolongational analysis would no longer be needed because adjacency within the event hierarchy is already specified at any given time-span level.
9. Some vowels are more relaxed than others, but the effect in terms of waves of tension and relaxation is slight compared to its musical counterpart.
10. I began to explore the idea of linear functions in the article "Timbral Hierarchies" (Lerdahl 1987), a study that builds small event hierarchies out of synthesized vowels of the same pitch and amplitude; only the vowel colors change. The study demonstrates that neighbor and passing events under these limited conditions are perceivable.
11. *Clos* breaks down into three functions—tonic (T), dominant (D), and subdominant (S). One or another of these functions, most often T, takes the place of *rpt* in figure 7.21(a). I mention this for readers familiar with *Tonal Pitch Space* (Lerdahl, 2001b) but leave further consideration of such musical details aside because this book is devoted to the sounds of poetry.
12. Theorizing about pitch space continues to be an active area of inquiry, see for instance, Cohn (2012) and Tymoczko (2023).
13. Shepard (1972) undertakes a pioneering study of this topic.
14. See Keyser (2020) for a stimulating discussion of the causes of these artistic revolutions. It is telling in this regard that Schoenberg thought of his new atonal harmonies as chord colors (Schoenberg, 1911). He was active as a painter and in close contact with Kandinsky, who at the time was creating his first colorful, nonrepresentational canvasses.

8. CODA

1. Fitch (2010) is a valuable resource on the evolution of language and its roots in animal communication.
2. Brown (2000) proposes a wide-ranging model along these lines. See Lerdahl (2020, chap. 3) for related discussion on the musical capacity, its connections to the sounds of poetry, and its origins in animal vocalization.

Bibliography

Adams, Stephen (1997). *Poetic Designs: An Introduction to Meters, Verse Forms, and Figures of Speech.* Broadview.
Attridge, Derek (1982). *The Rhythms of English Poetry.* Longman.
Balzano, Gerald J. (1982). "The Pitch Set as a Level of Description for Studying Musical Pitch Perception." In *Music, Mind, and Brain*, ed. Manfred Clynes. Plenum.
Bernstein, Leonard (1976). *The Unanswered Question.* Harvard University Press.
Bolinger, Dwight (1965). *Forms of English: Accent, Morpheme, Order.* Harvard University Press.
Bolinger, Dwight (1986). *Intonation and Its Parts: Melody in Spoken English.* Stanford University Press.
Bolton, T. L. (1894). "Rhythm." *American Journal of Psychology* 6: 145–238.
Brown, Steven (2000). "The 'Musilanguage' Model of Music Evolution." In *The Origins of Music*, ed. Nils L. Wallin, Björn Merker, and Steven Brown. MIT Press.
Chomsky, Noam (1957). *Syntactic Structures.* Mouton.
Chomsky, Noam (1965). *Aspects of the Theory of Syntax.* MIT Press.
Chomsky, Noam, and Morris Halle (1968). *The Sound Pattern of English.* Harper and Row.
Clough, John, and Jack Douthett (1991). "Maximally Even Sets." *Journal of Music Theory* 35: 93–173.
Cohn, Richard (2012). *Audacious Euphony: Chromaticism and the Triad's Second Nature.* Oxford University Press.
Cohn, Richard (2019). "Meter." In *The Oxford Handbook of Critical Concepts in Music Theory*, ed. A. Rehding and S. Rings. Oxford University Press.
Cooper, Grosvenor, and Leonard B. Meyer (1960). *The Rhythmic Structure of Music.* University of Chicago Press.
Corn, Alfred (2008). *The Poem's Heartbeat: A Manual of Prosody.* Copper Canyon Classics.
Cruttenden, Alan (1997). *Intonation.* 2nd ed. Cambridge University Press.
Crystal, David (1969). *Prosodic Systems and Intonation in English.* Cambridge University Press.
Cureton, Richard D. (1992). *Rhythmic Phrasing in English Verse.* Longman.

Darwin, Charles (1871). *The Descent of Man and Selection in Relation to Sex.* John Murray.
Dehaene, Stanislas (1997). *The Number Sense.* Oxford University Press.
Dell, Francois, and John Halle (2009). "Comparing Musical Texsetting in French and in English Songs." In *Towards a Typology of Poetic Forms.*, ed. J.-L. Aroui and A. Arleo. John Benjamins.
Dilley, Laura (2005). *The Phonetics and Phonology of Tonal Systems.* PhD diss., MIT.
Eliot, T. S. (1942). "The Music of Poetry." *The Complete Prose of T. S. Eliot: The Critical Edition*, vol. 6. John Hopkins University Press.
Fitch, W. Tecumseh (2010). *The Evolution of Language.* Cambridge University Press.
Friedmann, Michael (1985). "A Methodology for the Discussion of Contour: Its Application to Schoenberg's Music." *Journal of Music Theory* 29: 223–48.
Fry, Dennis B. (1958). "Experiments in the Perception of Stress." *Language and Speech* 1: 126–52.
Frye, Northrop (1957a). *Anatomy of Criticism.* Princeton University Press.
Frye, Northrop (1957b). "Introduction: Lexis and Melos." In *Sound and Poetry*, ed. Northrop Frye. Columbia University Press.
Fussell, Paul (1965). *Poetic Meter and Poetic form.* McGraw-Hill.
Fux, Johann Joseph (1725). *Gradus ad parnassum.* Joannis Petri van Gehlen. Trans. and ed. Alfred Mann. Norton, 1965.
Gardner, Helen (1949). *The Art of T. S. Eliot.* Faber.
Halle, John (1997). *A Grammar of Improvised Textsetting.* PhD diss., Columbia University.
Halle, John (2004). "Constituency Matching in Metrical Texts." Unpublished manuscript, available at https://johnhalle.com/musical.writing.technical/constituency.matching.pdf.
Halle, John, and Fred Lerdahl (1993). "A Generative Textsetting Model." *Current Musicology* 55: 3–23.
Halle, Morris, and Samuel Jay Keyser (1966). "Chaucer and the Study of Prosody." *College English* 28: 187–219.
Halle, Morris, and Samuel Jay Keyser (1971). *English Stress: Its Form, Its Growth, and Its Role in Verse.* Harper and Row.
Halle, Morris, and Jean-Roger Vergnaud (1987). *An Essay on Stress.* MIT Press.
Hallmark, Rufus, and Ann C. Fehn (2010). "Text and Music in Schubert's Settings of Pentameter Poetry." In *Of Poetry and Song: Approaches to the Nineteenth-Century Lied*, ed. Jürgen Thym. University of Rochester Press.
Hasty, Christopher (1997). *Meter as Rhythm.* Oxford University Press.
Hauser, Marc, and Elizabeth Spelke (2004). "Evolutionary and Developmental Foundations of Human Knowledge: A Case Study of Mathematics." In *The Cognitive Neurosciences III*, ed. Michael Gazzaniga. MIT Press.
Hayes, Bruce (1989). "The Prosodic Hierarchy in Meter." In *Phonetics and Phonology: Rhythm and Meter*, ed. Paul Kiparsky and Gilbert Youmans. Academic.
Hayes, Bruce (1995). *Metrical Stress Theory: Principles and Case Studies.* University of Chicago Press.

Hayes, Bruce (2009a). "Textsetting as Constraint Conflict." In *Towards a Typology of Poetic Forms*, ed. Jean-Louis Aroui and Andy Arleo. John Benjamins.
Hayes, Bruce (2009b). *Introductory Phonology*. Wiley-Blackwell.
Hayes, Bruce, and Abigail Kaun (1996). "The Role of Phonological Phrasing in Sung and Chanted Verse." *Linguistic Review* 13: 243–303.
Hayes, Bruce, and Margaret MacEachern (1998). "Quatrain Form in English Folk Verse." *Language* 64: 473–507.
Hayes, Bruce, Colin Wilson, and Anne Shisko. "Maxent Grammars for the Metrics of Shakespeare and Milton." *Language* 88, no. 4: 691–731.
Hayslett, Bryan (2019). *Theory of Prominence: Temporal Structure of Music Based on Linguistic Stress*. PhD diss., New York University.
Hopkins, Gerard Manley (1995). "Author's Preface." In *Hopkins: Poems and Prose*, ed. Peter Washington. Knopf.
Ito, John Paul (2021). *Focal Impulse Theory: Musical Expression, Meter, and the Body*. Indiana University Press.
Jackendoff, Ray (1989). "Comparison of Rhythmic Structures in Music and Language." In *Phonetics and Phonology: Rhythm and Meter*, ed. Paul Kiparsky and Gilbert Youmans. Academic.
Jackendoff, Ray (2009). "Parallels and Nonparallels Between Language and Music." *Music Perception* 26: 195–204.
Jesperson, Otto (1900/1933). "Notes on Metre." *Linguistica*. Danish original published in *Oversigt* 1900.
Kassler, Jaime C. (2005). "Representing Speech Through Musical Notation." *Journal of Musicological Research* 24: 227–39.
Katz, Jonah (2022). "Metre, Grouping, and Event Hierarchies in Music: A Tutorial for Linguists." *Language & Linguistics Compass*: e12472. https://doi.org/10.1111/.
Keyser, Samuel Jay (2020). *The Mental Life of Modernism*. MIT Press.
Kiparsky, Paul (1975). "Stress, Syntax, and Meter." *Language* 51: 576–616.
Kiparsky, Paul (1977). "The Rhythmic Structure of English Verse." *Linguistic Inquiry* 8: 189–247.
Kiparsky, Paul (1989). "Sprung Rhythm." In *Phonetics and Phonology: Rhythm and Meter*, ed. Paul Kiparsky and Gilbert Youmans. Academic.
Kirnberger, Johann Philipp (1771–76 [1982]). *The Art of Strict Musical Composition*. Ed. and trans. David W. Beach and Jürgen Thym. Yale University Press.
Krumhansl, Carol L. (1983). "Perceptual Structures for Tonal Music." *Music Perception* 1: 28–62.
Krumhansl, Carol L. (1990). *Cognitive Foundations of Musical Pitch*. Oxford University Press.
Ladd, D. Robert (2008). *Intonational Phonology*. 2nd ed. Cambridge University Press.
Lanier, Sidney (1880). *The Science of English Verse*. Scribner's.
Leithauser, Brad (2022). *Rhyme's Rooms: The Architecture of Poetry*. Knopf.
Lerdahl, Fred (1987). "Timbral Hierarchies." *Contemporary Music Review* 2: 135–160.
Lerdahl, Fred (1989). "Atonal Prolongational Structure." *Contemporary Music Review* 4: 65–87.

Lerdahl, Fred (2001a). "The Sounds of Poetry Viewed as Music." *Annals of the New York Academy of Sciences* 930: 337–54. Reprinted in *The Biological Foundations of Music*, ed. Robert J. Zatorre and Isabelle Peretz. Oxford University Press, 2001.
Lerdahl, Fred (2001b). *Tonal Pitch Space*. Oxford University Press.
Lerdahl, Fred (2013). "Musical Syntax and Its Relation to Linguistic Syntax." In *Language, Music, and the Brain: A Mysterious Relationship*, ed. Michael A. Arbib. Strüngmann Forum Reports, vol. 10, 257–272, J. Lupp, series ed. MIT Press.
Lerdahl, Fred (2020). *Composition and Cognition: Reflections on Contemporary Music and the Musical Mind*. University of California Press.
Lerdahl, Fred, and John Halle (1991). "Some Lines of Poetry Viewed as Music." In *Music, Language, Speech, and Brain*, ed. Johan Sundberg, Lennart Nord, and Rolf Carlson. Wenner-Gren International Symposium Series. Macmillan.
Lerdahl, Fred, & Ray Jackendoff (1977). "Toward a Formal Theory of Tonal Music." *Journal of Music Theory*, 21, no. 1: 111–71.
Lerdahl, Fred, and Ray Jackendoff (1983). *A Generative Theory of Tonal Music*. MIT Press.
Lerdahl, Fred, and Carol L. Krumhansl (2007). "Modeling Tonal Tension." *Music Perception* 24: 329–66.
Lewin, David (1974/2013). "Morgengruss." In *David Lewin's Morgengruss: Text, Context, Commentary*, ed. David Bard-Schwarz and Richard Cohn. Oxford University Press, 2013.
Liberman, Mark (1975). *The Intonational System of English*. PhD diss., MIT.
Liberman, Mark, and Alan Prince (1977). "On Stress and Linguistic Rhythm." *Linguistic Inquiry* 8: 249–336.
London, Justin (2012). *Hearing in Time: Psychological Aspects of Musical Meter*. Oxford University Press.
Marvin, Elizabeth, and Paul Laprade (1987). Relating Musical Contours: Extensions of a Theory for Contour. *Journal of Music Theory* 31: 268–74.
Mattheson, Johann (1739). *Der vollkommene Capellmeister*. Herold.
Mirka, Danuta (2009). *Metric Manipulations in Haydn and Mozart*. Oxford University Press.
Mirka, Danuta (2021). *Hypermetric Manipulations in Haydn and Mozart*. Oxford University Press.
Morris, Robert D. (1993). "New Directions in the Theory and Analysis of Musical Contour." *Music Theory Spectrum* 15, no. 2: 205–28.
Nespor, Marina, and Irene Vogel (1986). *Prosodic Phonology*. Foris.
Oehrle, Richard (1989). "Temporal Structures in Verse Design." In *Phonetics and Phonology: Rhythm and Meter*, ed. Paul Kiparsky and Gilbert Youmans. Academic.
Paschen, Elise, and Rebekah Presson Mosby (2001), eds. *Poetry Speaks: Hear Great Poets Read Their Work from Tennyson to Plath*. Sourcebook.
Patel, Aniruddh D. (2008). *Music, Language, and the Brain*. Oxford University Press.
Peretz, Isabelle, and Max Coltheart (2003). "Modularity of Music Processing." *Nature Neuroscience* 6: 688–91.

Pierrehumbert, Janet B. (1980). *The Phonology and Phonetics of English Intonation.* PhD diss., MIT.

Pierrehumbert, Janet B., and Julia Hirschberg (1990). "The Meaning of Intonational Contours in the Interpretation of Discourse." In *Intentions in Communication*, ed. Philip R. Cohen, Jerry Morgan, and Martha E. Pollack. MIT Press.

Pike, Kenneth (1945). *The Intonation of American English.* University of Michigan Press.

Poeppel, David, and M. Florencia Assaneo (2020). "Speech Rhythms and Their Neural Foundations." *Nature Reviews Neuroscience* https://doi.org/10.1038/s41583-020-0304-4.

Polansky, Larry, and Richard Bassein (1992). "Possible and Impossible Melodies: Some Formal Aspects of Contour." *Journal of Music Theory* 36: 259–84.

Prall, David W. (1936). *Aesthetic Analysis.* Crowell.

Prince, Alan (1983). "Relating to the Grid." *Linguistic Inquiry*, 14.1: 19-100.

Prince, Alan, and Paul Smolensky (1993/2003). *Optimality Theory: Constraint Interaction in Generative Grammar.* Rutgers Optimality Archive, vol. 537. Blackwell.

Quinn, Ian (1997). "Fuzzy Extensions to the Theory of Contour." *Music Theory Spectrum* 19: 232–63.

Rousseau, J.-J. (1760/1986). *Essai sur l'origine des langues.* In J. H. Moran & A. Gode, trans., *On the Origin of Language.* University of Chicago Press.

Ryan, Kevin M. (2022). "Syllable Weight and Natural Duration in Textsetting Popular Music in English." *English Language and Linguistics* 26, no. 3: 559–82.

Schachter, Carl (1980). "Rhythm and Linear Analysis: Durational Reduction." In *The Musical Forum*, vol. 4, ed. Felix Salzer. Columbia University Press, 1980. Reprinted in Carl Schachter, *Unfoldings*, ed. Joseph N. Straus. Oxford University Press, 1998.

Schenker, Heinrich (1921–24). *Der Tonwille.* A. Gutmann Verlag.

Schenker, Heinrich (1935). *Free Composition.* Trans. E. Oster. Repr. Pendragon, 2001.

Schlenker, Philippe (2017). "Outline of Music Semantics." *Music Perception* 35, no. 1: 3–37.

Schoenberg, Arnold (1911). *Theory of Harmony.* Trans. Roy Carter. University of California Press, 1978.

Schoenberg, Arnold (1954/1969). *Structural Foundations of Harmony.* Rev. ed. Norton.

Schulz, Johann A. P. (1794). "Takt." In Johann G. Schulz, *Allgemeine Theorie der schönen Künste*, 4th ed., ed. Johann G. Schulz. In der Weidmannschen Buchhandlung. Repr., Georg Olms, 1967.

Selkirk, Elizabeth O. (1984). *Phonology and Syntax: The Relation between Sound and Structure.* MIT Press.

Shepard, Roger N. (1972). "Psychological Representation of Speech Sounds." In *Human Communication: A Unified View*, ed. Edward E. David, Jr., and Peter B. Denes. McGraw-Hill.

Shepard, Roger N. (1982). "Structural Representations of Musical Pitch." In *The Psychology of Music*, ed. Diana Deutsch. Academic.

Slawson, Wayne (1981). "The Color of Sound: A Theoretical Study in Musical Timbre." *Music Theory Spectrum* 3: 132–141.
Smith, Barbara Herrnstein (1968). *Poetic Closure: A Study of How Poems End.* University of Chicago Press.
Steele, Joshua (1775). *An Essay Towards Establishing the Melody and Measure of Speech to Be Expressed and Perpetuated by Peculiar Symbols.* W. Bowyer and J. Nichols for J. Almon.
Temperley, David (1999). "Syncopation in Rock: A Perceptual Perspective." *Popular Music* 18, no. 1: 19–40.
Trager, George L., and Henry Lee Smith (1951). *Outline of English Structure.* Battenburg.
Tymoczko, Dmitri (2023). *Tonality: An Owner's Manual.* Oxford University Press.
van Heuven, Vincent J. and Alice Turk (2020). "Phonetic Correlates of Word and Sentence Stress." In *The Oxford Handbook of Language Prosody*, ed. Carlos Gussenhoven and Aoju Chen. Oxford University Press.
Wagner, Michael (2022). "Two-Dimensional Parsing of the Acoustic Stream Explains the Iambic-Trochaic Law." *Psychological Review* 129, no. 2: 268–88.
Weber, Gottfried (1821–24). *Versuch einer geordeneten Theorie der Tonsetzkunst.* B. Schotts Söhne.
West, Martin L. (1992). *Ancient Greek Music.* University of Oxford Press.
Wimsatt, William K., and Monroe C. Beardsley (1959). "The Concept of Meter: An Exercise in Abstraction." *PMLA* 74: 585–98.
Woodrow, Herbert (1909). *A Quantitative Study of Rhythm: The Effect of Variations in Intensity, Rate and Duration.* Repr. Kessinger, 2010.
Youmans, Gilbert (1983). "Generative Tests for Generative Meter." *Language* 59: 67–92.
Youmans, Gilbert (1989). "Milton's Meter." In *Phonetics and Phonology: Rhythm and Meter*, ed. Paul Kiparsky and Gilbert Youmans. Academic.
Yust, Jason (2018). *Organized Time: Rhythm, Tonality, and Form.* Oxford University Press.

Index

anacrusis, 8, 76
atonal music, 94, 150–51, 174
Attridge, Derek, 54, 168

beat: strong and weak, 5–8; upbeat and downbeat, 8
Bernstein, Leonard, 170
Bishop, Elizabeth, 124–27, 158, 166
blank verse, 39, 49, 120
British school of intonation, 95–96
Brodsky, Joseph, 172
"Burnt Norton" (Eliot), 115–18, 128, 137–40, 157, 166
Burton, Richard, 106–8

cadence, 38, 145–46
Chomsky, Noam, 167
clitic, 11; clitic group, 11–13; clitic host, 11, 16, 65, 71
closure: in music, 145; in poetry, 28, 39, 75–77, 87, 171
congruence, principle of, 25, 30, 57, 65, 76
content words, 11, 13–14
contour, 83–94, 99–100, 127; with bitonal syllables, 91–94; postulates of, 83–85; and prominence, 85–86; tiers of, 84–85
Cooper, Grosvenor, 38, 54
Corn, Alfred, 48, 168
Cureton, Richard, 54–55

Darwin, Charles, 1, 154
Dilley, Laura, 205
diphthong, 113, 117
Donne, John, 60–61, 78, 80
duration, 2, 30–31; neglect of, 37, 60; and stress, 13; and temporal precision, 17, 48–49

"Elegy Written in a Country Churchyard" (Gray), 33
Eliot, T. S., 48, 127, 169. *See also* "Burnt Norton"
enjambment, 38–40, 76, 106, 110, 124, 169
evenness, principle of, 15–17, 49, 168

Fiennes, Ralph, 118, 166
"Fire and Ice" (Frost) 40, 105–8, 156
"Fish, The" (Bishop), 124–27, 158, 166
focus, principle of, 15–17; for contrastive emphasis, 16
free verse, 115, 124, 150
Frost, Robert. *See* "Fire and Ice"; "Nothing Gold Can Stay"
Frye, Northrop, 53, 170
functions: line (beginning-middle-end), 77–78; linear (closure, departure, neighbor, passing, progression, repetition, return), 145–48
function words, 11, 13–14
Fussell, Paul, 48, 52

INDEX

Gardner, Helen, 172–73
Garrick, David, 44–45, 169
generative linguistics, 2–3, 56, 167
Gielgud, John, 109–10, 165
"God Save the King," 7, 141–42, 145–46, 172
Gray, Thomas, 33
Greek prosody, 33, 35, 37
grouping, 4; interacting with meter, 18; of poetic lines, 40; prosodic vs. syntactic, 11

Halle, John, 170; Halle and Lerdahl, 60, 66–67
Halle, Morris, and Samuel Jay Keyser, 56–60, 74
Hallmark, Rufus, and Ann Fehn, 170
Hayes, Bruce, 64–68, 96, 168, 171
Hayslett, Bryan, 173
hemiola, 104, 159
hierarchy: in grids, 5–6; of groupings, 4; headed, 65; in musical and linguistic syntaxes, 2
holy sonnets (Donne): sonnet #7, 78; sonnet #14, 60–61
Hopkins, Gerard Manley, 113, 169–70
"How Many Bards Guild the Lapses of Time" (Keats), 57–58
Hughes, Langston, 121–24, 157

iambic-trochaic law, 67–70
"Idea of Order at Key West, The" (Stevens), 118–21, 127, 157, 166
International Phonetic Alphabet (IPA), 149
interrogatives, yes-no, 89, 93–94

Jackendoff, Ray, 2, 141, 167, 170

Katz, Jonah, 170
Keats, John, 57–58, 80
Keyser, Samuel Jay, 174
Kiparsky, Paul, 57–58, 74, 78, 170

"Lake Isle of Innisfree, The" (Yeats), 113–15, 128, 157, 165
Lanier, Sidney, 45–48
Liberman, Mark, and Alan Prince, 61–64, 171
Leithauser, Brad, 169, 170, 173
length, principle of, 7, 25
linear (prolongational) analysis, 54, 143–44, 173–74

Macfadyen, Matthew, 108–9, 165
"Marseillaise, La" 8
McKellen, Ian, 108–9, 165
meaning: nonverbal, 96, 98, 127; poetic, 4, 75, 102, 105, 133
metrical grid, 5–7, 17; misnamed, 61; well- and ill-formed, 6, 18–20
Meyer, Leonard B., 38, 54
Milton, John, 78, 113, 169. See also *Paradise Lost*
Mirka, Danuta, 169
Mirren, Helen, 109–10, 165
monosyllabic word constraint, 57
Morris, Robert, 94
Mother Goose, 65–66

narrative, 75
network, 129, 173
"Nothing Gold Can Stay" (Frost), 15–16, 26–29, 64, 86–88, 92, 102–5, 129, 131–35, 146–48, 156
nuclear stress, 14–17, 65
nuclear tone, 95
nursery rhymes, 17, 49, 169

Olivier, Laurence, 169
"On First Looking into Chapman's Homer" (Keats), 80
optimality theory (OT), 58, 66

Paradise Lost (Milton), 39, 49–52, 73, 81–82, 110–12, 135, 155–56, 165
parallelism, principle of, 4, 12
periodicity, metrical, 5, 17, 26, 34, 53, 60

phase, in and out of, 8, 18, 69, 76
Pierrehumbert, Janet, 96–99
Poe, Edgar Allan, 70–71
poetic foot: foot/bar, 46–48; foot types (amphibrach, anapest, dactyl, iamb, pyrrhic, spondee, trochee), 32–33; in music, 37–38; problematic aspects of, 33–37; substitution, 34–35, 49, 77–78
poetic line, 38–40, 48; complexity or tension of, 42–43, 58–59, 74–75, 171; contraction or compression of, 43, 102–3, 169
Praat (program), 172
Prall, David, 52–53, 170
processing constraints, 168, 171
prominence (salience), 6–7; in contour, 85–87, 99; in grouping, 68; in music, 13, 150–51, 173; and tempo, 6; in sound color, 130, 140; and stress, 2, 16, 142, 144
prosodic hierarchy, 11–15, 161; categories of, 11; and feet, 33–35
prosody: against musical treatments of, 48–49; scholarly neglect of, 54
Prosogram (program), 172
proximity, principle of, 4, 25, 30, 65, 68–70

"Raven, The" (Poe), 70–71
reduction, meaning of, 171
rhythm rule, 61, 168
Richardson, Ian, 111–12
rules: preference, 3, 12, 58, 67; well-formedness, 18–20, 93
Ryan, Kevin, 168

Schenker, Heinrich, 173
Schoenberg, Arnold, 174
semantics, 2, 167; semantic nuance, 16, 83
Shakespeare, William, 39, 78; Hamlet's soliloquy, 44–45, 47, 77–78. *See* Sonnet #18; Sonnet #29; Sonnet #116

Shelley, Percy Bysshe, 49–50
Shepard, Roger, 174
Slawson, Wayne, 173
slots (syllabic), W S, 57, 59–61, 65, 74
Smith, Barbara Herrnstein, 171
Sonnet #18 (Shakespeare), 89–92, 98, 109–10, 165
Sonnet #29 (Shakespeare), 11–12, 14–15, 19, 21, 23, 27, 29, 34–38, 41–43, 64, 72, 74–75, 77, 88–89, 92–93, 108–9, 136–37, 146–47, 149–50, 155
Sonnet #116 (Shakespeare), 39
sound color, 128–41, 144, 149–50, 173
sound similarity: by traditional classifications (alliteration, assonance, contrast, identity, rhyme), 128; by degree of repetition, 130
"Star-Spangled Banner, The" 4–5, 8
Steele, Joshua, 44–45, 169, 172
Stevens, Wallace, 118–21, 127, 157, 166
stress maximum principle, 57
stress grid, 13–20, 161, 168; aligned with metrical grid, 20–30, 162; bracketed, 64, 67–68, 170; and poetic feet, 35–36; and sound color, 130, 140
stress, syllabic, 16–17; acoustic features of, 13, 172
syllable: bitonal, 91–94; extra-metrical, 60, 68; space, 149–50; and stress, 13–14, 16; as atom of analysis, 11
symmetry, principle of, 4, 12
syncopation, 8, 17, 169; anticipatory, 104
syntax, 2, 97; inverted, 80–82; timbral, 153

tactus, 6, 18–20, 30, 60, 167–68; sub-tactus, 23–25; supra-tactus, 28–29
template: deviation from, 42, 80–81; iambic, 43, 49, 69, 71–74; trochaic, 70–72
tension, 8, 54, 174; line (line complexity), 42, 49, 58, 71–75, 171; tonal, 74–75, 144, 150

text setting, 60, 64–67, 153, 168, 170
time-span reduction, 2, 54, 62, 141–44, 174; nondurational, 63–64, 152
"To a Skylark" (Shelley), 49–50
tonal space, 74, 150
tonal stability, 142, 146, 151
Tones and Break Indices (ToBI), 98–99
tree structures, 61–64, 171, 173

Wagner, Michael, 68, 171
"Weary Blues, The" (Hughes), 121–24, 157
Wimsatt, W. K., and Monroe Beardsley, 42, 48–53, 72

Yeats, William Butler, 113–15, 128, 157, 165
Youmans, Gilbert, 73–74, 80–81, 170

GPSR Authorized Representative: Easy Access System Europe, Mustamäe tee 50, 10621 Tallinn, Estonia, gpsr.requests@easproject.com

www.ingramcontent.com/pod-product-compliance
Lightning Source LLC
Chambersburg PA
CBHW022012290426
44109CB00015B/1143